Amazonian Quichua Language and Life

Amazonian Quichua Language and Life

Introduction to Grammar, Ecology, and Discourse from Pastaza and Upper Napo, Ecuador

Janis B. Nuckolls and Tod D. Swanson

LEXINGTON BOOKS
Lanham • Boulder • New York • London

Published by Lexington Books
An imprint of The Rowman & Littlefield Publishing Group, Inc.
4501 Forbes Boulevard, Suite 200, Lanham, Maryland 20706
www.rowman.com

6 Tinworth Street, London SE11 5AL, United Kingdom

Copyright © 2020 The Rowman & Littlefield Publishing Group, Inc.

All rights reserved. No part of this book may be reproduced in any form or by any electronic or mechanical means, including information storage and retrieval systems, without written permission from the publisher, except by a reviewer who may quote passages in a review.

British Library Cataloguing in Publication Information Available

Library of Congress Cataloging-in-Publication Data Is Available

ISBN: 978-1-7936-1619-7 (cloth)
ISBN: 978-1-7936-1621-0 (pbk.)
ISBN: 978-1-7936-1620-3 (electronic)

We dedicate this effort to all Amazonian Quichua–speaking Runa and their descendants, whose language and life are interwoven with intimate knowledge of their beautiful and complex environment

Contents

Acknowledgments	ix
Introduction	1

PART 1: SELF AND OTHER — 15

Lesson 1:	The Most Basic Verbal Interactions	17
Lesson 2:	Expressing Ideas of Being	23
Lesson 3:	Talking about Family	31
Lesson 4:	Types of Questions	39
Lesson 5:	Affirming, Negating, and Evading	49
Lesson 6:	Articulating the Perspectives of Self and Other	59
Lesson 7:	Human and Nonhuman Bodies	69
Lesson 8:	Expressing Thoughts, Feelings, Processes, and Enumeration	85
Lesson 9:	Suffixes of Instrumentality, Accompaniment, and the Imperatives	95
Lesson 10:	Suffixes of Togetherness, Separateness, and Exclusivity	107

PART 2: SPACE AND TIME — 119

Lesson 11:	Purpose, Directionality, Duration, Color	121
Lesson 12:	Attribution, Location, Past Tense	133
Lesson 13:	Habituality, Complex Movement Suffixes, Delimitation	145

Lesson 14: The Coreference Suffix *–sha*	157
Lesson 15: The Switch-Reference Suffix *–kpi*	167
Lesson 16: The Present Perfect *–shka*	175
Lesson 17: Talking about the Future	187
Lesson 18: Varieties of Compound Verbs	201
Lesson 19: Conditionality, Ordering, and Connecting Ideas	211
Lesson 20: Evidentiality, Speech Reports, Inchoative *–ya*, and Purposive *–chun*	221
Vocabulary	237
Bibliography	273
Index	275

Acknowledgments

We stand indebted to a number of people. Our work would have been impossible without the active collaboration and friendship of many *Runa* friends and relatives, especially those living in and around the Tena area within the community of Venecia. An enthusiastic *pagarachu*!, especially, to Tod Swanson's extended family. His wife Josefina Andi, her parents, sisters and brothers, and many extended kin have been willing interlocutors and helpful collaborators for us and for the many students who come to the Andes and Amazon Field School, otherwise known as *Iyarina*, for Quichua language immersion. We are particularly grateful to Josefina for her patience with our interminable questions, queries, and hypothetical sentences.

Both of our families have in fact supported us through several summers, while we worked on this grammar. Janis Nuckolls' husband Charles Nuckolls and three children have all been willing and often enthusiastic participants with us during extended stays at *Iyarina*. Nuckolls' closest Quichua friend and tireless consultant, Luisa Cadena, has been a significant voice in our work and in the ongoing Quichua instruction for countless numbers of students who come to *Iyarina* each summer. Her wisdom, humor, warmth, and detailed knowledge of her environment have deeply and positively influenced everyone she interacts with.

This grammar has been supported by Title VI funding from the US Department of Education and in particular the Title VI National Resource Centers at the University of Utah, Brigham Young University, the University of Wisconsin Madison, the University of Pittsburgh, and Florida International University, all of which have sent students to the Andes and Amazon Field School. Both authors received Title VI funding during the writing of the manuscript, and more than 180 Title VI Summer FLAS Fellowships for Quichua have funded the graduate students in our classes allowing us to invite expert Quichua narrators and artists as well as guest speakers.

Among our FLAS Fellows, a number of graduate students have been in residence at *Iyarina* during several field seasons. Alex Rice, Georgia Ennis, Brian Rupert, John Son, Lauren Dodaro, Travis Fink, Annie Preaux, Jarrad Reddekap, Chris Hebdon, Lisa Warren, Trisha Netsch Lopez, Chris Jarrett, Ernesto Benitez, Noah Diewald, and Barrett Hamp have all offered constant stimulation and enjoyable conversation. A special thanks to Barrett Hamp for his willingness to help with editorial work on this grammar.

It's been our privilege to work with Quichua teachers whose insights have contributed to our work. Armando Muyulema, Nely Shiguango, Luz Maria de La Torre, Martina Masaquiza, and Rosa Masaquiza have offered valuable insights to earlier iterations of this work. We have also been fortunate to spend many hours walking in the forest listening to the stories and songs and learning from the traditional artistry of Pedro Andi, Carmen Andi, Belgica Dagua, and Eulodia Dagua. Many extracts from their stories are featured in the grammar and Eulodia's ceramic *mukaha* bowl adorns our cover.

We are so grateful to colleagues who have collaborated with us or offered their expertise for guest lectures: Pieter Muysken, Lev Michael, Christine Beier, Connie Dickinson, Francesca Mezzenzana, Simeon Floyd, Martin Kohlberger, Bill Balee, Kathleen DeWalt, Will Waters, Wilma Freire, Juliet Erazo, Walter Carson, Lee Dyer, and in earlier years, Norman Whitten, Mike Uzendoski, Regina Harrison, and Frank Solomon. All have enriched and stimulated our thinking on grammar, ecology, health, and cosmology. We'd like to express a special 'thank you' to Pieter Muysken, whose visits are a highlight for us and for our students. His wide-ranging expertise has taught us much about Quichua and the larger family of Quechua languages. His elicitation sessions, guest lectures, and enjoyable company have made *Iyarina* an oasis of conversation, discussion, and debate.

Introduction

A goal of this pedagogical grammar is to open a door into a world of intimate meaning that knowledge of Quichua can make accessible. Increasingly, foreigners do not need to learn an indigenous language for reasons of basic communication. And many native speakers of indigenous languages already know an international trade language such as Spanish or English that they can use for basic communication. Language is more than a tool for basic communication, however. It also expresses the nuances of a person's socially and individually distinctive identity.

Every group has its inside jokes, its distinctive genres, styles, and shades of meaning that only insiders know. A language embodies the culture which makes possible the emergence of such genres, styles, and shades of meaning. It also carries within it an implicit philosophy or religious view of the world. Just as Sanskrit carries a history of Hindu thinking, Quichua carries within it a history of Andean and Amazonian thinking about the world. Because translations are only approximate when a word from one language is translated to another, there is always a remainder.

Although one can mechanically translate the Quichua past tense marker into the English tense system, one cannot so easily translate the distinctively Quichua understanding of history and past time into English notions of pastness. A good reason for studying Quichua, then, is to be able to understand this remainder, to communicate like an insider, to understand the distinctive ways that a Quichua dialect gives intimate and local shades of meaning to life. It is to understand the particular sensory flavor, the poetics, the cosmological overtones that are missed when talking to the same people in a trade language.

The reason foreigners learn Quichua should also be distinguished from the reasons Quichua children study Quichua in school. These children already know the language of local identity and are learning a unified variety for reasons of Pan-Andean identity.

Quichua is not only an abstract system but a cumulative history of people who speak it and of their complex knowledge of their environment, a knowledge which is based on the belief that birds, animals, plants, and water also have their *shimi* (speech) and their songs.

Historical Overview of Amazonian Quichua Dialects

Speakers of Amazonian Quichua number in the tens of thousands. Although their language is related to Highland Ecuadorian Quichua they are not migrants from the Andes nor do they share much with Andean culture. Rather, they represent diverse cultural and ethnic groups who underwent language shift to Quichua. Their memories, myths, and ancestor tales inevitably take them downriver and to the east, the direction in which their major rivers flow. Some people refer to their eastward origins with the term *sapi* which can be translated as 'root,' 'beginning,' and metaphorically implies 'origin.'

By way of historical background, speakers of Peruvian Quechua began moving northward into the Ecuadorian highlands only some 50 years before the Spanish conquest. Before that time, the communities in what is now Andean Ecuador spoke other languages, most likely Jivaroan in the south and Barbacoan in the north. Varieties of Quechua that spread northward with the Inca expansion included at least the *Chinchay Suyu* dialect of northern Peru as well as a separate administrative dialect from Cuzco (Adelaar and Muysken 2004). Because it was spread northward by elites, Quichua, which is what Ecuadorian varieties of Quechua are called, was initially a high-prestige language. Gradually, throughout the colonial period it became the native language of the conquered populations of Andean Ecuador. By the time of Ecuador's independence in 1830, Highland Andean Quichua became a low-prestige language associated with servants and hacienda workers who were bought and sold with the land.

By contrast with the low status of Highland Andean Quichua, speakers of Amazonian Quichua have never been a conquered population. Although the rubber boom did have a devastating effect on the region, Amazonian Quichua speakers were never subdued by colonialism in the way that Andean Quichua people were, and so they never absorbed the stigma that became attached to Highland dialects. Ethnohistorical accounts recorded by Muratorio (1991) include narratives recalling the inventive ways that Amazonian Quichua people were able to subvert attempts by rubber merchants and various government officials to corral their labor and time. Furthermore, in addition to manioc farming, they retained a lifestyle of hunting, gathering, and seasonal migration to remote areas for a much longer period of time than did their Andean counterparts, which created enormous difficulties for national-level governmental management and control.

Pastaza-Upper Napo Quichua

This pedagogical grammar will teach two closely related varieties of Amazonian Quichua associated with the Pastaza and Napo headwaters. These two dialects, which we will designate PQ (Pastaza Quichua) and NQ (Upper Napo Quichua) are classified as Quechua IIB dialects, which are northern variants because they are spoken in Ecuador and parts of Colombia, well north of the Incan capital of Cuzco, Peru. Quichua likely entered the eastern regions of Ecuador through the Pastaza Valley, and continued further into Amazonian Ecuador through networks of river systems, including the Ansuc, Arajuno, Villano, and Curaray. These river systems fan out toward the northeast into the Napo River, as well as the Puyo and Bobonaza Rivers that flow southeast into the Pastaza River (see map). During the colonial period the Quichua language was likely spread down these rivers causing language shift in communities which had previously spoken Jivaroan and Zaparoan languages.

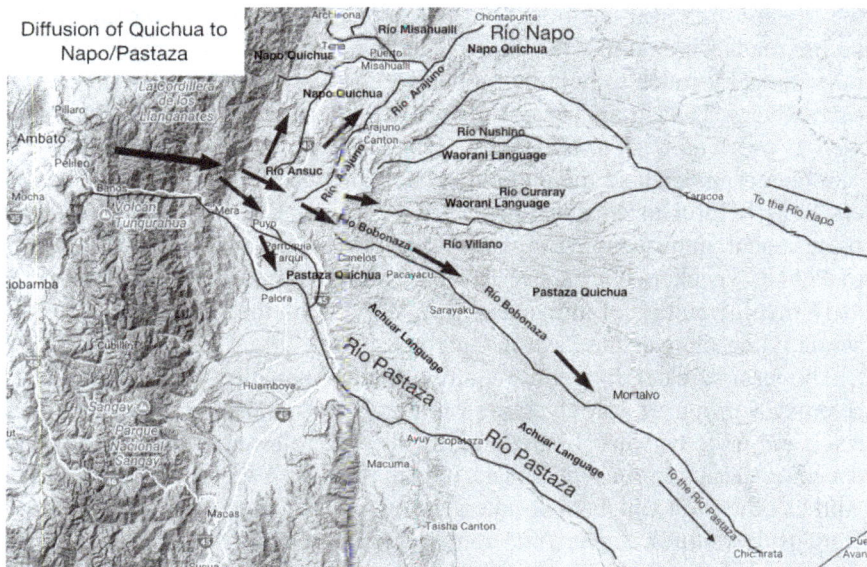

Diffusion of Quichua to Napo and Pastaza
TOD SWANSON

We do not yet completely understand the different modes of transmission of Quichua into Amazonian Ecuador. Adelaar and Muysken (2004) believe it highly unlikely that there was any Quichua spoken in Amazonian Ecuador at the time of the Inca conquest. Whitten (1976) has stated that Catholic missions have had an undeniable impact on the dominance that Quichua achieved in the lowlands of Ecuador by the mid-1800s. He also states that Quichua probably spread into the lowlands, in part, through a formative process consisting of intermarriages and alliances between Achuar and Zaparoan peoples who would adopt Quichua as a new mediating language which allowed them to be in contact with distant, highland sources of valued goods.

The speakers of Pastaza Quichua whose language provided the basis for this grammar are mostly from the Montalvo area near Ecuador's eastern border with Peru. They were raised in small settlements such as *Puka yaku*, *Hatun yaku*, and *Volvera*, near the military base in Montalvo, which is, as of this writing, not yet accessible by roads. Our older consultants who are now in their eighties, seventies, and sixties remember growing up during a time when clothes had to be made from tree bark, and steel axes had to be purchased from traders who plied their wares as they traveled along the networks of rivers, including the Bobonaza, and especially the Pastaza, which flows into the Marañon, which in turn reaches the Amazon River itself.

Our Napo Quichua sources reside in the communities of *Venecia* and *Santu Urku* on the South Bank of the Napo. Their family histories locate them in the Ahuano area near the mouth of the Arajuno River. They also recall a time before roads were built, when they hunted with blowguns and made seasonal migrations by canoe to hunting grounds at the mouth of the *Suno* and *Wataraco* Rivers. Their grandparents made long journeys by canoe to Iquitos as well as overland treks to trade with speakers living on the Bobonaza River.

To better understand the cultural connections between PQ and NQ speakers, it is helpful to consider the work of Rafael Karsten (1935), the first professional anthropologist to work in the region, who portrayed the culture of PQ/NQ speakers as 'greater Jivaroan' and noted during his fieldwork in 1916 that the culture of indigenous people living on the Upper Napo was essentially the same as the Pastaza Quichua.

The term 'greater Jivaroan' requires some explanation. We use it here to refer to a group of loosely shared cultural traits transmitted by intermarriage and trade between Jivaroan or, as they are referred to today, Chicham-speaking groups such as the Shuar, Achuar, Shiwiar, Awajun, and Wambiza as well as other non-Chicham speakers living around them, such as the Shapra, Kandoshi, Andowa, Zapara, and communities that underwent Quichua-zation from these languages. These communities shared a similar material culture including the design of blowguns, houses, feather ornaments, and ceramic vessels for serving chicha made of sweet manioc or peach palm. They also shared similar rituals, songs, and overlapping mythologies which were often translated across languages. Of course not all communities share these cultural traits in the same degree. Many have now been lost in Napo but they are remembered by older people and would have been obvious when Karsten carried out his research in 1916.

Historical Differences between Our Two Dialect Areas

Despite their probable common origins in the Pastaza headwaters and high degree of mutual intelligibility, the Upper Napo and Pastaza dialects have some differences which will be explained when relevant in the actual lessons. These differences were first distinguished in the 1950s when the Wycliffe Bible translators carried out surveys on what was then generically called "Jungle Quichua" or "Quichua del Oriente" to determine the boundaries of comfortable mutual intelligibility for a written text, namely translations of the Bible. The dialect we refer to as PQ was called Bobonaza Quichua by Orr and Wrisley (1981) because the majority of its speakers resided on the Bobonaza River. The Upper Napo dialect was called Tena Quichua because the majority of its speakers were oriented toward trade with Tena, the capital of Napo Province. Despite the fact that Wycliffe planned separate editions of the Bible for the two dialects, Upper Napo and Pastaza Quichua speakers communicate with each other easily without perceiving major difficulties. These two dialects should be distinguished from a third Amazonian dialect, designated Limoncocha by Orr and Wrisley (1981), which is spoken on the Coca River and its tributaries as well as on the Napo below the Coca. This dialect, which is not covered in our lessons, likely entered the Amazon through the Papallacta/Quijos valley at the headwaters of the Coca and so has ties to more northern Sierra dialects.

There are a number of complex historical reasons for the differences that do exist between PQ and NQ, but attempting to address those factors is outside of our main concerns for this pedagogical grammar. We will instead explain how our two groups of consultants differ in their backgrounds and experiences. Our Napo Quichua consultants have not had much contact with other indigenous languages although their parents and grandparents have. Our Pastaza Quichua consultants, by contrast, have vivid memories involving interactions with speakers of Zapara, Shiwiar, Shuar, and Spanish. Although older PQ speakers will sometimes profess ignorance of these languages, they are often aware, not only of what speakers of other languages are saying, but of how to produce grammatical utterances, and even more frequently, they can sing songs in these languages.

A second major difference between the Napo and Pastaza consultants lies in the degree of cultural loss due to depopulation during the rubber boom. Many of our older NQ sources (born in the 1920s, 1930s, and 1940s) do not know the names of their grandparents because they died or were taken away when their parents were still children. This break in generational continuity contributed to significant cultural loss of traditional songs, origin stories, ceramic arts, and face painting. Nevertheless the few older people who do remember these things recognize the songs sung by our PQ sources as similar to those their own grandparents once sang. To a certain degree then, the traditions still preserved by our PQ sources represent a cultural reservoir that was once more broadly shared by NQ and PQ speakers alike. We turn now to a brief discussion of first impressions made by Amazonian speakers upon early clergy and missionaries attempting to learn some of these languages.

Some Early Reflections on Quichua

Runa shimi, which is the term people use to refer to their language, means the speech or voice of *runa*. Although the meaning of *runa* is complex it can be roughly glossed as 'human beings.' Hence *runa shimi* means 'human speech.' *Runa shimi*, or Quechua, was the language of the Inca Tawantinsuyu (the four quarters) and is currently spoken in the Andean heartland of Ecuador, Peru, and Bolivia, and in parts of Argentina and Colombia as well as the western Amazon. With some 11,000,000 speakers, *Runa shimi* is the largest indigenous language of the Americas. In Ecuador alone, where Quechua is commonly referred to as Quichua, there are approximately 2 million speakers. Quichua is spoken in all of the Andean provinces of Ecuador (except Carchi) as well as the Amazonian provinces of Napo, Pastaza, Sucumbios, and Orellana.

Although Quichua has no genetic relation to Spanish or other Indo-European languages, it has shared the Andean environment with Spanish for over 500 years. A majority of Andean Spanish–speaking people have ancestors who once spoke Quichua. Hence, Quichua has deeply influenced Andean Spanish. The influence of Quichua is pervasive in the pronunciation of Andean Spanish as well as in the distinctive grammar and semantics of Andean Spanish.

Writing in 1773, the Jesuit priest Bernardo Recio offered a remarkable description of the influence of Quichua on the interior of the Spanish Quiteñan home. According to Recio, Quichua was so widely used in the capital city of Quito "that not only Indians speak it, but also mestizos and even the Spaniards but above all the women, even the *damas*. For since they suck it in with their milk and they learn it from those who nurse them, they retain it and use it so that when they go visiting or carry out their commerce they make use of it with the frankness with which here in Cataluna the ladies use their Catalan to speak amongst themselves." Recio wrote that Kichwa "is truly and of itself a language, the root and fount of many tongues; and one might hold the opinion that it was among the sixty-two of the tower of Babel."

First Impressions of Other Amazonian Languages

The indigenous languages of the Andean/Amazonian region have a preference for a concrete perspective that conflicts with the often abstract vocabulary of European and Middle Eastern languages (Adelaar and Muysken 2004, 234; Nuckolls and Swanson 2014). Dissonance between the concrete tendency of the native languages and the abstractions of western speech is something that has both fascinated and frustrated missionaries and visitors who have encountered native languages since earliest times. Consider the following testimony from Frank Drown.

In their 1961 book *Mission to the Head-Hunters*, Frank and Marie Drown describe the difficulties they encountered in learning Jivaro:

> We did not gain facility in this language as quickly as we had done in Spanish. . . . There were no words for salvation, grace, belief, or peace. After long and patient work, Ernest had discovered only a few which approximated thoughts of joy, comfort, patience, gentleness, goodness, and the many other virtues named in the Bible. When we spoke of the righteousness of God, we had to employ the same word the Indians used to describe a well-cleared garden patch. We had to face the fact that since the Jivaros did not know these things they felt no need to talk about them. But the more we studied the more we loved this strange jungle tongue. (Drown and Drown 1961, 53–54)

What is it exactly that frustrated the Drowns? We suggest that it was the near impossibility of communicating certain types of abstraction in the Shuar language. Biblical thinking is dependent on Greek concepts like "peace" or "grace" or perfect righteousness believed to exist timelessly in the mind of God quite apart from any particular historical instance. Such terms are abstract and free of perspective. Evidently the Drowns' Shuar interlocutors simply refused to think or to speak in these abstract terms. The closest they would come to contemplating what the Drowns meant by the righteousness of

God was to compare it to the comportment of a respected grandmother who kept her manioc garden free of weeds.

In Amazonian thinking there is a moral value attached to using concrete language which articulates a perspective. For example, in Amazonian Quichua it is not considered desireable to make the kinds of generic statements which are indispensible for scientific and social scientific discourse. If one were discussing nurturing habits of birds, for example, it would be strange to say something like 'The male guards the eggs.' Instead, a Quichua speaker would prefer to say something like 'It is said (by someone else) that the male guards the eggs,' or, 'I assert, from my perspective (having observed or experienced this), that the male guards the eggs.' We will see how Quichua suffixes very elegantly do the work of establishing a perspective, making the excessive wordiness of the English language examples unnecessary.

To speak truthfully, then, is to speak with awareness of a perspective, articulating its limits and advantages. One may use the perspectives of others (animals, plants, or humans) analogically but in doing so one must allow the interlocutors to imagine those perspectives. To do this is not easy. It takes discipline, strength, and skill to find the concrete analogies from nature. In Amazonian Quichua thinking a person who can speak this way is *sindzhi* (strong) and is the same kind of person who would keep a well-weeded garden patch.

Amazonian ideas of speaking well (*ali rimana*) also have an aesthetic quality. To speak beautifully is to speak with skillful analogies to nature using the sounds and movements of forest species to evoke concrete memories in the audience, which in turn give rise to thought. To illustrate an early European response to this quality of speech in the Ecuadorian Amazon we turn to another early missionary Francois Pierre. Like the Drowns, Father Pierre had difficulty communicating the abstract ideas of the Gospel so he let the Zaparo curaga of the Curaray speak for him. What impressed Pierre was the eloquent way in which the Zaparo chieftain held the attention of the people by using concrete analogies from nature:

> This elder, who did not know how to read or write, this Zaparo converted from infidelity, this savage confined in the deepest part of the woods, who does not have anyone with whom he could converse about holy things, who barely sees the missionary once every two years, explains without erring, difficult truths which are often inaccessible to reason alone. He does it simply; the terms, the formula are not things that interest him: nor would he even know what the words "define" or "distinguish" mean: he sees everything materially. But it is surprising how the idea shines resplendent through the painterly colors with which he dresses it. He makes the great trees and the rivers speak; he takes examples and comparisons from the flowers, the birds, and the savage beasts which turns the idea concrete until it is visible and palpable. (Pierre 1983, 83)

What is remarkable in these passages is the similarity in the experiences of the Drowns and Father Pierre. Both agree that abstractions like 'peace' or 'righteousness' have to be translated into the earthy concreteness of rivers and plants and garden patches. If speaking concretely by using the perspectives of nature corresponds to *ali rimana* there are also Quichua terms for expressing moral and aesthetic criticism of inappropriate speech. In Quichua the word *lala* is an adjective for someone who is 'soft.' A *lala runa* is someone who cannot stick to a task—the opposite of someone who is *sindzhi* or strong. *Lalana*, the verb formed from this adjective, means to exaggerate in the sense of speaking lazily or loosely. *Lalana* is to speak without the discipline of a properly limited perspective, and acting as though one had more perspective than one has. It is the way that 'softies' speak.

Even more reprehensible than *lalana* is *llullana*, a word which overlaps with the English meaning of 'to lie.' In Quichua however, an important meaning of *llullana* is the idea of deliberately speaking from a perspective that one does not have. Since there is no God's eye view from outside time and space, any speech from an abstract perspective would fall somewhere in this moral continuum between *lalana* and *llullana*. At best it is the speech of *quillas* (lazy people) and at its worst it is the speech of liars.

Related to the idea that one must speak from a perspective is the idea that language is not distinctive to humans but also characterizes all aspects of nature. In Quichua the word *shimi* has a broader range than the English word 'language.' It also means voice. A shared voice marks a collective identity, including voices of animal species. *Runa shimi* is often articulated by speakers wishing to enhance empathy (*llaquichina*) which creates emotional connections between those who share a common voice.

Teaching and Learning Goals

This grammar comes out of an ongoing collaboration between Nuckolls and Swanson at the Andes and Amazon Field School which began almost ten years ago. Each summer we have worked with speakers from the immediate Napo Quichua area as well as Pastaza Quichua speakers originating from Montalvo, but now residing nearby, for a period of seven weeks of intense linguistic research and language instruction. Observing interactions between speakers during targeted elicitation sessions as well as many kinds of less formal contexts has given us ample opportunities to evaluate the similarities and differences between the two dialects and to observe how their speakers interact. We have also been able to observe how similar and how distinctively Amazonian the culture of these two regions is.

What follows is a list of goals that a student may wish to achieve by studying this grammar:

1. To enable students to converse in Quichua with community members as quickly as possible, and thereafter to increase language competence in contexts of practical use.
2. To introduce the vocabulary and semantic fields of Quichua meaning for the areas of professional competence most likely to be used by students preparing to work with NGOs in Quichua communities. These areas include medical Quichua, Quichua for diplomacy, environmental Quichua, Quichua cultural terminology, etc.
3. To get the student to speak like an insider who can use subtle and polite forms of communication in certain contexts, and to be able to make and respond to humorous small talk.
4. To appreciate how Quichua as a language indigenous to the Americas works as a vehicle for cultural and religious identity including exploring semantic differences between Quichua and Indo-European languages such as Spanish or English.
5. To understand the social meaning of speaking Quichua in a country where Spanish is dominant.
6. To achieve proficiency appropriate to course level in the linguistic skills required to facilitate a successful social visit to a Quichua home. These include appropriate greetings and conversation designed to build relationships upon arriving and leaving, as well as skills in presenting the purpose of the visit.
7. To achieve proficiency appropriate to course level in the linguistic skills required to transcribe and translate a recorded oral text such as an origin story, a song, or a traditional narrative.
8. To achieve a level of conversational ability that will allow a linguist to conduct original research on this language by eliciting and discussing utterances with monolingual consultants, for the purpose of analyzing grammatical subsystems.

To begin studying Quichua, students may want to familiarize themselves with the consonants and vowels and the written symbols used to represent them, as well as the equivalent sounds in English. Before introducing these, a word about our written conventions will be helpful. Within Ecuador, Quichua is generally written as Kichwa in official documents of indigenous organizations as well as in materials produced by the Ministry of Education. We retain the older spelling Quichua here both because of its long history and because it continues to be used in many linguistic classification schemes.

It is also necessary to state our position with regard to the written forms of Quichua we have adopted. Although attempts to standardize written Quichua exist, it would be impossible to identify one set of conventions that is not controversial. Moreover, recent work has pointed not only to the emotionally charged dimensions of attempting to regulate written language (Haboud and Limerick 2017), but also to the counter-productive effect such regulating may have on indigenous language use in Ecuador.

Grzech, Schwarz, and Ennis (2019), Ennis (2019), and Wroblewski (2014) point out that despite Unified Kichwa's original function as a medium for written communication in formal educational settings, there has been a tendency for standardization to creep into spoken language in some public settings. Grzech et al. (2019) cite their ethnographically grounded case studies to argue that this has had a detrimental effect on peoples' speaking practices, inducing anxiety and pressure to conform to prescriptive ideologies of language production. Yet, as Ennis (2019) has demonstrated, social media and especially radio broadcasts have managed to avoid Kichwa Unificado because their content is dynamic, orally produced, and designed for local communities. The importance of orality and traditional speaking practices based on family members' local conventions has been convincingly articulated for Napo speakers by Uzendoski and Calapucha-Tapuy (2012).

We have attempted a compromise of sorts, by adopting some Unificado conventions, while trying to be flexible in order to accommodate unique features of PQ and NQ. For example, we use the traditional three vowels to represent *a*, *i*, and *u* sounds, but also include the *o* vowel for words borrowed from Spanish. The *o* vowel also appears in many ideophones, possibly because many Quichua ideophones tend to make use of the marginal sounds that rarely occur in ordinary words (Nuckolls, Stanley, Nielsen, and Hopper 2016). We also use the Unificado double *l* sound, written as *ll*, even though the PQ and NQ version of this sound is quite different from what Highland Quichua speakers would articulate. Unlike some versions of Unificado, we include the voiced consonants such as *d*, *b*, and *g*, where appropriate. We also include many unusual sounds that are used in ideophones, as well as in floral and faunal terms, and also in place names. These include, for example: *kw*, *ty*, *ky*, and *py*. Finally, although Unified Kichwa is written differently from the traditional spelling of 'Quichua,' we retain this traditional written form because it continues to be used in many linguistic classification schemes.

The following table displays the International Phonetic Association, or IPA, linguistic symbol in brackets [ ] as well as the equivalent written symbol used in our grammar for representing all Quichua words:

IPA and Written Symbols	Pronunciation	Quichua Example Words
[p] *p*	English *p* in *pat*	*pakana* 'to hide'
[b] *b*	English *b* in *but*	*bugyu* 'freshwater dolphin'
[t] *t*	More interdental than English alveolar *t*	*tunshi* 'type of bird'
[d] *d*	More interdental than English alveolar *d*	*dawa* 'type of bird'
[k] *k*	English *c* in *cat*	*kuti* 'again'
[g] *g*	English *g* in *goat*	*–guna* 'plural suffix'
[kʷ] *kw*	English *qu* in *quick*	*Kwankiri* 'name of a lake'
[pʲ] *py*	English *p* pronounced with an immediately following *y* as in *puny*	*pyulla* 'mold'
[tʲ] *ty*	English *t* pronounced with an immediately following *y* as in *tiara*	*tyukana* 'to spit'
[kʲ] *ky*	English *k* pronounced with an immediately following *y* as is the *cu* in *accuse*	*mikya* 'aunt'
[s] *s*	English *s* as in *sun*	*samana* 'to breathe'
[z]~[dz] *dz, z*	The *dz* sound as in English *heads* is unstable and easily loses the *d*, becoming simply *z*	*(d)zambulina* 'to immerse under water'
[ɕ] *sh*	English *sh* as in *she*	*shamuna* 'to come'
[h]~[ʔ] *h*	Word-initial *h* is often dropped, and may be replaced with a glottal stop, especially before vowels	*hapina* 'to take, grab hold' > *apina*
[ts] *ts*	English *ts* as in *lets*	*tsaka* 'bumpy'
[tɕ] *ch*	English *ch* as in *church*	*chay* 'that'
[dʑ] *dzh*	English *j*, *dg* as in *judge*	*mandzhana* 'to be afraid of something'
[m] *m*	English *m* as in *mother*	*mutyu* 'cut off'
[m̩] *m̩*	English *um*, as in negative '*um um*'	*m̩bwi* 'type of frog'

IPA and Written Symbols	Pronunciation	Quichua Example Words
[n] *n*	More interdental than English alveolar *n*	*nanana* 'to hurt, feel pain'
[ŋ] *ng*	Word final *n* is often pronounced as *ng* in English *sing*, except among ideophones, which vary	*polang* 'to emerge from underwater to the surface'
[ɲ] *ñ*	English *ny* words derived from Spanish ñ as *canyon*	*ñaña* 'sister of female'
[ɫ] *l*	English 'dark' *l*'s or velar *l*'s, as in *call*, *dull*, *role*	*lalana* 'to exaggerate'
[ʎ] *ll*	Said as if an *l* and *y* are simultaneously pronounced: *ly*	*llullana* 'to lie'
[ɾ] *r*	Spanish *r* in *perro*	*rikuna* 'to see'
[w] *w*	English *w* in *want*	*wawa* 'baby'
[β] *w*	A more fricativized version of a *w*, occurring before the *i* vowel	*wiwilang* 'plant based soap'
[j] *y*	English *yet*	*yaya* 'father'
[i] *i*	English *ee* in *beet* and *i* in *bit*	*rimana* 'to speak'
[u] *u*	English *oo* in *boot*	*ruku* 'old'
[a] *a*	English *a* in *ah ha*	*maki* 'hand'
[o] *o*	Spanish *ocho*. This vowel occurs in Spanish borrowings and also in ideophones	*polo* 'a puncture or piercing'

JANIS NUCKOLLS

Part 1

SELF AND OTHER

In this section we introduce fundamentally important skills for orienting oneself in relation to others within the Quichua-speaking world of *Runa shimi*. We introduce basic social moves such as greetings and leave-takings and the asking of several different types of questions for figuring things out in a new language world. You will learn how to form the simplest complete sentences, along with the most basic grammatical distinctions such as that between subjects and direct objects, and between statements made from a speaker's perspective and those made from the perspective of an 'other.' Pronouns and kinship terms for addressing the most significant others in your life are introduced, including members of one's nuclear family, kin terms for relatives by marriage, and terms for those you might choose to include in your family. Body part terminology for human selves and nonhuman others, impersonal verbs involving inner processes said to happen to one, concepts of possession, and numbers are all introduced. Suffixes for expressing thoughts, feelings, and processes, as well as instrumentality and accompaniment are taught. The final unit of this section introduces suffixes for distinguishing between togetherness and separateness.

Lesson 1

The Most Basic Verbal Interactions

Asina 'to smile, laugh'
TOD SWANSON

Greetings as Yes/No Questions

Among Quichua-speaking people there is a high value placed on demonstrating one's sociability toward others in everyday life. Humor is a key ingredient for sociable behavior and more will be said about this in lessons to come. More generally, there is a principle of conviviality which requires people to adopt a pleasant and friendly demeanor in interactions with others.

Not surprisingly therefore, greeting behavior is important, even though Quichua does not have dedicated words to greet others, such as the English forms 'Hello' and 'Hi' or the Spanish forms 'Hola' or 'Buenos dias,' etc. Instead, people greet each other quite often by asking a question such as 'Have you come?' or 'Are you living?' Such questions are similar to 'How are you?' except that they barely count as questions, since the answers are so obvious. They are quite important, nevertheless, for displaying your sociable self to others. We begin therefore with the most fundamental form of social behavior—the yes/no question. For now we will only explain how to respond to such questions affirmatively. Ways of responding negatively will be covered in Lesson 5.

When asking a yes/no question, the interrogative suffix *–chu* is added to the word which is the focus of the question. For example:

Conversational Model 1

Kawsangi-chu? 'Are you alive?'

The affirmative response then uses the *–mi* suffix to respond:

Kawsani-mi 'I'm alive'

Please note that for Quichua verbs, stress is usually placed on the next to last syllable which is accented below:

Kawsangí-chu? 'Are you alive?'
Kawsaní-mi 'I'm alive'

Without the *–chu* or *–mi* suffixes, however, the verbs' stress would be:

Kawsáni 'I'm alive'
Kawsángi 'you are alive'

As this yes/no question format is important generally for many types of conversations beyond simple greetings, it will be helpful to practice it below.

Practice 1

Practice the yes/no question of conversation model 1 using *–chu* on the first verb form and *–mi* on the second:

Example:

Waytangi 'you swim'/*waytani* 'I swim'
Waytangichu? 'do you swim?'/*waytanimi* 'I do swim'

Now, based on the example above, use the following sets of verbs to ask and answer yes/no questions:

1. *Paktamungi* 'you arrive'/*paktamuni* 'I arrive'
2. *Mikungi* 'you eat'/*mikuni* 'I eat'
3. *Puringi* 'you walk'/*purini* 'I walk'
4. *Tiyangi* 'you hang out'/*tiyani* 'I hang out'
5. *Yanungi* 'you cook'/*yanuni* 'I cook'
6. *Tarabangi* 'you work'/*tarabani* 'I work'
7. *Aswangi* 'you make *aswa*'/*aswani* 'I make *aswa*'
8. *Wasingi* 'you make a house'/'*wasini* 'I make a house'
9. *Chagrangi* 'you make an agricultural field'/*chagrani* 'I make an agricultural field'
10. *Puñungi* 'you sleep'/*puñuni* 'I sleep'

More Complex Yes/No Questions

The suffixes –*chu* and –*mi* can be attached to any type of word, whether a verb, noun, pronoun, or adverb. In the next exercise you will practice adding adverbs to basic sentences, and then add question and answer suffixes to these as well. Adverbs in English have a low status, especially among teachers of creative writing who often tell their students to avoid using them. In Quichua, however, adverbs are a very important, widely used class of words. They typically occur before the verb they modify, but may occur after as well. In the example below, a speaker asks a yes/no question by focusing on the adverb *alilla* 'well.' Note that unlike verbs, which shift stress with the addition of the suffixes –*mi* and –*chu*, adverbs (and also adjectives) retain their original penultimate (next to last syllable) stress even after these suffixes are added. The following conversational model also introduces the affirmative response words *nda* and *ari* which are comparable to saying 'yes.' *Nda* is typically used by PQ speakers while *ari* will be used by NQ speakers. However, this is not a hard and fast rule. There may be individual differences in usage patterns based on a person's life history, travels, parental origins, and current residential patterns.

Conversation Model 2

Alílla-chu paktamungi?
'Have you arrived well?' (That is, "Did you have a good trip?")

Nda. Alíllami paktamuni. (PQ)
Ari. Alíllami paktamuni. (NQ)
'Yes. I've arrived well.' (That is, "I've had a good trip.")

Practice 2

Reproduce the preceding dialogue using the following adverbs and verbs.

Example:

    alimánda 'slowly'/*tarabángi* 'you work'
    Alimándachu tarabángi? Nda/ari. Alimándami tarabáni.
    alimanda 'slowly'/*istudiangi* 'you study'
    ukta 'fast'/*mikungi* 'you eat'
    alilla 'well'/*tiyangi* 'you dwell in a place, you hang out'
    iridza 'ugly, bad'/*muskungi* 'you dream'
    sapalla 'alone'/*kawsangi* 'you live'
    wayra shina 'very fast,' literally: 'like the wind'/*yanungi* 'you cook'
    wayra shina 'very fast,' literally: 'like the wind'/*killkangi* 'you write'
    wayra shina 'very fast,' literally: 'like the wind'/*rimangi* 'you speak'
    sindzhita 'strongly'/*waytangi* 'you swim'
    sindzhita 'strongly'/*puringi* 'you walk, trek, or travel'
    chunlla 'quietly'/*tiyangi* 'you are located'
    chunlla 'quietly'/*puñungi* 'you sleep'
    waka waka 'crying and crying'/*puñungi* 'you sleep'
    kushilla 'happily'/*asingi* 'you laugh'

Culture Focus: The Sound of Laughter

Runa people place a lot of importance on sociability and cheerfulness even under difficult situations. Laughing in the face of danger or despair is an ability that people admire. Laughter in general, however, is positively valued and people enjoy reports about laughter, as well as talking about the sounds and qualities of laughter. Interestingly, *Runa* peoples' representations of laughter are not much different from an English-speaking person's. Laughter in Quichua is often expressed by the syllable *ha*, which is usually repeated multiple times.

Go to the following link:
http://quechuarealwords.byu.edu/?ideophone=ha

    Watch video 2 where a woman uses *ha* to describe the laughing sounds made by people who are gathered together to share food. She contrasts these happy social sounds to the melancholy sound of a bird called the *kukuli* bird, who is said by the happy people to be sad because of being alone.

Ha hay, a variant of *ha*, is sometimes used to describe extremely celebratory laughter occurring at festive occasions.

Go to video 1 at the following link:
http://quechuarealwords.byu.edu/?ideophone=hahay

Listen to a representation, from a traditional flood narrative, of celebratory laughter by intoxicated people who will not heed warnings about an impending flood.

Ending a Social Interaction

Just as Quichua has no dedicated greeting words such as 'hello,' it also has no dedicated word such as 'goodbye' to end a social interaction. Speakers will simply say *kayagama* 'until tomorrow,' or *riunimi* 'I'm going,' or *rishalla* 'I will just go.'

Speakers who are being left will sometimes anticipate another person's departure by observing their preparatory movements or by inferring their departure from the conversational context. This is what happens in the following conversational model between two people who are related to each other by *compadrazgo* ties. To be related by *compadrazgo* ties means that people see each other as having a significant relationship marked by mutually agreed upon obligations and responsibilities.

Conversation Model 3

Riungichu kumpari? 'Are you going compadre?'
Ari. Riunimi kumari, kayagama 'Yes, I'm going comadre. Until next time'

Translation Exercise

Go to the following link:
https://www.youtube.com/watch?v=zjzg-iGXWtA

Listen to an actual example of a response to leave-taking. Watch and listen to the speaker who notices North American students leaving for an extended hike in the forest. Notice how she says goodbye to them using informal Spanish *chao*, as well as with Quichua words (2:25–2:31). Identify and translate the Quichua words:

1. _____
2. _____

Culture Focus: Forest Resources: The *Piwi* Plant and Pottery

Regarding the comings and goings of Amazonian peoples, it is interesting to note the reference points for people as they travel. Fast growing second growth trees often dominate the skyline in previously deforested areas of the upper Amazon. People from that part of the world know they are home when they see the unmistakable branching of *Pollalesta discolor*, a member of the *Asteraceae* or aster family of flowering plants, against the evening sky. *Piwi*, (pictured below left), as it is referred to by Runa, is particularly valued by women as a wood for the firing of a *mukaha*, a type of ceramic polychrome drinking bowl pictured below.

Piwi plant

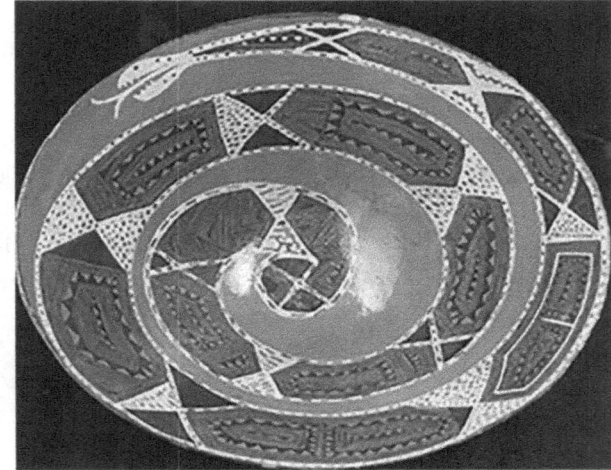

Mukaha 'drinking bowl'
TOD SWANSON

Lesson 2

Expressing Ideas of Being

Chunda muyu 'peach palm fruit'
TOD SWANSON

The Verb *Ana* 'to Be'

The Quichua verb is mostly regular. Verbs are conjugated by suffixing the person/tense morphemes to the root. The verb *ana* 'to be' is an important verb to know as its use is widespread for describing not only essential, permanent qualities that someone might want to claim, such as one's name or kinship status ('I am Rosa' or 'I am Fausto's sister'), but also for describing ascribed or temporary behaviors as well as habitual qualities ('He is an eater of meat,' or 'She is a hard worker').

Lesson 2

The root of the infinitive *ana* is just one sound: *a-*, and the infinitive suffix is *–na*, which basically means 'to ____.' The person/tense suffixes then replace the infinitive suffix *–na*. For the present tense, the suffixes are:

First person singular 'I': *–ni*
Second person singular 'you': *–ngi*
Third person singular 'he, she, it': *–n*

First person plural 'we': *–nchi*
Second person plural 'you-all': *–ngichi*
Third person plural 'they': *–nawn* (PQ)/*–nun* (NQ)

Personal Pronouns

Each present tense form of *ana* 'to be' occurs below with its pronoun.

Ñuka a-ni 'I am'
Kan a-ngi 'you are'
Pay a-n 'he, she, it is'
Ñukanchi a-nchi 'we are'
Kanguna a-ngichi 'You-all are'
Payguna a-náwn/a-nún 'They are' (PQ/NQ, respectively)

Note that stress is a bit irregular for the third person plural forms, shifting to the final, rather than to the penultimate syllable. The final syllable is marked with an accent to indicate its stressed status.

Practice 1

Conjugate the following verbs out loud, using the correct pronouns for each verb:

tarabana 'to work'
istudiana 'to study'
mikuna 'to eat'
tiyana 'to dwell, hang out (of people) be located, be available (of objects, resources)'
muskuna 'to dream'
kawsana 'to live'
yanuna 'to cook'

killkana 'to write'
rimana 'to speak'
waytana 'to swim'
purina 'to walk, trek, or travel'
puñuna 'to sleep'

Tips for Using Pronouns and Verbs

Although it is good practice to conjugate verb forms with their appropriate pronouns, it is important to remember that for Quichua, pronouns are not required when functioning as the subjects of sentences. Quichua is a Subject-Object-Verb language in principle, but subjects are often left out altogether, leaving listeners to infer the identity of a subject from context.

Another important consideration has to do with the way present tense is used. It is often used in a present perfect sense to indicate action that is complete as of the moment of speaking. For example, I may ask in English 'Did you eat?' A normal response would either be 'Yes, I ate' (past tense) or 'Yes, I've eaten' (present perfect). In Quichua there is a present perfect construction which will be learned in a later chapter, but the present tense is often used to express this meaning as well:

Ñuka mikuni 'I have eaten' or simply:
Mikuni 'I have eaten'

Practice 2

Use your new knowledge of verbs in the following conversational model, where the first speaker asks a second speaker about a third person or persons, leaving out the pronoun.

Example:

Mikunchu? 'Has he/she eaten?'
Nda/ari mikunmi. 'Yeah/yes. He/she has eaten.'

1. *puñuna* 'to sleep'
2. *waytana* 'to swim'
3. *muskuna* 'to dream'
4. *tarabana* 'to work'
5. *rimana* 'to speak'

Practice 3

Now go back to the same list of verbs (*puñuna, waytana, muskuna, tarabana, rimana*) and practice the same question/answer sequence using either of the third person plural ('we') forms.

Example:

Pastaza Quichua
  Mikunáwnchu? 'Have they eaten?'
  Nda, mikunáwnmi. 'Yeah, they've eaten.'

Upper Napo Quichua
  Mikunúnchu? 'Have they eaten?'
  Ari, mikunúnmi. 'Yes, they've eaten.'

Practice 4

Now go back to the same list of verbs (*puñuna, waytana, muskuna, tarabana, rimana*) and practice the same question/answer sequence using the second person ('you-all') and first person plural ('we') forms:

Example:

  Mikungichíchu? 'Have you-all eaten?'
  Nda/ari, mikunchími. 'Yes, we've eaten.'

Written Exercise 1

Complete the following sentences with the appropriate pronoun.

_____	ani
_____	mikun
_____	purinun
_____	llakinchi
_____	rimanchi
_____	killkangi
_____	angi
_____	rikunchi
_____	puñungichi
_____	waytangi

Practice 5

Construct questions with each of the following combinations of verbs and adverbs in any person/number that you have just learned, based on the situation described for each example. Attach the question suffix –*chu* to the adverb for each sentence.

Example:

ukta 'fast'/*rina* 'to go' (to a group of people):
Uktachu ringichi? 'Do you-all go fast?'

1. *Alimanda* 'slowly'/*purina* 'to walk, trek, travel' (to a person who has just had ankle surgery)
2. *ukta* 'fast'/*yanuna* 'to cook' (about a group of women)
3. *alilla* 'well'/*shamuna* 'to come' (to your neighbor)
4. *wayra shina* 'very fast,' literally: 'like the wind'/*kallpana* 'to run' (about yourself)
5. *sindzhita* 'strongly'/*awana* 'to make pottery' (to a group of pottery-makers)
6. *chunlla* 'quietly'/*tiyarina* 'to sit' (about a group of children)
7. *waka waka* 'crying and crying'/*puñuna* 'sleep' (about a baby)
8. *alilla* 'well'/*rimana* 'to speak' (to someone who has just told you something surprising)
9. *sindzhita* 'strongly'/*kalipana* 'to run' (about a group of adolescents)
10. *ukta* 'fast'/*waytana* 'to swim' (to your sister)

Written Exercise 2

Fill in the blanks for each of the following short sentences, using the correct present tense form of the verb in parentheses, which correctly translates the English into Quichua.

1. *Payguna aychata* _____ (*munana*). 'They want meat.'
2. *Ñuka bagrita* _____ (*hapina*). 'I catch a catfish.'
3. *Kanguna lagartota* _____ (*kasana*). 'You-all hunt a caiman.'
4. *Pay charapata* _____ (*rikuna*). 'He/she sees a turtle.'

Charapa 'turtle'
ALEXANDER RICE

5. *Kan alillami* _____ (*kawsana*). 'You live well.'
6. *Wawa chunlla* _____ (*puñuna*). 'The baby sleeps quietly.'
7. *Ukta* _____ (*tarbana*)! 'You work quickly!'
8. *Payguna wasiichu* _____ (*awana*)? 'Do they make pottery in the house?'
9. *Kanguna alillachu* _____ (*muskuna*)? 'Do you-all dream well?'
10. *Ñuka hachi kayutui* _____ (*puñuna*). 'My uncle sleeps in a bed.'
11. *Ñukanchi lomochata* _____ (*apamuna*). 'We bring a *lomocha*.' (large edible rodent)
12. *Ñukanchi apayaya wasita* _____ (*wasina*). 'Our grandfather makes a house.'
13. *Ñukanchi* _____ (*puñuna*) *wasi ukui*. 'We sleep inside the house.'
14. *Payguna hatun chagrata* _____ (*chagrana*). 'They make a big *chagra*.' (agricultural field)
15. *Ñukanchi* _____ (*mingana*) *domingo pundzha*. 'We have a *minga* (work party) on Sunday day.'
16. *Payguna wayra shinachu* _____ (*istudyana*). 'Do they study fast (literally: like the wind)?'
17. *Kanguna runa* _____ (*ana*). 'You-all are *runa*.' (people, members of the Quichua-speaking community)
18. *Ñuka saksakta* _____ (*mikuna*). 'I eat until completely full.'
19. *Sindzhitachu* _____ (*purina*)? 'Do you walk fast?'
20. *Sacha wagratachu* _____ (*kasana*)? 'Do you-all hunt tapirs?'

Culture Focus: Forest Resources: *Chunda muyu*

The first image of this lesson, a photo of peach palm fruit, called *chunda muyu* and classified as *Bactris gasipae*, has historically been an important source of nutrition for indigenous Amazonians. It is boiled and eaten, or boiled and fermented into a mild beer. The wood from its tree is valued for its strength and it has been used for weapons such as spears.

Transcription Exercise 1: The Historical Present

Go to the following link:
https://www.youtube.com/watch?v=X5Z97bfn6LM

Listen as the speaker (0:27–0:33) describes preparations for a traditional peach palm fruit festival that she heard reports about from her father. The following verbs are used: *pallagrina* 'to go and harvest,' *yanuna* 'to cut firewood,' *warkuna* 'to hang.' Although the speaker is describing events from long ago, she uses present tense forms of verbs in a historical present sense. The nouns *chunda* 'peach palm fruit' and *ashanga* 'basket' are also used, as well as an evidential suffix *–shi* (to be discussed in Lesson 6), and a locative suffix *–i* (to be discussed in Lesson 12). Write as accurately as possible the three sentences you hear her say:

_____

_____

_____

Note whether any of them has an explicit subject pronoun.

Lesson 3

Talking about Family

Ayllu 'family'
TOD SWANSON

In conversation model 3 at the conclusion of Lesson 1, there was a brief exchange between two people who had a type of relationship, the *compadrazgo* relation, which anthropologists refer to as 'fictive kinship.' The *compradazgo* system originated in European Spanish culture as a way of establishing bonds between nonrelatives through godparenting practices. However, it has become embedded into Quichua culture in unique ways. For example, Quichua people who are already closely related as siblings may decide to further strengthen their ties through godparenting each others' children, rather than asking an outsider to do so. As a consequence of this, it is not uncommon to hear the following exchange between two sisters:

Riungichu kumari? 'Are you going comadre?'
Ari. Riunimi kumari, kayagama. 'Yes, I'm going comadre; until next time.'

Fictive kinship, as the term implies, allows people to construct meaningful social relationships with others who are not part of their families. Another way to do this, is, obviously, is to establish affinal relationships through marriage. Terms for in-marrying relatives are discussed in Lesson 6. For Quichua people, social relationships are most meaningful when based on family ties. Words for friend such as *amigo/amiga* are borrowings from Spanish which are used, but not invested with as much significance as family relationships. In Quichua social interactions, it is most likely that a first question asked of someone will not be 'what is your name?' but rather 'whose son/daughter are you?'

The extended family or *ayllu* is the most important unit of Quichua society. We know from earliest records, such as that of Juan de Betanzos, that the Inca empire, called *Tawantinsuyu*, was organized around *ayllus*. Kinship terms were also used to express the relationship between the Inca and their deities. Inca Yupanque was the first to be given the title *Indichuri*, which can be translated as 'the sun's son' or 'son of the sun.'

Family and Kinship Terms for Consanguineals (Blood Relations)

Although it is probably true for all human cultures, Quichua speakers place a strong emphasis on family relationships, and feel a very poignant sadness at the prospect of not having one's family around them. Look at the following list of kin terms and then go to the following link:
https://www.youtube.com/watch?v=l1ECt5i2U2c

Listen to the first 20 seconds. The speaker tells about all of the family members who have passed from her life. She lists each kinship category that she does not have, and calls herself a *wakcha* 'orphan.' She uses the impersonal verb *illana* 'to lack' (Lesson 7), which is suffixed with the attributive suffix *–k* (Lesson 12). She also uses the despitative suffix *–was* (Lesson 9), shortened to *–s* on each kinship term.

Try to pick out as many kin terms mentioned by the speaker, as you can from the following list:

ayllu 'family (blood kinship)'
wakcha 'orphan'
yaya 'father'

mama 'mother'
mikya 'aunt,' also used as a term of respectful address by a younger person to an older, unrelated woman
hachi 'uncle'
apa yaya (PQ) 'grandfather'
apa mama (PQ) 'grandmother'
ruku 'old, big'
ruku yaya (NQ) 'grandfather'
ruku mama (NQ) 'grandmother'
musu (PQ) 'adolescent male'
wambra (NQ) 'adolescent male'; (PQ) 'adolescent male or female,' 'boyfriend' or 'girlfriend"
churi 'son, small boy'
churiguna 'little boys'
ushushi (*ushi*) 'daughter, small girl'
turi 'brother of a female'
wawki 'brother of a male'
ñaña 'sister of a female'
pani 'sister of a male'
wawa 'baby, young child, toddler'
llulluku 'newborn'
kari 'male' (adjective), 'husband' (noun)'
kari wawa 'boy baby, child'
warmi wawa 'girl baby, child'

Asking Questions about Family with *–yuk*

Although questions to others about their families might be considered overly personal in some cultural contexts, the same is not true for Quichua-speaking people who freely discuss their family matters, including illnesses, deaths, traumas, break-ups, and many other kinds of issues as well.

One of the most basic questions one can ask is a question that clarifies which family members a person actually has. The easiest way to do this is to ask a question using the possessor suffix *–yuk* along with the verb *ana* 'to be':

Mama-yuk-chu angi? Literally: 'Are you a mother-possessor?'
Nda/Ari. Mama-yuk-mi ani. Literally: 'Yes. I'm a mother-possessor.'

When a form of the verb *ana* is preceded by a word ending in *–mi* or *–chu*, however, there is a slight change in the resulting spoken form. In such an utterance, the suffixes *–chu* and *–mi* seem to 'jump over' to the verb, rather than staying on the original word they were attached to. Therefore, rather than pronouncing the question as follows:

Mama-yuk-chu angi?

The speaker will combine the *–chu* and whatever form of *ana* 'to be' follows, into one word: *changi*:

Mama-yuk-chu angi? > *mamayuk changi?*

It is as if the suffix *–chu* has hopped over to the next word. However, this 'hopping over' only happens when the next word is some form of the verb *ana* 'to be.' Another aspect of this process is that the vowel of the suffix *–chu* is deleted. This process happens no matter which form of the verb *ana* is used:

'I' First person singular: *–chu* + *ani* = *chani*
'you' Second person singular: *–chu* + *angi* = *changi*
'he/she/it' Third person singular: *–chu* + *an* = *chan*
'we' First person plural: *–chu* + *anchi* = *chanchi*
'you-all' Second person plural: *–chu* + *angichi* = *changichi*
'they' Third person plural: *–chu* + *anawn* = *chanawn;* *–chu* + *anun* = *chanun*

The very same process takes place when a word ending in the *–mi* suffix is followed by a form of *ana* 'to be':

First person singular: *–mi* + *ani* = *mani*
Second person singular: *–mi* + *angi* = *mangi*
Third person singular: *–mi* + *an* = *man*

First person plural: *–mi* + *anchi* = *manchi*
Second person plural: *–mi* + *angichi* = *mangichi*
Third person plural: *–mi* + *anawn* = *manawn;* *–mi* + *anun* = *manun*

Practice 1

Construct questions and answers about which *ayllu* members your conversationalists may have, using the preceding model.

Example:

Wawayuk changi? 'Do you have children?'
Nda, wawayuk mani. 'Yes, I have children.'

1. *Yaya* 'father'
2. *Apa yaya* (PQ) 'grandfather'
3. *Ruku yaya* (NQ) 'grandfather'
4. *turi* 'brother of female'
5. *wawki* 'brother of a male'
6. *pani* 'sister of a male'
7. *ñaña* 'sister of a female'
8. *mikya* 'aunt'
9. *hachi* 'uncle'
10. *ushushi* 'daughter'
11. *churi* 'son'
12. *warmi wawa* 'girl baby'

Telling about One's Family with *Charina* 'to Have' and Direct Object Marker *–ta*

We now introduce a fundamentally important new grammatical relation, that of the direct object. The ideal direct object is something that is in some way directly affected by the action of a subject, but the notion of being 'affected by' has to be interpreted rather broadly. In the following examples, the direct object is italicized:

I kicked *the ball*.
I drink *aswa*.
I saw *my friend*.

Although the ball is certainly affected by being kicked (it is moved from one place to another), it is arguable whether the *aswa* is affected by being drunk or whether a person is affected by being seen. Nevertheless, English speakers would consider these noun phrases to be direct objects, which must occur after a verb.

If you are still struggling to conceptualize direct objects, think of the most important part of a sentence that remains after a subject and verb are expressed. If that leftover part is not expressing locational ideas, it is more than likely a direct object.

Quichua direct objects generally occur before the verb. In PQ the direct object marker is the suffix *–ta*, which is pronounced as *–da* when it follows a voiced sound, such as *n*:

aswa-ta upini 'I drink *aswa*'
lulun-da mikuni 'I eat eggs'

For simplicity, we will represent all direct object markers as *–ta*.

Yaku aycha-ta hapini. 'I catch fish.' (Literally: 'I catch water meat.')

The direct object marking system for Napo Quichua is a bit more complex because the direct object marker has, in addition to *–ta* and *–da*, another variant form *–ra*, which occurs after a vowel:

Aswa-ra upini. '(I) drink *aswa.*'
Lumu-ra mayllangi. '(You) wash the manioc.'
Wasi-ra pichan. '(He/she) sweeps the house.'

Besides the *–yuk* plus *ana* 'to be' construction, the verb *charina* 'to have' may also be used to ask about which family members a person may have. In this construction, the family member becomes a direct object and is suffixed with *–ta* or one of its variants:

Mama-ta charingichu? 'Do you have a mother?' (PQ)
Mama-ra charingichu? 'Do you have a mother?' (NQ)

Practice 2

Construct questions using *charina* and a kinship term suffixed with a direct object marker.

Example:

Pastaza Quichua
  Apa yaya-ta charingichu? 'Do you have a grandfather?'
  Nda. Apa yaya-ta charinimi. 'Yes. I have a grandfather.'

Upper Napo Quichua
  Apa yaya-ra charingichu? 'Do you have a grandfather?'
  Ari. Apa yaya-ra charinimi. 'Yes. I have a grandfather.'

1. *yaya*
2. *apa yaya*
3. *ruku yaya*
4. *turi*
5. *wawki*
6. *pani*
7. *ñaña*
8. *mikya*

9. *hachi*
10. *ushushi*
11. *churi*
12. *warmi wawa*

Written Exercise 1

Draw lines connecting the Quichua kinship term in the first column below to its English language equivalent in the second column.

1. *yaya* — 'aunt'
2. *apa yaya* — 'sister of female'
3. *ruku yaya* — 'son'
4. *turi* — 'grandfather' (NQ)
5. *wawki* — 'father'
6. *pani* — 'brother of male'
7. *ñaña* — 'daughter'
8. *mikya* — 'sister of male'
9. *hachi* — 'grandfather' (PQ)
10. *ushushi* — 'brother of female'
11. *churi* — 'girl baby'
12. *warmi wawa* — 'uncle'

Written Exercise 2

Construct sentences about the most important kinship relations you have, using Quichua terms. You may use either the direct object + *charina* 'to have' construction, or the *–yuk* construction.

Example:

   Ñuka yayata charini, wawata charini, turita charini . . .

Or:

   Ñuka yayayuk mani, wawayuk mani, turiyuk mani . . .

Romantic Love: *Llakichina*

Although love for one's family is very important, Runa also invest a great deal of energy in romantic love, which is seen as a kind of natural force that is in need of proper channeling and focusing through magical means. The closest term to English 'love' is *llaki*, although it has important differences in sense and connotation. For Runa, *llaki* involves notions of tenderness, affection, empathy, and can even involve sadness if one's feelings are not reciprocated. If the object of one's feelings of *llaki* are not reciprocated, then magical practices may be used.

Love magic may involve the singing of songs, possibly along with the use of special substances from plants, animals, or insects. Peoples' explanations for why a particular substance is chosen vary. For example, animals judged to be very successful at love include the freshwater dolphin, *bugyu*, said to travel in male/female pairs, and the toucan bird, *sikwanga,* who, upon losing a partner, will seek another one that very day.

Listening and Writing Exercise

Go to the following link and listen to approximately the first 30 seconds while the speaker explains how attached to each other toucan birds are:
https://www.youtube.com/watch?v=_lrLznnM6gI&feature=youtu.be

Although this short narrative has been translated into English, see if you can listen and find ten Quichua words that you recognize and write them down. There are also a number of kinship terms from this lesson. New verbs from the video include: *wañuchina* 'to kill,' *kantana* 'to sing,' *kayana* 'to call,' *sakirina* 'to remain, stay,' *shamuna* 'to come.'

Try to write each word as you hear it, even if you don't yet understand all of its suffixes:

_____   _____

_____   _____

_____   _____

_____   _____

_____   _____

Lesson 4

Types of Questions

Lomo chagra 'manioc garden'

Asking Information Questions

Dialogue:

Speaker 1: *May-ta riŋgi kumpari*? 'Where are you going *kumpari*?'
  may 'where'
  –ta information question marker

Speaker 2: *Chagra-ma rini kumari. Kan-ga?* 'I'm going to the *chagra kumari.* And what about you?'
 –ga topicalizing suffix

Speaker 1: *Wasi-ma rini.* 'I'm going home.'
 wasi 'house'
 –ma directional suffix meaning 'toward,' 'to'

Speaker 2: *Yuyangi! Pita lala ruku ñambi-i sirin.* 'Watch out! There's a big old pit viper lying on the path'
 yuyana 'to be aware, think, reflect' (PQ)
 iyana 'to be aware, think, reflect' (NQ)
 pita lala 'pit viper'
 ruku 'big'
 ñambi 'road, path'
 –i location suffix meaning 'in, on, near'

Speaker 1: *May-ta?* 'Where?'

Speaker 2: *Chay-ma! Chunda ruya laro-i.* 'Over there! Beside the peach palm tree.'
 chunda 'peach palm'
 ruya 'tree' (PQ)
 yura 'tree' (NQ)
 laro 'beside, next to'

Speaker 1: *Wañuchingichu?* 'Have you killed it?'
 wañuchina 'to kill'

Speaker 2: *Hah ow. Uma-ta chyuw pitini!* 'Yeah, I cut its head right off *chyuw*!'
 uma 'head'
 pitina 'to cut'
 chyuw 'expressive adverb for a complete severing or cutting through something. Usually occurs with verb *pitina* 'to cut'
 hah ow 'informal way of saying yes, similar to yup, yeah, etc.'

The preceding dialogue illustrates the use of the information question marking suffix *–ta*, which becomes *–ra* for Napo speakers. It is typically suffixed to a question word, such as 'who,' 'what,' 'where,' 'why,' 'how,' 'how much,' etc. Although it is identical to the direct object markers *–ta/–ra*, it is probably historically unrelated. Interrogative *–ta* is most likely a variant of Highland Ecuadorian question marker *–tak*, which lost its final consonant in Amazonian varieties. There is no need to worry about possible confusion between the question suffix and direct object marker, however, as context

Types of Questions

always makes clear which suffix is being used. The interrogative *–ta/–ra* is attached to a question word which is usually the first word of a sentence.

Besides *may* 'where' which is used in our dialogue, other Quichua question words that are useful to know include: *pi* 'who' and *ima* 'what.' An additional point concerning information questions is that they may be a bit more complex. The questions *Mayta ringi?* (PQ) or *Mayra ringi?* (NQ) can both be translated as 'Where are you going?' They could, however, be made more complex by adding the directional suffix *–ma*, to be discussed in Lesson 11. This additional suffix would result in: *Maymata ringi?* (PQ) or *Maymara ringi?* (NQ).

Similarly, the question 'Where do you live?' uttered as *Mayta kawsangi?* (PQ) or *Mayra kawsangi?* (NQ), could be additionally elaborated with the locative suffix *–i/–bi*, to be discussed in Lesson 12: *Maybita kawsangi?* (PQ) or *Maybira kawsangi?*, which would literally be translated as 'In where do you live?' Finally, *Pita rikungi?* (PQ) and *Pira rikungi?* (NQ) 'Who do you see?' could be additionally specified with Lesson 3's direct object marker *–ta/–ra*: *Pitata rikungi?* (PQ), or *Pirara rikungi?* (NQ) 'Whom do you see?'

Practice 1

Practice answering the following information questions which ask *ima* 'what?'

Example:

Mikuna 'to eat' (*aycha* 'meat')
  Imata mikungi? 'What have you eaten/do you eat?'
  Aychatami mikuni. 'I've eaten/I eat meat.'

  1. *upina* 'to drink' (*aswa* 'manioc beverage')
  2. *uyana* 'to hear' (*pishku* 'bird')
  3. *mikuna* 'to eat' (*chunda* 'peach palm fruit')
  4. *rikuna* 'to see' (*wasi* 'house')
  5. *munana* 'to want' (*aswa* 'manioc drink')
  6. *apamuna* 'to bring' (*wangana* 'wild pig')
  7. *charina* 'to have' (*bagri* 'catfish')
  8. *taksana* 'to launder' (*llachapa* 'clothes')
  9. *tarpuna* 'to plant' (*papachina* 'small potato')
  10. *apana* 'to take' (*aswa maytu* '*aswa* pulp that is wrapped in a leaf')

Practice 2

Practice answering the following information questions which ask *pi* 'who?' Remember to add the direct object suffix.

42　　　　　　　　　　　　*Lesson 4*

Example:

Llachapa 'clothing' *taksana* 'to launder' (*ñaña* 'sister of female')
Pita llachapata taksan? 'Who washes clothes?'
Ñañami llachapata taksan. '(My) sister washes clothes.'

1. *wasi-ma* 'house-to' *rina* 'to go' (*mikya* 'aunt')
2. *aycha* 'meat' *pitina* 'to cut' (*hachi* 'uncle')
3. *aswa* 'manioc beverage' *upina* 'to drink' (*wawki* 'brother of male')
4. *chunda* 'palm fruit' *pallana* 'to harvest' (*ruku mama* 'grandmother')
5. *ashanga* 'basket' *awana* 'to make' (*yaya* 'father')
6. *wangana* 'forest pig' *kasana* 'to hunt' (*kari* 'man')
7. *pita lala* 'pit viper' *rikuna* 'to see' (*ushushi* 'daughter')
8. *chagra-manda* 'agricultural field-from' *shamuna* 'to come' (Antoñia)
9. *puñuna* 'to sleep' (*wawa* 'baby')
10. *asina* 'to laugh' (*kushillu* 'spider monkey')

Gesturing While Speaking

There is a common view of gesturing while speaking which considers it to be an indication of someone's inability to express oneself properly with language. This 'deficit' view of gesture is increasingly coming under fire as more and more research by linguists and psycholinguists reveals that

Makiwan rimana 'to speak with hands'
TOD SWANSON

gestures accompanying speech are integrated with language at the deepest levels of cognition.

You may have already noticed while watching audiovisual sources that Quichua speakers, both male and female, are often exuberant with their gesturing. This is particularly noticeable when they use expressive adverbs known as ideophones, a word class that will be discussed in more detail in Lesson 7. Although Quichua speakers gesture a lot while speaking, they will often use special gestures while articulating ideophones. The ideophone introduced in this lesson, *chyuw*, is quite often accompanied by a cutting-like gestural motion. Go to the following link:
http://quechuarealwords.byu.edu/?ideophone=chyuw

Watch the short video clips featuring *chyuw*. Try to listen for the verb *pitina* 'to cut,' which is the verb that occurs with *chyuw* most often. How many times can you hear some form of this verb?

The Syntax of Questions

Yes/no questions suffixed with *–chu* need not undergo a change in their syntactic position. However, it often sounds better to put the word suffixed with *–chu* as close to the beginning of the sentence as possible. For example:

Alitachu kawsan kariwan? 'Does she live well with (her) husband?'

This is far more natural sounding than:

**Kariwan alitachu kawsan*? 'With her husband does she live well?'

This is because yes/no questions, and any kind of question for that matter, are a natural focus for a sentence. And typically, whatever is of most topical interest will come earlier in a sentence rather than later.

Information questions, for example, always place the information question word at the beginning of a sentence. For example:

Imata kuchungi? 'What (tree) do you chop down?' (the verb '*kuchuna*' presupposes that it is a tree that is being cut)

If the information question requires a complement, then that complement is transposed behind the verb:

Imata kuchungi hachawan? 'What (tree) have you chopped down with the ax?'

But not:

*Hachawan imata kuchungi? 'With an ax, what (tree) do you chop down?'

If the subject of an information question is specified, it will often be the last, rather than the first element of the sentence:

Imata kuchunawn payguna? 'What (tree) do they cut?'

Practice 3

Practice asking and answering the following information questions for third person plural subjects, which you will insert in your answers.

Example:

mikuna 'to eat'/*aycha* 'meat'/*wawaguna* 'children'
Imata mikunawn wawaguna? 'What do the children eat?'
Aychatami mikunawn wawaguna. 'The children eat meat.'

1. *upina* 'to drink'/*aswa* 'manioc beverage'/*hachiguna* 'uncles'
2. *uyana* 'to hear'/*pishku* 'bird'/*churiguna* 'boys'
3. *mikuna* 'to eat'/*chunda* 'peach palm fruit'/*apayayaguna* 'grandfathers'
4. *rikuna* 'to see'/*wasi* 'house'/*aylluguna* 'family members'
5. *munana* 'to want'/*aswa* 'manioc drink'/*apamamaguna* 'grandmothers'
6. *apamuna* 'to bring'/*wangana* 'wild pig'/*kariguna* 'men'
7. *hapina* 'to catch'/*bagri* 'catfish'/*ushushiguna* 'daughters'
8. *taksana* 'to launder'/*llachapa* 'clothes'/*kumariguna* 'comadres'
9. *tarpuna* 'to plant'/*papachina* 'small potato'/*wawaguna* 'children'
10. *apana* 'to take'/*aswa maytu* 'aswa pulp'/*wawkiguna* 'brothers of males'

Non-Immediate Imperatives and the Politifying Suffix *–pa*

A commonly used imperative or directive is the same verb form as the second person forms of verbs. The second person singular occurs in the preceding dialogue when Speaker 2 says *Yuyangi!* which is literally 'you think!' but is better translated here as 'Watch out!'

This is the non-immediate imperative, which is used for non-urgent actions that a speaker would like another speaker to accomplish. It takes the same form as the second person suffix *–ngi*. For example:

apamungi 'you bring (something)'

Since an imperative is a form of speech designed to manipulate other peoples' behavior, it is often softened with the suffix *–pa*, which indicates a tone that is similar to the English word "please." This suffix is used quite a lot in Highland dialects of Quichua but in Pastaza and Napo its use is more restricted to commands that might be interpreted as rude if not softened. It is the last suffix occurring before the person/tense/number suffixes:

apamuna 'to bring' > *apamu-pa-ngi* 'you please bring'

Practice 4

Practice turning the following commands into polite imperatives.

Example:

Ali 'good' *aycha-ta* 'meat-direct object' *apamuna* 'bring'
Ali aychata apamu-pa-ngi 'please bring nice meat'

1. *Ñuka* 'my' *wasi-i* 'at-home' *sakiringi* 'you stay'
2. *Kamba* 'your' *turi-ta* 'to brother' *rimangi* 'you speak'
3. *Ñuka* 'my' *wasi-ma* 'house-to' *shamungi* 'you come'
4. *Ñuka* 'my' *wasi-manda* 'house-from' *llukshingi* 'you leave'
5. *Apa mama-ta* 'grandmother-direct object' *aswa-ta* 'aswa-direct object' *upichingi* 'you give to drink'
6. *Chuchawasa-ta* 'medicinal tree bark-direct object' *kachangi* 'you send'
7. *Lomo-ta* 'manioc-direct object' *yanungi* 'you cook'
8. *Lagarto-ta* 'lizard-direct object' *mikungi* 'you eat'
9. *Wawa-ta* 'child-direct object' *likcharingi* 'you wake up'
10. *Chay* 'that' *ñambi-ta* 'path/road-direct object' *apanakungi* 'you follow'
11. *Yaku* 'water' *uray-ta* 'downriver-adverbializer' *waytangi* 'you swim'
12. *Wasi* 'house' *ukuy* 'inside' *tiyaringi* 'you remain'

Culture Focus: Orienting Oneself by Way of Rivers

The flow of rivers is of fundamental importance for Runa peoples' spatial orientation. Go to the following link:
https://www.youtube.com/watch?v=SDTZMO3DivY

Listen to the ambient sounds of the rainforest. One bird in particular, the *waktaway*, is heard calling. Watch, in particular, the flow of the water as it heads *urayta* 'downriver.'

The Causative Suffix –*chi*

The opening dialogue featured a new suffix –*chi*, occurring in the verb *wañuchina* 'to kill,' which is formed from *wañuna* 'to die.' To kill, therefore, is literally translated as 'to cause to die.' Any verb suffixed with causative –*chi* will take a direct object. This is a very productive suffix that will greatly increase your vocabulary.

Examples of –*chi* suffixed verbs show how this suffix affects a verb's meaning:

rikuna 'to see' > *rikuchina* 'to show'
upina 'to drink' > *upichina* 'to give someone to drink'
wañuna 'to die' > *wañuchina* 'to kill'
puñuna 'to sleep' > *puñuchina* 'to put a baby or a child to bed'
purina 'to walk' > *purichina* 'to make someone walk, take someone around'
yachana 'to know' > *yachachina* 'to teach'
kuyuna 'to move oneself' > *kuyuchina* 'to make something move'
tukuna 'to become' > *tukuchina* 'to finish something'
nuspana 'to dream' > *nuspachina* 'to cause someone else to dream'
kushiyana 'to become happy' > *kushiyachina* 'to make someone become happy'
piñarina 'to be angry' > *piñachina* 'to anger someone'
llakina 'to love' > *llakichina* 'to make someone feel tender emotions, including love, sadness, or empathy; also the name for a genre of songs meant to inspire such feelings'
llukshina 'to leave or to emerge' > *llukshichina* 'to cause to emerge, chase out (of an animal from a hole)'
hapina 'to catch, grab hold of an object, animal, a person for romantic relationship' > *hapichina* 'to cause something to be caught, especially of a fire being lit'

Written Exercise 1

Draw a line to the best translation:

Ñambita rikuchin.   'He kills (literally: "finishes off") the agouti.'
Ñambita rikun.   'He's caught fish.'
Chi sisata wañuchin.   'The baby sleeps.'
Chi sisa wañun.   'I've made the baby sleep.'
Sikuta tukuchin.   'She looks at the path.'
Siku tukun.   'I've lit the fire.'

Ñambimanda llukshin.	'He makes it come out of a hole.'
Uktumanda llukshichin.	'It emerges from the path.'
Wawata puñuchini.	'He/she/it kills the flower.'
Wawa puñun.	'That flower dies.'
Ninata hapichini.	'She becomes an agouti.'
Yaku aychata hapin.	'He shows the path.'

Open-Ended Questions with Topicalizer –*ga*

We have learned about two types of questions, the polar, or yes/no question and the information question. We now consider a type of open-ended question with topicalizer –*ga*, which occurs in our dialogue. –*Ga* is a topicalizing suffix which can occur on any word to indicate focus. We will discuss its focusing function more in future lessons. A secondary use of its focusing function is to ask a 'what about?' question, which occurs in our opening dialogue. Speaker 2 asks Speaker 1 in a very friendly and informal way about what she is doing:

Speaker 2: *Chagra-ma rini kumari.* 'I'm going to the *chagra, kumari.*'
Kan-ga? 'And what about you?'

Open-ended questions are found throughout dialogues between people who wish to convey casual, friendly messages with each other. Their open-endedness gives speakers ample options to respond in ways that vary from straightforward to light-hearted and humorous.

Practice 5

Practice the open-ended question by having someone read each of the following statements and then ask you about what you are doing. You should then respond by either substituting the word in parentheses with an appropriate response, or by making up your own response.

Example:

Ñuka chagra-ma rini. Kanga? (*wasi*) 'I'm going to the *chagra*. What about you?'
Ñuka wasi-ma rini. 'I'm going to the house.'

1. *Ñuka aswa-ta upini.* 'I drink *aswa.*' (*muyu* 'fruit'[1])
2. *Ñuka uray-manda shamuni.* 'I come from downriver.' (*hanak* 'upriver')

3. *Ñuka ushushi-ta charini.* 'I have a daughter.' (*churi* 'son')
4. *Ñuka wangana-ta kasani.* 'I hunt for forest pig.' (*lagarto* 'lizard')
5. *Ñuka bagri-ta aysani.* 'I pull (i.e., "catch") a catfish.' (*chulla shimi*, literally: 'uneven mouth,' used for a type of fish with differently sized upper and lower lips)
6. *Ñuka mukaha-ta awani.* 'I make a *mukaha*.' (*ashanga* 'basket')
7. *Ñuka mikya-ta tupani.* 'I meet up with my aunt.' (*hachi* 'uncle')
8. *Ñuka apa yaya-yuk m-ani.* 'I am a grandfather-possessor.' (*apa mama* 'grandmother')
9. *Ñuka Tena-ma purini.* 'I travel to Tena.' (*Puyo*)
10. *Ñuka llachapa-ta taksani.* 'I wash clothes.' (*plato* 'dishe[es]' *mayllana* 'to wash')

Culture Focus: In the *Chagra*

The agricultural field is more than a place to work. It is a site for people to take care of the land that will sustain them and to watch over what they've planted. Weeds are always competing for nutrients. Various rodents attempt to eat manioc even before it is harvested. Birds may even try to steal corn kernels off of their cobs. The *chagra* is also a place for couples to have private time, for children to be educated about subsistence activities, and for family members to strengthen their ties by working together. Go to the website's chapter 4 page and complete the writing exercise based on an activity involving a *sawli* 'machete,' which is one of the most valuable tools for working in one's *chagra*.

Note

1. Note that certain fruits, particularly juicy ones, are 'drunk' rather than eaten.

Lesson 5

Affirming, Negating, and Evading

Tinahaguna 'tinajas'
JANIS NUCKOLLS

More on Yes/No Questions

The yes/no question suffix *–chu* may be attached to any type of word in a sentence, whether it is a noun, pronoun, proper name, adjective, adverb, or verb. The decision over where to put the *–chu* suffix depends on what a speaker wishes to focus on with that question. For example, by placing *–chu* on the word for *lomocha*, the following question focuses upon that word:

Lomochata-chu hapingi? 'Have you caught a *lomocha*?'

This question focuses on the word for the animal, to emphasize that this particular animal, rather than another, was the one caught.

Another way of asking this question is to focus on the verb instead:

Lomochata hapingi-chu? 'Have you caught a *lomocha*?'

This question, by contrast, focuses on the verb, to emphasize that it was catching rather than perhaps just seeing it.

Practice 1

Practice varying the focus of each of the following questions by placing *–chu* onto a different word than the one given for each of the sentences.

Example:

Given sentence:

Kay wasiichu puñungi? 'Is it in this house that you sleep?'

Varying focus sentence:

Kay wasii puñungichu? 'Is sleeping what you do in this house?'

1. *Shigratachu awangi?* 'Is it a *shigra* that you've made?'
2. *Canoata awangichu?* 'Is it the case that you've made a canoe?'
3. *Hamangaichu puñungichi?* 'Is it in a hammock that you-all sleep?'
4. *Lomochatachu mikungichi?* 'Is it a *lomocha* that you-all eat?'
5. *Tinahatachu awangi?* 'Is it a *tinaha* that you have made?'
6. *Kuchatachu rikungi?* 'Is it a lake/pond that you see?'
7. *Sindzhita tarabanchu?* 'Is it working that he/she does strongly?'
8. *Paychu lomochata hapin?* 'Is he/she the one who has caught a *lomocha*?'
9. *Kandzhu hamangata awangi?* 'Are you the one who has made a hammock?'
10. *Lomocha yakui kawsanchu?* 'Is it the case that the *lomocha* lives in water?'
11. *Indillamatachu mikunawn?* 'Is it sloth (meat) that they eat?'
12. *Chagramandachu shuwanawn?* 'Is it from the *chagra* that they steal?'

Negation

Negative statements and negative responses to questions are both formed with a combination of the adverb *mana* and the negative suffix *–chu*. The use of *mana/–chu* negation involves surrounding whatever element of a sentence is the focus of the negation, with *mana* preceding it and *–chu* following it. Please note that when *–chu* follows an *n* or any other voiced sound, its pronunciation changes to *–dzhu*.

The following example illustrates this. It is from a traditional story about the *bullukuku* hawk. This hawk tells little children that one of their parents is not yet asleep, by first making its characteristic sound, namely: *bullukuku*, and then the narrator 'translates' its sound into the human utterance 'He is not yet asleep.' The word for 'yet' is *chara*. *Mana* and *–chu* surround the verb 'he sleeps': *mana puñun-chu*, and are pronounced as follows:

Bullukuku~kuu~kuu~kuu~kuu, chara mana puñundzhu, chara mana puñundzhu.
Bullukuku~kuu~kuu~kuu~kuu (which meant) 'He is not yet asleep; he is not yet asleep'

An audiovisual clip of this sentence may be heard at the following link: http://quechuarealwords.byu.edu/?ideophone=bulyukuku

Practice 2

Make negative 'not yet' statements out of the following verbs using the model from the traditional story. Vary your person and number.

Example:

Mikuna > chara mana mikundzhu. 'He/she/it has not yet eaten.'

1. *hapina* 'to catch'
2. *upina* 'to drink'
3. *rimana* 'to speak'
4. *shamuna* 'to come'
5. *likcharina* 'to wake up'
6. *tigramuna* 'to return'
7. *llukshina* 'to emerge'
8. *mingana* 'to have a work party'
9. *rikurina* 'to appear'
10. *chayana* 'to cook until done'

Replying to a Yes/No Question with a Negative Statement

When responding negatively to a yes/no question, it is considered polite to supply the questioner with whatever correct information is available. This is a basic cooperative principle of conversational practice that is probably universal. Similarly, a speaker of English will not simply answer a question negatively. He or she will also elaborate the response whenever appropriate. For example, if asked "Have you lived here a long time?" a polite response would be "No. I've only lived here a month."

The following short dialogues illustrate polite negative responses to yes/no questions. Notice that both the question and the answer have no pronouns. It is quite common for speakers to leave them out of an utterance, which can, nevertheless, be understood through context cues.

Question: *Lomochatachu hapingi?*
  'Have you caught a *lomocha*?'

Answer: *Mana lomochatachu hapini; wagratami hapini.*
  'I haven't caught a *lomocha*; I've caught a tapir.'

The preceding response, while quintessentially correct, is not usually used. The following more abbreviated response is more typical.

Question: *Lomochatachu hapingi?*
  'Have you caught a *lomocha*?'

Answer: *Mana. Wagratami hapini.*
  'No. I've caught a tapir.'

Practice 3

Practice your negative responses by using the shorter answer.

Example:

  Mikungichu? 'Have you eaten?'
  Mana. Upinimi. 'No. (But) I've drunk.'

  1. *Wasingichu?* 'Are you building a house?' (*chagrana* 'to make an agricultural field')
  2. *Mikunawnchu?* 'Have they eaten?' (*upina* 'to drink')
  3. *Tushungichichu?* 'Do you-all dance?' (*istudiana* 'to study')

4. *Uktachu shamungi?* 'Do you come quickly?' (*alimanda* 'slowly')
5. *Shigratachu awangi?* 'Do you make a bag?' (*ashanga* 'basket')
6. *Wasiichu puñungi?* 'Do you sleep in the house?' (*chagrai* 'in the *chagra*')
7. *Hamangaichu puñungichi?* 'Do you-all sleep in a hammock?' (*kayutui* 'in the bed')
8. *Chagranawnchu?* 'Are they making a *chagra*?' (*wasina* 'to make a house')
9. *Yanunchu?* 'Does he/she cook?' (*tarabana* 'to work')
10. *Lomochatachu mikungichi?* 'Do you-all eat *lomocha*?' (*charapa* 'tortoise')
11. *Tinahatachu awangi?* 'Have you made a *tinaja*?' (*mukaha* 'drinking bowl')
12. *Kuchatachu rikungi?* 'Do you see a lake?' (*wasi* 'house')
13. *Wayra shinachu taraban?* 'Does he/she work like the wind, i.e., very fast?' (*alimanda* 'slowly')
14. *Paychu lomochata hapin?* 'Is he/she the one who has caught a *lomocha*?' (*ñuka* 'I')
15. *Kandzhu hamangai tiyaringi?* 'Are you the one who sits in the hammock?' (*pay* 'he/she/it')
16. *Lomocha yakuichu kawsan?* 'Does the *lomocha* live in water?' (*pambai* 'in the ground')

Evasion and Echo Questions

There are a couple of options for answering an information question. Either the information is supplied, or it is not. Quichua speakers may not supply information either because they do not have it, or because they may not feel that a listener is entitled to know the answer to their question. To avoid answering an information question for whatever reason, speakers can simply say *mana yachanichu* 'I don't know,' or, and this is *far* more common: they answer by first making '*hm hm*' sounds with the first sound lower and the second higher in pitch. They then echo all or part of the question, often adding the adverb *chari* 'perhaps' to the reply.

Speaker 1: *Mayta rin Masha Cervantes?* 'Where has brother-in-law Cervantes gone?'

Speaker 2: *Hm hm . . . Mayta chari rin?* '. . . Where, perhaps, has he gone?'

Such answers may be regarded as 'performances of uncertainty,' which illustrate a cultural orientation on the part of Quichua speakers that does not stigmatize a lack of knowledge. In Quichua-speaking culture it is far better to express uncertainty than to speak presumptively without really knowing. When speakers echo another person's question with the '*hm hm*' construction, they may be expressing an empathetic stance toward that question, as if to say 'I wish I could tell you what you want to know, but unfortunately, I can't. I'm therefore adopting it as my question as well.'

Practice 4

Practice answering questions using the *hm hm* construction.

Example:

> *Mayta rinawn payguna?* 'Where have they gone?'
> *Hm hm . . . Mayta chari rinawn payguna?* 'Hm hm . . . Where, perhaps, have they gone?'

> 1. *Pita pita lala umata chyu pitin?* 'Who cut the *pita lala*'s head right off?'
> 2. *Imamandata mana shamunawnchu, payguna?* 'Why do they not come?'
> 3. *Maymandata llukshin lomocha?* 'Where did the *lomocha* emerge from?'
> 4. *Maymandata paktamun Masha Elario?* 'Where did brother-in-law Elario arrive from?'
> 5. *Imamandata aswan Kachun Antonia?* 'Why does sister-in-law Antonia make *aswa*?'
> 6. *Imamandata llullan payba wawa?* 'Why does his/her child lie?'
> 7. *Imamandata mana likcharinchu kamba hachi?* 'Why does your uncle not wake up?'
> 8. *Imamandata wakan, kamba wawa?* 'Why does your child cry?'
> 9. *Imamandata sakirin payba mikya?* 'Why does your aunt remain?'
> 10. *Maymandata shamun apa yaya?* 'Where does grandfather come from?'

The Plural Suffixes –*guna*/–*una*

The plural suffixes –*guna*, used in PQ, and –*una*, used by NQ speakers when a word ends in a vowel, are used with several categories of words. Most often they pluralize nouns:

> *Charapa* 'turtle' > *charapaguna* (PQ) 'turtles'
> *Wawa* 'child' > *wawaguna* (PQ) 'children'
> *Ñaña* 'sister of a female' > *ñañaguna* (PQ) 'sisters of a female'

Suffixation with *–guna* (PQ) or *–una* (NQ) may have the effect of changing an adjective into a noun:

ichilla 'little' > *ichillaguna* 'the little ones'
kuska 'straight' > *kuskaguna* 'the straight ones'
puka 'red' > *pukaguna* 'the red ones'

–Guna is also used to pluralize demonstrative pronouns:

kay 'this' > *kayguna* 'these'
chay 'that' > *chayguna* 'those'

To make phrasal constructions plural, *–guna* or *–una* is suffixed only to the head of the phrase, rather than to modifiers.[1] For example, in a phrase consisting of a demonstrative and noun, only the noun is pluralized:

chay wawa 'that child' > *chay wawa-guna* (PQ) *chay wawa-una* (NQ)

Note that when *–una* is added to a word ending in the vowel *a*, as in *wawa*, there is a slight change in pronunciation. The *a* from *wawa* and the *u* from *–una* combine into one *au* sound: *wawAUna*.

Practice 5

Practice making plural forms for the following phrases.

Example:

ñukanchi wasi 'our house' > *ñukanchi wasiguna* (PQ) *ñukanchi wasiuna* (NQ)

1. *ñukanchi ñaña* 'our sister'
2. *chi sacha wagra* 'that tapir'
3. *kay wagra* 'this cow'
4. *ñuka hachi* 'my uncle'
5. *chi mana ali wawa* 'that not well-behaving child'
6. *kay ichilla* 'this little one'
7. *kay ali* 'this good (one)'
8. *chi sindzhi* 'that strong one'
9. *kay chunda ruya* 'this peach palm tree'
10. *chi hatun kucha* 'that big pond'
11. *chi mana kuska ñambi* 'that not straight path'
12. *kay tullu runa* 'this boney person'

–*Guna* and –*una* can also pluralize proper names to designate a group of people. For example, speakers frequently take the name of one person among a group and add a plural to designate the group as a whole:

Faustoguna shamunawn. 'Fausto (and the people with him) have come.'

Practice 6

Practice turning the following singular sentences into plural sentences. Pluralize the subject and then make the verb agree with that subject in each sentence.

Example:

Cervantes shamun. > Cervantesguna shamunawn.

1. *Wawa wakan.* 'The child cries.'
2. *Kan shamungi.* 'You come.'
3. *Pay shuwan.* 'He/she/it steals.'
4. *Ñuka apa yaya taraban.* 'My grandfather works.'
5. *Leopoldo bagrita hapin.* 'Leopoldo catches a catfish.'
6. *Kanoa yakui shayarin.* 'The canoe stands in the water.'
7. *Pay aychata mana kasanchu.* 'He doesn't hunt for meat.'
8. *Ñuka wawki pugllan.* 'My brother plays.'
9. *Ñuka masha shamun.* 'My brother-in-law comes.'
10. *Payba mikya paktamun.* His/her aunt arrives.'
11. *Ñuka ruku yaya chagrai taraban.* 'My grandfather works in the field.'
12. *Wawa kayutui sirin.* 'The baby lies in bed.'
13. *Ñuka turi sachamanda tigramun.* 'My brother returns from the forest.'
14. *Ñuka pani tinahata awan.* 'My sister makes a *tinaha*.'
15. *Pay tukuta mikun.* 'He/she eats grubs.'
16. *Pay kuska ñambita apanakun.* 'He/she follows the straight path.'
17. *Leopoldo mana ali ñambita apanakun.* 'Leopoldo follows the not good path.'
18. *Chunda ruya pukun.* 'The *chunda* tree ripens.'

Culture Focus: Traditional Festival: *Hista*

A traditional festival or *hista/ista*, originally a borrowing from Spanish *fiesta*, is celebrated over several days.[2] It involves drinking massive quantities of *aswa*, which is the staff of life for many Amazonian Quichua people. Women spend weeks preparing the *aswa*, which is made from cooked manioc tubers that have been mashed, masticated, and allowed to ferment for a couple of days. The result is a mildly fermented substance with a mashed potato-like consistency that is mixed with water and drunk. Women also make new drinking bowls, called *mukahas*, for this celebration, many of which are ceremonially smashed after being drunk from. Festival etiquette requires that anyone who is offered *aswa* must accept it and drink the entire quantity from the *mukaha*. Not doing so gives the offerer license to pour the *aswa* all over the person who did not drink it. Go to the website's chapter 5 page and complete the writing exercise based on such an event that took place during a *hista* celebration.

Notes

1. The head of a phrase is the word which carries the most important meaning, without which, the phrase would make no sense. For example, considering the phrase 'those little children' in the sentence 'Those little children played,' one could simply say 'Children played,' but not 'Those little played.' 'Children' is therefore the head of the phrase 'those little children.'

2. Although written in this grammar, many word-initial *h*'s are no longer being pronounced in PQ or NQ.

Lesson 6

Articulating the Perspectives of Self and Other

Kanoaimi purinawn 'It's in a canoe that they travel'
JAREN WILKEY

We have discussed the use of the suffix *–mi* for responses to yes/no and information questions. This chapter introduces a related but distinctive function for *–mi*, as well as a new suffix *–shi*. While *–mi* and *–chu* form a pair of suffixes, *–mi* also 'pairs off' with another suffix *–shi*. Suffixes *–mi* and *–shi* are part of a subsystem of the grammar called 'evidentiality,' which is found in languages throughout the world. In Quichua, evidential suffixes mark one's knowledge source as stemming either from a speaker/articulator/utterer, or from the perspective of an 'other.'

The Speaking Self –*mi*

Speakers of Quichua are careful to clarify the sources of their statements because there is a cultural preference for contextualizing statements within a particular perspective. This means that even the simplest statements are in need of some marker of perspective. Although speakers of English can simply say 'John arrived from Montalvo,' a Quichua speaker would have to perspectivize such a statement as based on the speaker's or someone else's perspective:

Juan-mi Montalvo-manda paktamun.
'(from my perspective) John (is the one who) has arrived from Montalvo.'

It is also important to remember that when using *–mi* or *–shi* in their evidential functions to mark perspective, any word within a sentence may have the *–mi* or *–shi* suffix attached, depending on where the main focus is supposed to fall. An alternative way of stating the sentence about Juan's arrival would be the following:

Juan Montalvo-manda-mi paktamun.
'(I assert from my perspective) that it is from Montalvo (and not from somewhere else) that John has arrived.'

When marking statements with speaker perspective *–mi*, there is often an implication of strong, possibly exaggerated certainty that may be enhanced with intonation and emphasis. This can result in a variety of speech act effects, such as accusing, blaming, and criticizing. Although such speech acts are not usually observed in the typically convivial atmosphere of everyday Quichua conversations, they occur quite commonly in narrative discourse. The following examples illustrate accusations from narrative conversations:

Kan-mi kurita shuwangi!
'You have stolen the gold from me!' i.e.: I assert from my perspective that you are the one who has stolen the gold from me!

Kan-manda-mi kasna tukunchi.
'Because of you we have become like this.' i.e.: I assert from my perspective that it is your fault that we are like this!

–mi + *ana* = *mi-ana* > *mana*

As was first introduced in Lesson 3, a word suffixed with *–mi* occurs immediately before the verb *ana*, the *m-* from *–mi* 'hops' over to *ana* turning the verb into *mana*. The vowel *–i* then drops off of the *–mi* form. Despite the fact that this new-ish verb resembles the negative form *mana*, it has the opposite semantic sense. We may consider the form *mana* 'asserted by speaker to be the case that . . .' as a kind of evidentially specified verb, which is opposed to evidentially neutral *ana* which merely means 'to be.'

Practice 1

Practice constructing evidential *mana* from a *–mi* +*ana* combination.

Example:

Paymi an Juan. > *Pay man Juan.* 'He is Juan.'

1. *Ñukanchimi anchi Runa.* 'We are Runa.'
2. *Kangunami angichi ayllupura.* 'You-all are the same family.'
3. *Kanmi angi wakcha wawa.* 'You are an orphan child.'
4. *Ñukami ani sindzhi warmi.* 'I am a strong woman.'
5. *Paygunami anawn ali hapik runa.* 'They are good hunters.'
6. *Ñukanchimi anchi Puka Yaku runa.* 'We are Puka Yaku people.'
7. *Kangunami angichi Canelos runa.* 'You-all are Canelos people.'
8. *Ñuka ayllumi an Cuhi.* 'My family (name) is Cuhi.'
9. *Kanmi angi sindzhi runa.* 'You are a strong man.'
10. *Paygunami anawn apayayayukguna.* 'They have grandfathers.' (Literally: 'They are grandfather possessors.')

The Voice of the 'Other' –*shi*

Let us now consider the suffix *–shi*, which indicates that a statement is made from someone else's perspective. The following example illustrates a simple statement about a person's departure.

Faviola-shi rin.
'Faviola (is the one who) has gone (according to someone).'

In discourse contexts from everyday life, a speaker uttering such a *–shi* suffixed statement will often add qualifying remarks such as: 'She told Uncle Venancio that she was going' or 'Somebody said that somebody else saw her leave early this morning,' which would clarify where the claim originated. Despite the fact that a *–shi* suffixed statement indicates that someone else's knowledge underlies the assertion, there is not necessarily any implication that the statement is unreliable.

If, however, a translational equivalent of this statement were attempted in English, it might be represented as any of the following variations:

'Apparently it is Faviola who has left.'
'It is alleged that Faviola is the one who has left.'
'Faviola has, according to someone, left.'

All of these create implications of uncertainty for speakers of English, even though, as we just stated, they are not necessarily uncertain for Quichua speakers. The semantic 'otherness' encoded in *–shi* makes it an appropriate suffix for use in traditional narratives of all kinds. These narratives are meaningful for people and are not considered 'not true' because of being based on someone else's perspective. The *–shi* suffix used in such narratives clarifies their basis in traditional knowledge or in ancestors' experiences. Among speakers of the Upper Napo area, and in other dialects of Quichua as well, the phrase *nishka nin*, which literally translated means 'it is said that it was said,' is often used instead of the suffix *–shi*.

The following example is typical of a PQ traditional narrative that employs *–shi*. It uses the phrase *kallari timpu* 'beginning times,' as well as a special narrative past tense marker *–shka*:

Kallari timpu shuk wakcha wawa-shi kawsa-shka sachai.
'In beginning times an orphan child (it is said) lived in the forest.'

In order to translate the perspective of the traditional, authoritative 'other' marked by *–shi*, the phrase 'it is said' is used.

–Shi may also be suffixed onto expressive adverbs, as happens in the following traditional narrative describing an encounter between a man and a forest spirit. The man is alerted to the presence of the forest spirit by the sound of the spirit's ax hitting trees as it moves through the forest. This sound is described at the following link with repetitions of *ton*:
http://quechuarealwords.byu.edu/?ideophone=ton2

Ton ton ton ton ton-shi waktan.
'It hit (the trees), (apparently going) *ton ton ton ton ton*.'

The framing of a story as based in traditional knowledge, however, does not cast doubt on its meaningfulness or truth. Moreover, *–shi* suffixed forms are often used to discuss happenings in the contemporary lived world. In the following example, a description of a fight is given with a *–shi* suffixed form because the speaker heard about the fight's events from someone else:

Fernando-shi Sergiota makan.
'Fernando (is the one who) has hit Sergio.'

Again, it must be emphasized that the use of *–shi* does not necessarily call into question a claim that is being made. Instead, it frames a claim as arising from an 'other.' In upcoming chapters we will discuss instances of *–shi* suffixation creating possible implications that may lead to doubt or uncertainty. For now, however, it is best to think of *–shi* as simply a suffix used to indicate a perspective other than that of the speaker. As such, it is typically observed with sentences *about* someone or something, and is therefore most 'at home' with third person sentences involving a 'he/she/it' or a 'they.'

Practice 2

Make up sentences using either the *–mi* or *–shi* evidential suffixes in the following pairs of words, and explain why you chose the suffix you did for a particular example.

Example:

Hapina 'to catch' (*bagri*) 'catfish
Payshi bagrita napin. 'He/she (apparently) has caught a catfish.'

1. *kachana* 'to send' (*shimi* 'word')
2. *awana* 'to make' (*ashanga* 'basket')
3. *mikuna* 'to eat' (*yaku aycha* 'fish,' literally: 'water meat')
4. *upina* 'to drink' (*aswa* 'manioc beverage')
5. *wañuchina* 'to kill' (*pita lala* 'pit viper')
6. *yanuna* 'to cook' (*lomo* 'manioc')
7. *pitina* 'to cut' (*kaspi* 'stick')
8. *rikuna* 'to see' (*lagarto* 'lizard')
9. *rimana* 'to speak' (*Runa shimi* 'Quichua')
10. *pichana* 'to sweep' (*wasi* 'house')

Questions with *–shi*

The use of *–shi* to acknowledge the perspective of an other is extended, at times, to express feelings of puzzlement, wondering, or perplexity. When people wonder about matters that are beyond their grasp, they will sometimes ask a question with question words such as *ima* 'what,' *imawa* 'why,' or *pi* 'who' which are suffixed with *–shi*. Such questions, which are often unanswerable, can be translated as 'What/why on earth?' 'Who in the world?' 'What the heck?' etc. When speakers use *–shi* to ask an unanswerable question, the *–shi* replaces the information question marker *–ta* which was introduced in Lesson 4:

Ima raygushi rin Masha Elario? 'Why (in the world) has brother-in-law Elario left?'
Imatashi kapari-n allku? 'What (in the world) is the dog barking at?'
Pishi chasna wakan? 'Who (on earth) is crying like that?'

Evidential *–shi* is used to express questions that are unanswerable, perhaps because unanswerable or unknown questions or musings have a quality of otherness, due to the fact that they are outside of the speaker's capacity to know.

Written Exercise 1

Translate the following *–shi* questions.

1. *Imatashi munan wawa?*

2. *Ima raygushi mana shamundzhu masha Fausto?*

3. *Pishi paktamun?*

4. *Ima raygushi wakanawn wawawaguna?*

5. *Pishi bagrita hapin?*

6. *Pishi kurita shuwan?*

Culture Focus: Forest Resources: Cacao

Theobroma cacao, a member of the *Steruliaceae* family, consists of many varieties of trees that yield a fruit which is highly valued and enjoyed. Runa harvest the large pods, whose shape resembles an acorn squash, break them open, and suck the sweet pulp from the bean pods. The bean pods themselves are a source of chocolate. Ecuadorian cacao beans are now exported around the world and used in high quality 'boutique chocolate' markets.

According to Runa, all trees have a spirit, but it is usually the most important or largest trees whose spirits become the subjects of mythic narratives. The following exercise features a fragment from a traditional narrative about a wild cacao tree, whose spirit becomes angry with a human man for presuming to harvest the wild cacao without asking the spirit of the tree for permission first. The story was recorded by Tod Swanson and features the speaker recounting the story. You will listen to a portion of the story which features the words of the man's wife who does not yet know that he has been killed and is wondering why he hasn't returned home. She expresses her wondering by asking unanswerable questions with –*shi*. The fragment occurs at 1:58 and lasts until 2:11 at the following link:
https://www.youtube.com/watch?v=5SbQ4CKWyIE&feature=youtu.be

Please listen to this fragment which is partially transcribed below. Your assignment is to fill in the missing portions which feature two unanswerable questions using –*shi*:

Transcription Exercise 1

Mana rikurishka, mana rikurishka, mana . . .

1. _____

   'He didn't show up, and didn't show up, (and so she said/thought) "Why on earth has he not come?"'
   Ña kasnai shamuna mara indi, ñaaa yaykushkay.

   'Now it was about this (time) when he was supposed to come, and the sun nowww it had entered (gone down).'
   Chi yaykukpi _____ *nishka pay.*

   'As it entered, "why on earth has he not come?" she said.'

Affinal 'Others'

In addition to one's nuclear family, there are terms for the families a person is related to by marriage. Relatives related by marriage, called 'affines' by anthropologists, have distinctive terms and rules for address.

awlla 'all extended family of someone who marries into your family'
warmi 'wife, also woman'
kari 'man, husband'
kusa 'husband'

> *masha* 'a man who marries into a family; primary sense: son-in-law; secondary sense: brother-in-law; tertiary sense: any man who has married into one's extended family'
> *kachun* 'a woman marrying into a family; usual meaning is sister-in-law'
> *warmi yaya* 'man's father-in-law'
> *warmi mama* 'man's mother-in-law'
> *warmi ñana* 'wife's sister'
> *warmi turi* 'wife's brother'
> *kari yaya* 'woman's father-in-law'
> *kari mama* 'woman's mother-in-law'
> *kari wauki* 'husband's brother'
> *kari pani* 'husband's sister'

Although terms like *masha* 'brother-in-law' and *kachun* 'sister-in-law' may seem neatly and unproblematically the same as the English language terms, they are not exactly the same. In English the terms 'brother-in-law' and 'sister-in-law' are reciprocal terms. In *Runa shimi* they are not.

For example, in the context of her husband's family a woman is called *kachun*. The term is respectful and endearing. In Napo it is usually appended to the woman's first name.

Example:

> NQ: *Maria kachun shamun.* 'Daughter- or sister-in-law Maria has come.'
> PQ: *Kachun Maria shamun.* 'Daughter- or sister-in-law Maria has come.'

In the context of her husband's family a *kachun* is of a different status than her husband's sisters. Although in English she would call her husband's sister 'sister-in-law,' in *Runa shimi* she would not call refer to them as *kachun* but rather as *kari pani* 'husband's sister.' Her husband's brother is her *kari wawki* 'husband's brother.'

In the context of his wife's family a man is called *masha*. It is usually appended to the man's first name.

Example:

> NQ: *Pedro masha shamun.* 'Brother- or son-in-law Pedro has come.'
> PQ: *Masha Pedro shamun.* 'Brother- or son-in-law Pedro has come.'

In the context of his wife's family a *masha* is of a different status than his wife's brothers. Although in English he would call his wife's brothers 'brother-in-law,' in *Runa shimi* they are not his *masha* but rather his *warmi turi* 'wife's brother.' His wife's sister is his *warmi naña* 'wife's sister.'

To summarize, then, in the context of one's in-laws, a woman will be addressed as a *kachun* by her sister-in-law, or mother-in-law, but it is not appropriate for her to address her mother or sister-in-law as *kachun*. A man will be addressed as *masha* by his father-in-law or brother-in-law, but he should not address either of them with the term *masha*. The asymmetry of such terminological restrictions reveals the tension inherent in affinal relations, a tension found throughout the world's cultures.

Practice 3

Have a conversation with a classmate about family. Tell the names and kinship relations of the most important members of your nuclear and extended family. You may use the following sentences to structure your conversation.

Examples:

    Ima shuti-ta angi? 'What is your name?'
    Ñuka shuti-mi an Rosa. 'My name is Rosa.'
    Ñukaga kusa-ta charinimi. '(as for me) I (do) have a husband.' Or '*Ñuka kusa-yuk mani.* 'I am a husband-possessor.'
    Ñuka kusa shuti Carlos-mi an. 'My husband's name is Carlos.'

Another Kind of 'Other': Fictive Kinship

Quichua fictive kinship provides another set of relationships that allow people to extend their social network beyond nuclear family and affinal relations. Fictive kinship uses the Spanish *compadrazgo* system discussed in Lesson 3, which allows adults to 'co-parent' a baptized child. For *Runa*, co-parenting may involve helping to provide necessities for a child that parents are unable to afford. However, the relationship is also important for the adults, as it allows them a new basis for interaction. When a child is 'co-parented' by another adult, that person is addressed by the child's parents as *compadre* (which is pronounced *kumpari*) if male, and *comadre* (pronounced *kumari*) if female. The following terms are used for the relationship between the co-parent and the child:

marka yaya 'godfather'
markamama 'godmother'
marka ushushi 'god daughter'
marka churi 'god son'

Lesson 7

Human and Nonhuman Bodies

Amarun kaspi ruya 'anaconda stick tree'
TOD SWANSON

Dialogue 1

1. Antoñia: *Shamungichu kumpari*? 'Have you come, kumpari?'
2. Leopoldo: *Nda. Shamunimi.* 'Yes. I've come.'
3. Leopoldo: *Ima raygvta kasna hamangai siringi*? 'Why do you lie in the hammock like this?'

4. Antoñia: *Wiksami yapa nanawan; chaki tak pungiwan.* 'My stomach hurts a lot (and my) feet are completely swollen *tak*!'

   wiksa 'stomach'
   yapa 'a lot'
   nanana 'to hurt, be painful'
   tak (ideophonic adverb) 'completely swollen'
   pungina 'to swell'
   –wa (first person direct object) 'to me'

5. Leopoldo: *Chuchawasata upingi. Chimanda ali tukungi!* 'Drink some *chuchawasa* (broth). Then you'll get well.'

   chuchawasa 'type of tree bark with medicinal value'
   tukuna 'to become, to happen'

6. Antoñia: *Apamupangi kumpari!* 'Please bring some, *kumpari!*'

   –pa 'politifying suffix'

7. Leopoldo: *Ña.* 'Okay.'

The foregoing dialogue reveals some of the ways in which the body is talked about, especially when it is not well. This chapter concerns some of the ways in which Quichua conceptions of the body differ from European conceptions. When people become ill, for example, they often seek treatments from plants in their surroundings. This is possibly related to the observation that Quichua speakers do not see a fundamental difference between their own bodies, and those of the living species that surround them. Perhaps the first thing to notice is that Quichua uses many of the same words for human and animal body parts:

kiru 'teeth; beak'
(w)illma 'human body hair; feathers; fur'
maki 'hand; paw'
chaki 'foot; hoof'
rigra 'arm of a human; wing of an animal'
sillu 'fingernail; claws'
shimi 'the mouth; voice or language of any living thing'

This may seem strange to speakers of European languages who take it for granted that their bodies differ qualitatively from those of plants and animals.

The reasons for this are complex, but may be understood as, in part, related to the European split between culture and nature. Human bodies are different because they are believed to express a moral and cultural personality which is traditionally understood in Judeo-Christianity as made in the image of God. By contrast plants and animals are pure nature.

Consider, for example, how the following expressions and usages create a different set of associations for human vs. nonhuman bodies: hands pray and create art while paws and claws carry out instinctive acts; humans speak but animals bark, howl, or chirp; humans kiss, caress, and make love while animals mate; humans shed tears while trees drip sap. In English the attribution of animal bodies to humans is most commonly in the form of insult such as: 'He fell into her claws' or 'Don't put your paws on me.'

By contrast Quichua culture does not make a split between culture and nature, and comparing human and animal bodies is common in compliments. Therefore, unlike English or Spanish, Quichua often uses the same terms for the human body as it does for the bodies of plants or animals. For example, the roots of a tree are its *angu* 'tendons or veins.' The stem is its *tullu* 'bones.' The smaller stem of a leaf is its *maki* 'hand.' The nodes of its stem are its *muku* 'knuckles.' The base of a tree is its *siki* 'buttocks.' If its *kara* 'skin/bark' is cut, the sap that it sheds is its *wiki* 'tears.'

This interchangeability of terms reflects differences in the way Quichua people speak about plants and animals. In Quichua the human body is frequently used to speak analogically about plant and animal experience. Consider the following brief narrative by one of our linguistic consultants.

> This is a fig tree. When we are about to cut any tree. the tree gets harder. Why does it tense up? Because it is a living being. . . . It stands there tightening up because it does not want to be cut. When we cut it *tak* with a knife, do tears (*wiki*) not come out? It cries then. Those tears/sap (*wiki*) are crying. To sing (to trees) you have to know this.

Her comparison works, in part, because the Quichua word *wiki* means both sap and tears. In English such a narrative might be understood to be merely poetic, but this feature of the Quichua language reflects a deeper confidence that a plant's experience can be known by analogy to human feelings. Furthermore, it expresses a belief that the boundaries between human and nonhuman bodies are porous, and that bodily qualities are transmutable across the species barriers.

The following is a very basic list of the body part terms you will most likely need to use. The list is generally organized by a top down logic beginning with the upper parts of the body and working downward toward the feet. More specific terms for internal body parts are available in the website supplement for this lesson.

akcha 'hair'
uma 'head'
rigri 'ear'
ñawi 'face'
ñawi lulun 'eye'
singa 'nose'
kara 'skin'
shimi 'lips, mouth'
sillu (PQ) 'fingernail; claws'
kiru 'teeth'
kallu 'tongue'
kunga 'neck, throat'
rigra 'upper arm (down to the elbow)'
rigra muku 'shoulder'
maki 'hand, forearm (area up to elbow)'
maki muku 'wrist'
luki maki 'left hand'
ali maki 'right hand'
maki riru 'finger'
shillu (NQ) 'nail (of finger or toe)'
hatun shungu 'heart'
chuchu 'breast'
pupu 'navel'
tintili 'side'
siki 'buttocks'
kangik 'hips'
changa 'upper leg, thigh'
kunguri 'knee'
pingullu 'lower leg'
chaki muku 'ankle'
chaki 'foot'
chaki riru 'toe'
tullu 'bone'

Practice 1

Hamangai tiyarin 'In a hammock he sits'
JANIS NUCKOLLS

Describe what you see in this picture. What is this man doing? How many parts of his body can you name?

Practice 2

Using the following model, point to five different parts of your body, using Quichua words.

Example:

   Kay man maki. 'This is (my) hand.'

Note: Quichua body part terms are rarely modified by possessive pronouns when a speaker refers to his or her own body part. Moreover, it is not necessary to pluralize body part terms because they can refer either to one member of a set of body parts, such as one finger, eye, etc., or to the collective members of fingers, eyes, etc. This is exemplified in the dialogue at the beginning of this chapter in line 4. The speaker uses the singular form *chaki* even though both of her feet hurt.

Ideophones for Bodily Movements and Configurations

In PQ there are many expressive adverbs called 'ideophones' that depict visually observable movements and configurations of the body as well as other kinds of sensory perceptions. Ideophones are words that are difficult to define within a traditional dictionary format. They occur in many languages and language families throughout the world, although European languages such as English do not have nearly as many as are found in Asian and African languages. They may also be referred to as 'mimetics' and 'expressives' by linguists who study them. Whatever term is used, they have a lot in common with each other, no matter which language they are part of.

They are most often used as adverbs, although they may take over the role of the verb they are supposed to be modifying. They tend to be performatively foregrounded with an intonational emphasis that marks them off as distinctive from their surrounding utterances. They often use sounds, syllable structures, or stress patterns that are atypical for their language. They are frequently accompanied by their own gestures which causes the rest of the utterance's syntax to just 'stop what it's doing,' in a sense, so that the ideophonic performance may take center stage.

The cultural significance of ideophones is enormous. Quichua speakers use ideophones in a way that enhances their own animistic view of the world. Ideophones are a way of letting nonhuman forms of life speak for themselves. When someone moves through thick underbrush and describes the sound of that rustling movement with the ideophone *taras*, that person is not simply adding a vivid detail. The ideophone is, in a sense, a depiction of the voice of the bushes reacting to the presence of human movement. The ideophone, then, allows nature to speak from its own perspective.

Allowing nature to speak is significant aesthetically and cosmologically. Quichua narrative style is therefore rather sparse, tending toward minimalist in terms of figurative usages such as metaphor. The goal of narrative skill seems to be to evoke for a listener the event itself in a kind of cinematic 'you-are-there' experience. The tendency to use ideophones may be motivated by the same urge we all have to share photographs and videos of our experiences. Ideophones are tools for pointing the imagination to the polysensory world of experience.

Mastering ideophones will help you achieve a much greater authenticity when you speak Quichua. We introduce one of them here. The ideophone *ang* describes a mouth that is widely and completely opened. It combines with the following verbs:

ang paskana 'to open the mouth as widely as possible, e.g., to yawn; to nurse (of a baby); to open the mouth of an animal, e.g., a baby bird, to feed it.'

ang chapana 'to wait with mouth wide open, e.g., baby birds waiting to be fed.'

ang sirina 'to lie with mouth wide open, e.g., an anaconda trying to disgorge what it has swallowed, a person trying to drink an entire pond (myth).'

ang puñuna 'to sleep with mouth wide open, e.g., several types of fish.'

ang rikuna 'to stare with mouth wide open, e.g., an alligator menacing someone.'

ang sambayana 'to become so tired that one's mouth hangs wide open.'

As is apparent from the definitions, most of the time, *ang* is part of an adverbial phrase that is best translated as 'with mouth wide open.' The pronunciation of *ang* is sometimes extended, its pitch is sometimes raised, and it is often followed by a pause, all of which serves to dramatize and foreground the image being described. An audiovisual example of *ang* may be viewed at the following link:
http://quechuarealwords.byu.edu/?ideophone=ang

In video 1, the speaker explains how a tortoise that had become lodged in a jaguar's teeth became dislodged by a man who was able to remove it from the animal because of its wide open mouth.

Written Exercise 1

Complete the following sentences with the correct form of the verb that occurs with *ang*.

1. *Llulluku wawa shimita ang* _____ (*paskana* 'to open').

2. *Bagri shina ang* _____ (*puñuna* 'to sleep').

3. *Ñuka ang* _____ (*sambayana* 'to become tired').

4. *Lagarto ñukanchita ang* _____ (*rikuna* 'to look at, stare').

5. *Amarun ang* _____ (sirina 'to lie') *chagra ñambii*.

6. *Pishku wawaguna ang ang kiruta* _____ (*paskana* 'to open').

Impersonal Verbs

This section introduces impersonal verbs. These are verbs that mostly concern bodily functions which are described as happening to a speaker, as if the speaker has relinquished control over his or her own body. They include: *nanana* 'to hurt,' *pungina* 'to swell,' *raykanayana* 'to hunger' (PQ), *yarkanayana* 'to hunger' (NQ), *upinayana* 'to thirst,' and *shikshina* 'to itch.' One frequently used impersonal verb that does not involve bodily functions is *illana* 'to be lacking.'

Impersonal verbs are easy to use because they only occur in the third person singular form. Impersonal verbs that refer to bodily functions and processes often take a special direct object suffix *–wa* that is reserved for the first person. This suffix may be translated with the word 'me' because its function is analogous to that word's function in English. In English, 'me' is a special, direct object pronominal form, as are 'him' and 'her.'

First Person Object Suffix *–wa*

In Quichua, the first person 'me' form is the only person to have its own special direct object suffix form. No other pronoun has such a special form. As stated above, this suffix is used with impersonal verbs. It may also, however, be used with other kinds of verbs as in some of the following examples:

kuna 'to give'
   kuwangi 'you give me'
   kuwan 'he/she gives me'
   kuwangichi 'you-all give me'

rimana 'to speak'
   rimawangi 'you speak to me'
   rimawan 'he/she speaks to me'
   rimawangichi 'you (plural) speak to me'

shikshina 'to itch'
   shikshiwan 'it itches me'
   shikshichiwan 'it makes me itch'

wañuchina 'to kill'
   puñuy wañuchiwan 'sleep is killing me' (i.e., I am dying of sleepiness)
   raykay wañuchiwan 'hunger is killing me'
   chiri ima shina wanuchiwan! 'how the cold is killing me!'

Transcription Exercise

Go to the following link:
https://www.youtube.com/watch?v=FJg2pXNb55Y
  Listen to the segment from a personal experience narrative (found at 1:19–1:30). She mentions various *llakichina* 'love songs' that were taught to her by a friend, using *yachachina* 'to teach,' with the first person object marker *–wa*. She also uses a past tense form of *yachachina* that will not be discussed until Lesson 12. Listen and transcribe the sentences as best you can. She mentions titles of five songs, each of which is named after plants, birds, or forest spirits.

Kantota yachachina 'to teach songs'

1. _____
2. _____
3. _____
4. _____
5. _____

Written Exercise 2

Translate the following forms of the verb:

tapuna 'to ask'

  tapuwangi _____

  tapuwan _____

  tapuwangichi _____

tupana 'to meet'

  tupawangi _____

  tupawan _____

  tupawangichi _____

killkana 'to write'

  killkawangi _____

  killkawan _____

  killkawangichi _____

  killkawanawn _____

Practice 3

Use the following impersonal verbs, along with *–wa*, to tell about some physical problem you may have.

Example:

   nanana 'to hurt,' *wiksa* 'stomach' > *Wiksa nanawan*. 'My stomach hurts.'

1. *chaki, nanana*
2. *maki, pungina*
3. *ñawi, pungina*
4. *maki muku, nanana*
5. *kallu, pungina*
6. *kara, shikshina*
7. *upinayana*
8. *raykanayana*
9. *sawli, illana*
10. *ashanga, illana*

Culture Focus: Forest Resources: Bitter Trees

In the Ecuadorian Amazon the bark of the *Cespedesia spathulata* tree is widely used as a remedy for stomach problems as well as for aches and pains. Runa believe that their ancestors lived longer and had more endurance than people have now because they drank daily doses of tinctures made from *Cespedesia spathula* and other bitter trees. This practice is called *ayakta upina* 'to drink bitters' because of the bitter alkaloids contained in the bark. Drinking bitters is believed to impart the long life and strength of the hardwoods to the drinker. The tree is also said to be a person who heals in a cross-gender fashion. Female patients drink medicine taken from the male tree, recognized by the reddish color of its new leaves. By contrast, male patients drink medicine taken from the female tree, recognized by the pale green color of its new leaves. The night after the patient drinks the bitter tea the tree may appear in a dream as a human medicine woman or man to sweep away the sickness of the patient.

Practice 4

Pain, swelling, and itching are the most common physical complaints one hears people discussing. Answer each of the following yes/no questions in the affirmative, using the impersonal verbs *nanana* 'to hurt,' *pungina* 'to swell,' and *shikshina* 'to itch.' Assume that someone is asking each question about your own anatomy, which will make use of the *–wa* suffix necessary.

Example:

Kungurichu pungin? 'Is (your) knee swollen?'
Nda. Kungurimi pungiwan. 'Yes. (My) knee is swollen.'

1. *Makichu pungin?*
2. *Ñawichu pungin?*
3. *Chakichu tak nanan?*
4. *Karachu shiksin?*
5. *Kungurichu pungin?*
6. *Kungurichu shikshin?*
7. *Rigrichu pungin?*
8. *Kiru yapachu nanan?*
9. *Changa yapa nananchu?*
10. *Ñawi yapa punginchu?*
11. *Kara yapa shikshinchu?*
12. *Ñawi lulun yapa punginchu?*

Written Exercise 3

Answer each of the following questions in the negative, and then supply whatever correct information is called for. If the question concerns a body part, assume that it concerns your own anatomy.

1. *Umachu shikshin?* _____
2. *Ñawi lulundzhu pungin?* _____
3. *Makichu tak nanan?* _____
4. *Pupuchu shikshin?* _____
5. *Maki mukuchu nanan?* _____
6. *Maki pambachu tak pungin?* _____
7. *Chaki mukuchu shikshin?* _____
8. *Kungurichu nanan?* _____
9. *Kamba hachi Cervantes kayutui sirindzhu?* _____
10. *Paybawawapuñundzhu?* _____
11. *Ringichu kumari Estella?* _____
12. *Chuchawasatachu upingi?* _____

Possessive Markers

Dialogue 2

1. Asevero: *Shamungi kumari! Wawata puñuchingi! Kamba llulluku yapa wakawan.* 'Come, comadre! Put the baby to sleep! Your infant is crying (at me) so much.'

   llulluku 'newborn baby'
   puñuchina 'to cause, put to sleep'

2. Valenciana: *Ciertomi ningi kumpari. Wakaysiki man payga. Kangunawa wawagunaga?* 'You're right, compadre. He's a crybaby. What about your-all's children?'

   cierto 'certainly'
   kangunawa 'your-all's'

3. Asevero: *Mana wakanawnchu. Ali wawaguna manawn.* 'They don't cry. They're good children.'

4. Valenciana: *Atsatsay! Yanga ningi!* 'I don't believe you. You're talking nonsense!'

   atsatsay (exclamative) meaning roughly, 'I don't believe you.'
   yanga 'useless, for nothing, without value'

5. Asevero: *Mana llullanichu. Chasna manawn ñukanchi wawaguna.* 'I'm not lying, that's the way our children are.'

   chasna 'like that'
   ñukanchi 'we, our'

6. Valenciana: *Kirumi nanan. Chi raygumi wakan.* 'His teeth hurt. That's why he's crying.'

   chi raygu 'that's why'

7. Asevero: *Kiru yapa nanachik man.* 'Their teeth cause them a lot of pain (literally: their teeth are such pain causers).'

   nanachina 'to cause pain'

Possessive pronouns in Quichua are slightly irregular. The paradigm follows:

First person singular: *ñuka* 'mine'
Second person singular: *kan-ba* 'yours,' pronounced *kamba*
Third person singular: *pay-ba/paywa* 'his, hers, its'

First person plural: *ñukanchi* 'ours'
Second person plural: *kangunawa* 'your-all's'
Third person plural: *paygunawa* 'theirs'

The only irregularity occurs in the third person singular form. Whenever any object, entity, or person is used in a plural possessive form, it will be suffixed with *–wa* rather than *–ba*, if it ends in a vowel. Note that the *–y* sound is treated as a consonant. For example:

pay 'he/she/it' > *payba* 'his/hers/its'
Camilla 'Camilla' > *Camillawa* 'Camilla's'

When a construction consists of more than one term that is capable of taking a possessive suffix, speakers only mark with a possessive the terms immediately modifying the word that is possessed. For example:

payba hachi 'his/her uncle'

but not:

**payba hachiwa ushushi* 'his/her uncle's daughter'

Instead, speakers leave the possessive marker off of *pay* because it does not immediately precede the word *ushushi*. They would say instead:

pay hachiwa ushushi 'his/her uncle's daughter'

Practice 5

Modify each of the following nouns with the correct possessive form of the word in parentheses.

Example:

(*pay*) *wawa* > *payba wawa*

1. (*Antonia*) *sawli* 'machete'
2. (*Fernando*) *chagra* 'garden, agricultural field'
3. (*ñuka*) *ushushiguna* 'daughters'
4. (*kanguna*) *wawkiguna* 'brothers of a male'
5. (*payguna*) *mikya Lola* 'Aunt Lola'
6. (*ñukanchi*) *llakta* 'place, nucleated settlement such as village or town'

7. (*ñuka hachi Fernando*) *kanoa* 'canoe'
8. (*kan*) *hamanga* 'hammock'
9. (*ñuka mikya*) *churiguna* 'sons'
10. (*kanguna ñaña*) *mukahaguna* 'drinking bowls'
11. (*kanguna*) *yaku aycha* 'fish'
12. (*pay yaya*) *wawki* 'brother of male'
13. (*ñuka turi*) *churiguna* 'sons'
14. (*payguna*) *minga* 'work party'
15. (*ñukanchi masha Leopoldo*) *chagra ñambi* 'garden path'
16. (*kan*) *apa mama* 'grandmother'

Practice 6

Go back and make each of the above phrases into any statement that would make sense. A good way to do this would be to turn the possessive phrase into a direct object and use verbs such as *mikuna* 'to eat,' *rikuna* 'to see,' *llakina* 'to love,' *gustana* 'to enjoy,' or *uyana* 'to hear.'

Example:

Kangunawa yaku aycha 'you-all's fish' > *kangunawa yaku aychata mikuni.* 'I eat your-all's fish.'

Written Exercise 4

Fill in each of the following blank spaces with any possessively marked pronoun or noun that makes sense.

1. _____ *pani man Irmilinda.*
2. _____ *turi shamun.*
3. _____ *llaktama rinchi.*
4. _____ *wawkiguna hapinawn wanganata.*
5. _____ *yayaguna purinawn Kwankiri yakuma.*
6. _____ *chagrai tarabangichichu?*
7. _____ *pani mana kawsanchu.*
8. _____ *yaya llaktai tiyan.*
9. _____ *chagra ñambita apanakunchi.*
10. _____ *ashangata mana apamunichu.*

Written Exercise 5

Modify each of the following nouns with the correct possessive form of the word in parentheses, then use the phrase in a complete sentence.

Example:

(pay) hachi Cervantes > payba hachi Cervantes > Payba hachi Cervantes paktamun.

1. *(ñukanchi) apayaya* _____
2. *(payguna ñaña) churi* _____
3. *(kanguna turi Cezar) masha* _____
4. *(kan) wasi* _____
5. *(ñuka) ushushi* _____
6. *(pay) hatun chagra* _____
7. *(payguna mikya Lucinda) sawli* _____
8. *(kanguna) ali aswa* _____
9. *(kan) wawaguna* _____
10. *(pay) hachiguna* _____

Lesson 8

Expressing Thoughts, Feelings, Processes, Actions, and Enumeration

Manduru pod and seeds
TOD SWANSON

The Polyfunctional Suffix *–ri*

The suffix *–ri* has several interrelated meanings. The first two sentences below illustrate the verb *aspina* 'to scratch, scrape':

1. T: *Imata aspingi masha?* 'What are you scraping, *masha*?'

    aspina 'to scrape'

2. M: *Ayawaskata aspini kumari, tuta upingaw.* 'I'm scraping the *ayawaska* (root), *kumari*, in order to drink (it) tonight.'

85

1. Reflexive –*ri*

In the next two sentences, by contrast, the verb *aspina* is suffixed with –*ri* to describe the reflexive action of scratching oneself:

3. A: *Ima rayguta kasna aspiringi wawa?* 'Why, child, are you scratching yourself like that?'

    aspirina 'to scratch oneself'

4. S: *Karami yapa shikshiwan.* 'My skin itches me a lot.'

    shikshina 'to itch'

There are several other verb pairs which feature this reflexivizing –*ri*. Some of the more commonly used verbs are listed below:

apana 'to take something' > *aparina* 'to carry something on one's body'
pakana 'to hide or store something away' > *pakarina* 'to hide oneself'
allsana 'to pull or lift something' > *allsarina* 'to pull oneself, e.g., to lift one's foot out of a muddy hole'

Some reflexive –*ri* verbs have no corresponding non-*ri*-derived verb. For example:

awirina 'to paint oneself, e.g., with *wituk* (*Genipa Americana*) juice or with cosmetics.'

2. Cognitive –*ri*

In another of its functions, –*ri* indicates that a verb refers to inwardly directed cognitive processes. Consider the difference between examples 5 and 6 below, which feature the verbs *yuyana* 'to pay attention to' and *yuyarina* (PQ) and *iyarina* (NQ) 'to think, consider, remember':

5. F: *Sachai purisha, pumata yuyangichi*! 'When walking in the forest, watch out for jaguars (you-all)'

    puma 'jaguar'
    yuyana 'pay attention, watch out for, be heedful of something'

6. D: *Yuyaringi! Ima shinata upichini tukuy runata? Mana charinichu aswata.* 'Think! How will I give all the people something to drink? I have no *aswa*.'

yuyarina 'to consider, remember, realize'

In sentence 5, the verb *yuyana* has an implied object of attention or consideration, namely the jaguar. However, in sentence 6, *yuyarina* focuses on an inwardly directed process of thought, namely the problem of how to make a small amount of *aswa* serve a large number of people. The following pairs of verbs further illustrate this inwardly directed *–ri*.

yachana 'to know, be familiar with something' > *yacharina* 'to become accustomed to something, i.e., to know inwardly'
mandzhana 'to be afraid of something' > *mandzharina* 'to be frightened or surprised'
piñana 'to speak, or act angrily toward someone' > *piñarina* 'to feel angry'

There will occasionally be a cognitive *–ri* verb which cannot be shown to match any other verb:

kungarina 'to forget'

3. The *–ri* of Bodily Configuration

The next meaning of the *–ri* suffix specifies bodily movements which may happen suddenly, or may be marked by a distinctive bodily configuration. In examples 7 and 8, the verb *tiyana* 'to settle, be in a place' contrasts with its *–ri* suffixed form *tiyarina* 'to sit down':

7. *Ñukanchi Puka Yaku llaktai tiyanchi.* 'We live (dwell) in Puka Yaku town.'
8. *Kanguna tiyaringichi! Samangichi!* 'You-all sit down, rest!'

Many bodily configurational verbs exist only in *–ri* forms:

sirina 'to lie down'
hatarina 'to get up'
kungurina 'to kneel down'

kumurina 'to bend over'
kushparina 'to shake, thrash, move back and forth'
llushkarina 'to slip, slide'

4. The *–ri* of Low Animacy Actions

The final group of *–ri* verbs is exemplified by models 9 and 10:

9. T: *Kay wawaga wiñangami!* 'This baby will grow!'

   wiñana "to grow, thrive"

10. G: *Kay papa dzas wiñarin; chimanda kuti wañurin.* 'This potato sprouts quickly; then again it withers.'

    wiñarina 'to sprout, e.g., plants, hair'
    wañurina 'to wither, die out, e.g., plant, fire'

In this function, the *–ri* suffix is used to refer to processes where agentivity, or animacy, is relatively low. This means that it is often difficult to identify a specific animate agent or actor that is responsible for the verb's action. In example 9, the baby is doing the growing, but in example 10, it is a potato plant, which is a less active, volitional, capable being than a human. Animacy is a very important feature of many grammatical categories and processes, not just in Quichua, but in all languages. This function of *–ri* is quite important, as is evident by the numerous other pairs which rely on *–ri* for this distinction:

wañuna 'to die, e.g., people, animals' > *wañurina* 'to wither, die out, e.g., a fire; to wither or lie dormant, e.g., a plant, or vine'
samana 'to rest, to breathe' > *samarina* 'to subside, e.g., any pain, sore, illness, or infection'
hambina 'to cure, to treat a river or pond with venom' > *hambirina* 'to heal, e.g., an infection or illness'
allsana 'to pull or lift something' > *allsarina* 'to be pulled, lifted, or configured in a certain way; e.g., the way the tips of a crescent moon appear to be pulled in different directions'
rikuna 'to look at someone, something' > *rikurina* 'to appear'
uyana 'to listen to something' > *uyarina* 'to be heard, to sound'
chakichina 'to dry something' > *chakirina* 'to dry up'
tukuna 'to become' > *tukurina* 'to be used up, finished, or deleted'

Although these four functions of *–ri* have been presented as fairly distinct, there are cases of overlap. For example, *allsarina* can be both a reflexive *–ri* and also, in another use, an inanimate *–ri* verb:

Reflexive *–ri*: *allsarina* 'to lift oneself, e.g., a foot from a muddy hole'
Low animacy *–ri*: *allsarina* 'to be lifted, e.g., the tips of a crescent moon'

In other words, be aware of these different functions, but do not be too concerned if you are unable to pick out precisely which function is being used in a particular context.

Written Exercise 1

Match the pairs by drawing a line to the best translation:

Ñambi rikurin.	He shows the path.
Ñambira rikuchin.	She looks at the path.
Ñambira rikun.	The path appears.
Chi sisa wañurin.	That flower wilts.
Chi sisata wañuchin.	That flower dies.
Chi sisa wañun.	She kills the flower.
Sikura tukuchin.	She becomes an agouti.
Siku tukun.	He kills (finishes off) the agouti.
Siku aicha tukurin.	The agouti meat is finished.

Practice 1

Make up simple sentences for each of the following verbs, using kinship terms, pronouns, or any basic vocabulary.

Example:

Llakina 'to love': *Pay wawata llakin.* 'He/she loves the baby.'

llakina 'to love'
llakirina 'to be sad'
churana 'to put something somewhere, to impregnate someone'
churarina 'to put on clothes'
aysana 'to pull, to catch fish with hooks and lines, pulling them in'
aysarina 'to go down (a swelling) or recede (a cresting river)'
hapina 'to take; to grab something'

hapirina 'to light or turn on'
hapichina 'to light or turn something on'
takana 'to pound'
takarina 'to bump into something without meaning to'
kawsana 'to live'
kawsarina 'to revive'
kawsachina 'to cause someone to revive'
pitina 'to cut'
pitirina 'to cut oneself'
rikuna 'to see'
rikurina 'to appear, to look-like'
rikuchina 'to show'
sakina 'to leave something or someone behind'
sakirina 'to stay'
tukuna 'to become; to be transformed into something else'
tukurina 'to run out'
tukuchina 'to finish'

Written Exercise 2

Choose the best verb to complete each sentence, and add the correct ending for the present tense.

1. (*chakichina, chakirina*)

    Ñalla allpa _____.

    Kamba llachapagunata _____.

2. (*samana, samarina*)

    Kunan ñuka maki nanay _____.

    Tarabangichu o _____ -chu?

3. (*rikuna, rikurina*)

    Yaku hawai _____ wagraga.

    Ñuka payta _____.

4. (*pakana, pakarina*)

    Ñuka _____ kanoai.

    Alita kulkita _____.

Expressing Thoughts, Feelings, Processes, Actions, and Enumeration

Written Exercise 3

Choose from among two possible verbs to correctly complete the following sentences.

1. *(llakina, llakirina)*

   _____ kamba wawata?

2. *(aspina, aspirina)*

   Ñuka karata shikshiwan. Chi raygu _____.

3. *(samana, samarina)*

   Payguna sindzhita tarabanawn chagrai. Chi raygu kunan _____.

4. *(piñana, piñarina)*

   Ñuka wawki saman. Chi raygumi payba chaki nanay _____.

5. *(hambina, hambirina)*

   Ñukanchi yakuta_____.

6. *(yachana, yacharina)*

   Ñuka tukuyta _____.

7. *(hapina, hapirina)*

   Pay lomokuchita _____.

8. *(tukuna, tukurina)*

   Ñukanchi aswa ña _____.

9. *(allsana, allsarina)*

   Ñuka chaki turui pambarin. Amarun shamun! Ukta _____!
   [+ –wa]

10. *(wiñana, wiñarina)*

    Ñawpaga ñuka akcha urman. Kunan kuti _____.

Culture Focus: Forest Resources: Red and Black Dyes

Wituk and *manduru* are primary agents of beauty in the traditions of the Runa and Shuar communities of eastern Ecuador. Their fruits produce vivid black and red dyes that are used to beautify one's body and hair. According to tradition, toucans owe the red color of their feathers to *manduru*. Elderly people tell about blackening their teeth with *wituk* to beautify and protect teeth from decay. So beautiful and mysterious are these colors that they are integral to creation stories. In Amazonian Quichua, Zaparo, and Shuar origin stories *wituk* (*Genipa*) was once a sensuous human girl. After *wituk* and her sister *manduru* mature through a series of amorous misadventures they turn into the trees that impart beauty and mystery to other species: *Bixis orellana*, the source of red face paint, and *Genipa americana*, the source of black face paint. The two sisters then transform the various beginning times people into different species of plants and animals by painting each of them with their own distinctive red, reddish brown, and black designs.

Numbers

Although Quichua speakers are increasingly using the Spanish number system for economic transactions, there is a set of numbers from 1 through 10, and unique numbers for 100 and 1,000 as well. Every quantity that a person would need to express in practical everyday life is expressed with some combination of the following:

1 *shuk*
2 *ishkai* PQ/*ishki* (T)
3 *kimsa* PQ/*kinsa* (T)
4 *chusku*
5 *pichka*
6 *sukta*
7 *kanchis*
8 *pusak*
9 *iskun*
10 *chunga*
100 *patsak*
1,0000 *waranga*

From these numbers, all other quantities up to ninety-nine can be expressed through compounding. For example:

Expressing Thoughts, Feelings, Processes, Actions, and Enumeration

11 *chunga shuk*
20 *ishkay chunga*
21 *ishkay chunga shuk*
22 *ishkay chunga ishkay*
100 *patsak*
101 *patsak shuk*
107 *patsak kanchis*
121 *patsak ishkay chunga shuk*
999 *iskun patsak iskun chunga iskun*

Information about numerical quantities may be asked with the information question *masna* 'how much, how many?' plus the information question suffix *–ta*. For example:

Masnata shamunawn? 'How many have come?'

If a specific quantitative question is being asked, the information marking *–ta* suffix is added to whatever *masna* modifies. For example:

Masna wawata shamunawn? 'How many children have come?'

If *masna* modifies a word that is a direct object, then that direct object may receive both the *–ta* interrogative as well as the *–ta* direct object marker:

Masna wawatata charingi? 'How many children do you have?'

Or, more commonly, speakers will simply drop one of the *–ta*'s, allowing context to make clear what the question means:

Masna wawata charingi? 'How many children do you have?'

Written Exercise 4

Answer the following questions using Quichua numbers.

1. *Masna rukuzunata paktamunawn?*

   _____

2. *Masna ñawi luluntata charin, kamba allku?*

   _____

3. *Masna pundzhata tiyan shuk semana?*

   _____

4. *Masna pundzhata tiyan, shuk wata?* (*wata* 'year')

   _____

5. *Masna watayukta an kanba mama?*

   _____

6. *Masna watayukta an kamba yaya?*

   _____

7. *Masna watatata charin kamba mama?*

   _____

8. *Masna killata puringi?* (*killa* 'month')

   _____

9. *Masna wangutata rangi?*

   _____

10. *Masna kullkitata munangi?*

    _____

Written Exercise 5

Translate the following into Quichua numbers:

1. 455
2. 1,001
3. 67
4. 789
5. 19
6. 345
7. 1,056
8. 2,000
9. 611
10. 20,000

Lesson 9

Suffixes of Instrumentality, Accompaniment, and the Imperatives

Maytuna 'to wrap in leaves and roast'
JANIS NUCKOLLS

The Instrumental and Comitative *–wan*

The instrumental *–wan* is suffixed to a noun, pronoun, verb, or adverb, to designate inclusion, accompaniment, or instrumentality. Below is an example of its instrumental use:

Hachawan ruyata kuchuni. 'I chop down the tree with an ax.'

In its comitative function, the *–wan* suffix encodes an idea of accompaniment rather than instrumentality:

Faviolawan rini. 'I go with Faviola.'

Practice 1

Practice making sentences with the instrumental *–wan* by suffixing it to the appropriate noun in each of the following sets of words. Vary your person/number usage and be sure to add the direct object marker *–ta* wherever necessary.

Example:

kullki 'money'/*llachapa* 'clothing'/*randina* 'to buy'
Kullkiwan llachapata randini. 'I buy clothing with money.'

1. *pacha* 'blanket'/*kayutui* 'in bed'/*puñuna* 'to sleep'
2. *kaspi* 'stick'/*palo* 'snake'/*waktana* 'hit'
3. *waska* 'fiber rope'/*ashanga* 'basket'/*watana* 'to tie'
4. *chaki* 'foot'/*ñambii* 'on the path'/*purina* 'to walk'
5. *sawli* 'machete'/*panga* 'leaf'/*pitina* 'to cut'
6. *lomo* 'manioc'/*aycha* 'meat'/*karana* 'to give food'
7. *pay* 'he/she/it'/*shimi* 'word'/*kachana* 'to send'
8. *illapa* 'shotgun'/*pawa* 'turkey'/*wañuchina* 'to kill'
9. *hacha* 'ax'/*yuyu* 'heart of palm'/*yuyuna* 'to harvest heart of palm'
10. *yaku* 'water'/*lomo* 'manioc'/*mayllana* 'to wash'
11. *manga allpa* 'pottery clay'/*mukaha* 'drinking bowl'/*awana* 'to make'
12. *garabatu* 'a forked stick used to harvest fruit'/*muyu* 'fruit'/*pallana* 'to harvest'
13. *linterna* 'flashlight'/*wawa* 'child'/*maskana* 'to search'
14. *kiru* 'tooth'/*muyu* 'fruit'/*kanina* 'to bite'
15. *ashanga* 'basket'/*yaku aycha* 'fish'/*hapina* 'catch'
16. *pillchi* 'hollow drinking gourd'/*masha Leopoldo* 'brother-in-law Leopoldo'/*upichina* 'to give to drink'
17. *kanoa* 'canoe'/*yakui* 'in water'/*purina* 'to travel'
18. *panga* 'leaf'/*aycha* 'meat/fish'/*maytuna* 'to wrap with leaves and roast over a fire'

Culture Focus: Forest Resources: Cooking Leaves

Throughout the western Amazon, *llaki panga*, which are also called *maytuna panga* (see website images), are the preferred leaves for steaming food. Fish, mushrooms, or other delicacies are folded into the leaf, tied off, and placed over a fire. Once steamed, the bacteria are killed, leaving the food sealed in a sterile packet. Until opened, the food remains protected from bacteria and so does not spoil quickly. Even steamed fish will keep for a few days in a *maytu* packet without refrigeration. *Llaki panga* leaves are also used to store and heat up leftovers. For this reason, they are usually grown just outside the kitchen where they can be picked at a moment's notice.

Although other species in the *Marantaceae* family can also be used to steam food, *llaki panga* are preferred because of the delicate aroma they impart. Thus they also function as a kind of seasoning.

The Despitative –*was*

The inclusive/despitative –*was* is different in function from –*wan*. The main difference between –*wan* and –*was* is that when a speaker uses –*wan* its meaning is simply inclusive. The suffix –*was* also has inclusivity as part of its meaning. However, an additional dimension of its meaning is that it conveys a sense of discordance or unexpectedness as well. For example, the sentence *Paywas shamun* could be translated with any of the following:

'Even he/she has come.'
'Surprisingly, he/she also has come.'
'Despite what you may have thought would be the case, he/she has come.'

The pronunciation of –*was* is often shortened to –*s* by speakers An additional variation of this suffix is its alternate form –*bas*, which occurs after a consonant or diphthong.

Written Exercise 1

Fill in the blanks below by suffixing the word indicated with the most appropriate suffix, using either –*wan* or *was*.

1. *Payguna aychata, lomota, llachapata, pukunata-_____ shuwanawnmi.*
2. *Kan payta kungi! Ñukata-_____ kuwangi!*
3. *Chagramanda shamusha, ashanga-_____ lomota apani.*
4. *Sawli-_____ wañuchi motolota!*
5. *Manga allpa-_____ awani ali mukahata.*
6. *Ñukanchi kushillu aycha, pawa, pawshi, sikwanga, charapa aychata-_____ apamunchi.*

The Immediate Imperative Forms

Although Quichua-speaking people are generally reluctant to forcefully manipulate and control the actions of others, there are occasions when this becomes necessary. If someone is behaving dangerously, or if immediate action is required, then speakers ignore politeness conventions and issue direct commands to each other. Rather than using the non-immediate imperative with its politifying suffix *–pa*, which was learned in Lesson 4, speakers will instead use a direct order. Such direct commands are appropriate for parents telling their children to do something right away ('Go and get my machete!'), for anyone warning someone else about an immediate threat to their safety ('Watch out for that snake!'), or for directing someone to do something requiring immediate action for their own benefit ('Come and eat!').

The immediate imperative is easily formed for verbs whose root vowels end in the *i* vowel, by taking the infinitive form of the verb and simply removing the infinitivizing *–na* suffix:

hapina 'to take, grab, attach to oneself romantically' > *hapi!* 'take!'
upina 'to drink' > *upi!* 'drink!'
sakirina 'to stay, remain' > *sakiri!* 'stay!'
pitina 'to cut' > *piti!* 'cut!'

If the verb root's final vowel is *a* or *u*, then an *-i* is added to that final vowel:

kallpana 'to run' > *kallpai!* 'run!'
shamuna 'to come' > *shamui!* 'come!'

Written Exercise 2

Go to the following link:
https://www.youtube.com/watch?v=WsYD743QOw0&list=PLLRu2Lfj1Zib S3uTdbPNLEvA3qOPMdpmM&index=2

The recording is taken from a story about the power of a love charm to help a man who was not attractive to women. After using the love charm, however, the man is besieged by requests from women who suddenly want him. In the brief excerpt (found at 2:37–2:42), you will hear a voice quoting two women who use the immediate imperative to convince this man to take them. Their directives have been translated into English. Write the Quichua you hear the narrator say.

Suffixes of Instrumentality, Accompaniment, and the Imperatives   99

1. _____ 'Take me! (said one);
2. _____ 'Take me! (said another);
3. _____ 'I (am the one who) wants you.'

Written Exercise 3

The next recording is taken from a Quichua story about a flood that destroyed the earth, possibly a version of the Biblical flood story. In this version, however, the ending of the story includes an episode about the woodpecker's gift of fire to humans. As the earth had been drenched with rain for so many days, fire was unavailable for cooking, and people were starving. In the following short excerpt, desperate people use the immediate imperative to ask the woodpecker to give them fire. Their request is ultimately granted and the woodpecker pecks at a tree until sparks of fire appear. Listen to the recording (at 2:48–2:55):
https://www.youtube.com/watch?v=9WBoORq9SYc
Now translate the following into English:

1. *Ninata kuwai carpintero!* _____
2. *Ninata kuwai!* _____
3. *Ñuka raykaywanmi wañuni!* (*nishashi nin:* 'saying, they say, he said)

Culture Focus: Sociable Visiting

Working with people and visiting together are part of the fabric of everyday life. In such contexts, immediate imperatives are often used for hospitable invitations where someone is asked to do something that would facilitate their own comfort, such as sitting down, or eating and drinking what is offered. Sharing *aswa* is the ultimate sign of good hospitality. The following ideal dialogue is a model for visiting the home of someone else. Such visits make use of immediate imperatives that order someone to do something for their own comfort.

1. Host: *Don Pedro Buenos dias!* 'Good morning Don Pedro.'
2. Host: *Pasiyai* 'Come in.' Literally: Pass time (with us), from verb *pasiyana*
3. Host: *Tiyari*. 'Sit down.'

Sacha tarabana 'forest work'
TOD SWANSON

4. Host: *Aswata upi.* 'Drink some *aswa.*'
5. Host: *Alilla changi?* 'Are you well?'
6. Visitor: *Alilla mani.* 'I am well.'
7. Host: *Kamba warmiga?* 'And what about your wife?'
8. Visitor: *Paywas ali.* 'She is also well.'
9. Host: *Kamba wawagunaga?* 'And what about your children?'
10. Visitor: *Tukuy ali manchi.* 'We are all well.'
11. Visitor: *Kanga?* 'And what about you?'
12. Host: *Ñukas ali mani.* 'I am also well.'

13. Visitor: *Wawagunanchi?* 'And all of the children?'
14. Host: *Ari, tukuy ali manchi.* 'Yes we are all well.'

The preceding dialogue contains several examples of the singular form of the immediate imperative. To make an immediate imperative form plural, simply add the second person plural imperative form *–ichi*:

apamuna 'to bring' > *apamu-ichi* '(you-all) bring!'
randina 'to buy' > *rand-ichi* '(you-all) buy!'
maskana 'to search' > *maska-ichi* '(you-all) look for!'

Practice 2

Practice the immediate imperative by transforming the list of verbs to follow, along with their possible direct objects, or adverbs, into immediate imperative statements.

Example:

tapuna 'to ask'/*ruku mama* grandmother'

Ruku mamata tapui! 'Ask grandmother (right now)!'

Or:

Ruku mamata tapuichi! 'You-all ask grandmother (right now)!'

1. *tapuna* 'to ask'

   pay
   apa yaya
   ñuka kumari
   payba ushushi

2. *ñawpana* 'to lead'

   kucha-ta
   kucha-ma
   hawa llakta-ma
   purun ñambi-ta

3. *pitina* 'to cut'

   waska
   maki riru
   pita lala uma
   muyu

4. *tigrana* 'to go back'

> *ukta*
> *chagra-ma*
> *llakta-ma*
> *wasi-ma*

5. *waktana* 'to hit'

> *taylla ruya*
> *hatun ruya*
> *lomocha aycha*
> *ruya kaspi*

6. *karana* 'to give food'

> *lomo*
> *yaku aycha*
> *aycha*
> *papa*

Negating the Immediate Imperative Forms

The negative imperative is similar to the use of "don't" in English. It is formed with *ama* and the negative suffix *–chu*. The negative imperative simply takes the imperative form of a verb and surrounds it. For example:

> *Tiyari!* 'Sit down (right now)' > *Ama-tiyari-chu!* 'Don't sit down!'
> *Tiyaringi!* 'Sit down (at some point)' > *Ama-tiyaringi-chu!* 'Don't sit down!'

The negative imperative is typically constructed around a verb, but it may also include an adverb, a noun, or a noun phrase. For example:

> *Ama sapalla tarabaichu!* 'Don't work alone!'
> *Ama paywan purichu!* 'Don't travel (go around) with him/her!'

Practice 3

Now practice the negative imperative with the verbs and objects below.

Example:

> *tapuna* 'to ask'/*ruku mama* 'grandmother'
> *Ama ruku mamata tapuichu!* 'Don't ask grandmother (right now)!'

Suffixes of Instrumentality, Accompaniment, and the Imperatives 103

Or:

Ama ruku mamata tapuichichu! 'Don't you-all ask grandmother (right now)!'

1. *watana* 'to tie'

    kanoa
    kay sindzhi waska 'this strong rope'
    ismu ashanga 'rotted basket'
    ñuka maki

2. *upichina* 'to give to drink'

    aswa anzi
    ayag aswa
    mana ali yaku
    trago

3. *yanuna* 'to cook'

    dzas
    wayra shina
    payba lomo-ta
    kay palanda

4. *saltana* 'to leap'

    kucha yaku-i 'in deep water'
    nina-i 'in the fire'
    kayutu-i 'in the bed'
    pangaguna-i 'on the leaves'

5. *kallpana* 'to run'

    sacha ñambi-ma
    ñuka wasi-ma
    payba chagra-ma
    hista wasi-ma

6. *rikuchina* 'to show'

    kamba ali mukaña
    kamba ali tinaha
    ismu hacha
    amarun

Kamachina 'to Advise'

Runa speakers tend to shy away from generalizations. There is a type of situation, however, where general statements are appropriate. This situation involves advising people, especially parents giving advice to children, about how to behave or not to behave. There are ways of advising people by telling them not to do something specific, which we have just illustrated with imperatives. However, another form of advice-giving involves generalizations that make use of the infinitive form of a verb. This kind of advice is often given in the form of a negative statement:

Amarun-da mana mikuna. 'Anacondas/boas are not for eating.'
Aswa anzi-ta mana upina. 'The dregs of *aswa* are not for drinking.'
Turu llachapata mana churarina. 'Muddy clothes are not for putting on.'

Written Exercise 4

Turn the following statements into advice-giving *kamachina* statements.

Example:

Ñuka sapalla kawsani. 'I live alone'
sapalla mana kawsana. '(a person) is not to (i.e., should not) live alone.'

1. *Kay ismu wasii puñunchi.* 'We sleep in this rotted house.'

   _____

2. *Purun ñambita purini.* 'I walk along weedy paths.'

   _____

3. *Ayag aswata upichinchi.* 'We give bitter *aswa* to drink.'

   _____

4. *Ismu hachawan kuchunchi.* 'We chop (trees) with a rotten ax.'

   _____

5. *Ashka karamelota chupanawn.* 'They suck on (eat) lots of candy.'

   _____

6. *Lluchu chakiwan sachai purini.* 'With bare feet I walk in the forest.'

   _____

7. *Ñuka mushuk hachata shuwanawn.* 'They have stolen my new ax.'

8. *Payguna llullagunawan purinawn.* 'They go around (hang out) with liars.'

9. *Amarun aychata mikun.* 'He/she eats anaconda meat.'

10. *Kay ichushka wasii puñushun.* 'Let's sleep in this abandoned house.'

The First Person Plural Imperative *–shun*

The first person plural imperative is similar to the "Let's + a verb" construction in English. It is formed with a verb root that is suffixed with *–shun*.

Example:
  hapina 'to catch' > *hapishun* 'let's catch'

Practice 4

Turn the following sets of words into first person plural imperative sentences using *–shun*. If your *–shun* verb occurs with a noun, it may need a direct object suffix or an instrumental suffix.

Example:

  ali aswa/upina > *Ali aswata upishun.* 'Let's drink good *aswa*.'

  1. *wira pawa/wañuchina*
  2. *mushuk llachapa/churarina*
  3. *aspirina* 'aspirin'/*randina*
  4. *wira wangana/maskana*
  5. *Kwankiri yaku/hambina*
  6. *llullu apangura/mikuna*
  7. *chi tullu allku/karana*
  8. *mushuk hacha/ruya/ruchuna*
  9. *kullki/anzelo/randina*
  10. *muru bagri/aysana*

11. *hawa llakta/purigrina*
12. *ashka aswa/upina*
13. *payba kullkiyuk turi/tapuna*
14. *ñañawa sawli/kuchuna*
15. *kay panga/yaku aycha/maytuna*
16. *hawa llakta shimi/rimana*
17. *maytuna panga/maskana*
18. *yana bagri/hapina*
19. *lomo kaspi/tarpuna*
20. *ashanga/lomo/aparina*

Lesson 10

Suffixes of Togetherness, Separateness, and Exclusivity

Pugllanakuna 'to play together'
JAREN WILKEY

Narrative: "To catch a *killpundu*"

1. *Ñuka yaku wawata hambini; Hambini ñuka, sapalla.* 'I was treating a small pond; I was treating (it) alone.'
2. *Chiga ñuka rikuni killpundugunata; hrrrr hrrrrr hrrrr kantanawn.* 'Well then I notice some *killpundu* (birds); they are singing *hrrrr hrrrr hrrrrrr*.'

   hrrrrrr 'sound of birds singing or chirping'
   killpundu 'a small bird with a large beak'

3. *Ñuka tay* (pause) *ruya sapii mitikuni.* 'So then I hide *tay* (not moving) against the tree trunk.'

   mitikuna 'to hide'
   tay 'a complete absence of motion'

4. *Chiwan pariul purururururu pawan, kirui amulin.* 'And at that moment, flying *purururururu* it (the mother bird) comes, holding (food) in its beak.'

   pururururururur 'sound of bird flying'
   pawana 'to fly'
   amulina 'to hold in the mouth'
   kiru 'tooth, beak'

5. *Chiga garararararara garararararara gararararararara. Mikunata mitsanakunawn. Chasna uyarin.* 'And so then (I hear) *garara.* . . . They are being stingy with each other over food. That's how it sounds.'

   gararararara 'sound of birds fighting'
   mitsana 'to be stingy'
   –naku [reciprocal morpheme]

6. *Chusku wawata rikuni*! '(Upon looking), I see four baby (birds).'

Language and Culture Focus: Ideophones and Their Gestures

The preceding narrative features several ideophones: *gara*, the sound of birds fighting with each other over food; *puru*, the sound of birds flying; and *tay*, a complete absence of motion. When Quichua speakers use ideophones, they will often deploy a gesture for that ideophone, especially if the ideophone is depictive of some kind of motion. However, one of the ideophones featured in the opening narrative of this chapter, *tay*, is somewhat unusual in that it depicts a complete lack of movement. Nevertheless, even a lack of movement can be gestured. While uttering *tay*, speakers may gesture its meaning with the entire upper body, in a way that indicates stasis, often by bringing the hands and arms into a position of stillness that is then held for a moment. Go to the following link:
http://quechuarealwords.byu.edu/?ideophone=tay

Watch videos 1 and 3. Listen to the short fragments of speech, and watch the speakers bring their bodily postures into a stillness that occurs simultaneously with their pronunciation of *tay*. You will also notice a slightly higher pitch on *tay* followed by a brief pause before the rest of the utterance is resumed.

The Reciprocal Suffix –*naku*

The reciprocal suffix –*naku* is used to describe actions performed by two agents upon each other, or with their mutual cooperation. Not every verb can take this suffix. It tends to occur when actions are performed by agents inhabiting the same spatial arena. Verbs such as *shuwana* 'to steal' and *muskuna* 'to dream,' therefore, are not good candidates for this suffix. This suffix is different from the causative –*chi* suffix because the causative suffix can be used when only one entity is responsible for an action, event, or process. People do, for example, talk about being caused to dream with the verb *muskuchina*. For the suffix –*naku*, however, it is necessary for there to be actions, events, or processes that are mutually brought about. –*Naku* is added to a root before any tense or aspect morphemes:

makana 'to hit'
maka-naku-na 'to fight/hit together'
payguna maka-naku-nawn/nun 'They fight with each other.'

Verbs suffixed with –*naku* are only used in the plural persons, because –*naku* requires joint action brought about by two or more agents:

First person plural: *Ñukanchi makanakunchi*. 'We hit each other.'
Second person plural: *Kanguna makanakungichi*. 'You-all hit each other.'
Third person plural: *Payguna makanakunawn*. 'They hit each other.'

Besides these examples, the following verbs are among the most likely to take the –*naku* suffix:

kwintana 'to talk, recount' > *kwintanakuna* 'to talk, recount together'
rimana 'to speak' > *rimanakuna* 'to speak together'
llullana 'to lie' > *llullanakuna* 'to lie to each other'
piñana 'to speak angrily with/at someone' > *piñanakuna* 'to argue'
kipina 'to make into a bundle' > *kipinakuna* 'to hug together'
tupana 'to find, encounter' > *tupanakuna* 'to meet up with someone'
apana 'to take' > *apanakuna* 'to follow'
purina 'to walk' > *purinakuna* 'to walk together'

hapina 'to catch, hunt, become romantically attached to' > *hapinakuna* 'to be in a romantic relationship together'

puñuna 'to sleep' > *puñunakuna* 'to engage in sex'

Practice 1

Make simple sentences with each of the following *–naku* verbs, using the given pronoun.

Example:

Ñukanchi/asinakuna 'to laugh' > *Ñukanchi asinakunchi.* 'We laugh together.'

1. *payguna/apanakuna* 'to follow (literally: to take together)'
2. *kanguna/asinakuna* 'to laugh together'
3. *payguna/aspinakuna* 'to scratch each other'
4. *payguna/ichunakuna* 'to mutually abandon/break up with each other'
5. *kanguna/kipinakuna* 'to hug each other'
6. *payguna/llakinakuna* 'to love/feel affection for each other'
7. *ñukanchi/makanakuna* 'to hit/fight each other'
8. *payguna/mitsanakuna* 'to be stingy with each other'
9. *payguna/muktinakuna* 'to sniff each other'
10. *payguna/piñanakuna* 'to speak angrily with each other'
11. *payguna/rimanakuna* 'to speak with each other'
12. *kanguna/tandarinakuna* 'to gather together'
13. *ñukanchi/tanganakuna* 'to shove each other'
14. *kanguna/tapunakuna* 'to ask each other'
15. *ñukanchi/tupanakuna* 'to meet up with, run into someone (literally: to find each other)'
16. *kanguna/yanapanakuna* 'to help each other'

Practice 2

Using the following set of *–naku*-suffixed verbs, study each of the images of people doing various activities on the website supplement and decide which of the following verbs would be most appropriate to describe the main activity that you see in each image. Then write three sentences which tell a mini-story about why the individuals in each set of pictures is doing what they are doing. You may need to use one verb for more than one picture. Each picture is labeled with a word describing the main actor or actors engaged in activities. Finally, share your sentences with your classmates or instructor.

Suffixes of Togetherness, Separateness, and Exclusivity 111

Verb list:

pugllanakuna 'to play with each other'
apanakuna 'to follow each other'
kipinakuna 'to hug each other'
upichinakuna 'to give each other to drink'
samanakuna 'to rest together'

List of people pictured

A. *ñañaguna*

 1. _____
 2. _____
 3. _____

B. *kariguna*

 1. _____
 2. _____
 3. _____

C. *warmiguna*

 1. _____
 2. _____
 3. _____

D. *istudianteguna*

 1. _____
 2. _____
 3. _____

E. *istudianteguna*

 1. _____
 2. _____
 3. _____

F. *wawaguna*
   1. _____
   2. _____
   3. _____

The Conjunctive Suffix *–ndi*

The suffix *–ndi*, which is added to nouns, works in many ways like the conjunction "and" in English, but the fit is not perfect. The most common use is to express the idea of natural pairs such as husband and wife, mother and child, etc. The Highland dialects' suffix *–ntin* and its variants *–ndi/–ndin* have been used by anthropologists to argue that the cosmology of Quichua speakers has a distinctive view of wholeness or pairedness. In his book *Mountain of the Condor*, Bastien (1978) wrote, "Andeans understand their body as a gestalt, and the suffix *–ntin* of *uqhuntin* expresses this completeness. When Andeans add *–ntin* to a word it means that two separate entities have been transformed into something complete and whole."

Tawantinsuyu was the Andean name for the Inca empire. It meant the four places *tawa-ntin-suyu* (literally: four-united-place) that were distinct yet united. Many native languages have technical terms for this complementarity. Ruth Moya (1981, 72) saw in *–ntin* the notion of that which is paired in a complementary fashion. Complementary foods are joined with this suffix:

lumu aychandi 'manioc and meat'
lumundi uchundi 'manioc and hot pepper'

When *–ndi* is appended to kinship terms it may express the completion that a couple achieves as a pair, or the togetherness of a parent and child.

When there is a series of nouns, the suffix *–ndi* can be appended to the end of each noun:

Yayandi mamandi wawandi sachama purinawn. 'Father, mother, and children walked to the forest.'

When appended to the number two, *ishki* (NQ) or *ishkay* (PQ), *–ndi* has the meaning of 'both':

Ishkandi shamun. 'They both have come.'

When added to other numbers, it means something like 'the _____ of them':

Chuskundi rin. 'The four of them have gone.'

The opposite of *–ntin* is *chulla* which expresses the idea of a broken pair. A type of fish which has an asymmetrically shaped mouth, consisting of a top half that is much larger than the bottom half is called *chulla shimi*, which means 'uneven mouth.'

The Exclusive Suffix *–pura*

The suffix *–pura*, which is another nominal suffix, is used to indicate action that occurs among an exclusive group. The difference between *–pura* and *–ndi* is that when the suffix *–pura* is used, there is an implication of exclusivity, while with *–ndi*, the implication is that there are parts making up a whole.

Examples:

Wawapura pugllanaku-nun/nawn. 'The children are playing with each other.'
Warmipura kwintanaku-nun/nawn. 'The women talk among themselves.'
Karipura tandarinaku-nun/nawn. 'The men are meeting with each other.'
Warmipuralla yakuma taksa-nawn/-nun. 'Just the women wash clothes together.'
Karipura sachama ri-nawn/-nun. 'The men, together go to the forest.'

Writing Exercise 1

Choose the best suffix, *–ndi* or *–pura* for each of the following sentences:

1. *Kachi uchu-_____ mikunchi aychata.*

2. *Warmi-_____ aswanawn.*

3. *Kari warmi-_____ kawsanawn.*

4. *Wawa-_____ pugllanawn.*

5. *Kari-_____ aychata kasanawn.*

6. *Ayllu-_____ chagrai tarabanawn.*

7. *Mama wawa-_____ chagrama purinawan.*

8. *Warmi-_____ mukahata awanawn.*

9. *Yaya mama-_____ kiwata allmanawn.*

10. *Kari wawki-_____ wasita wasinawn*

The Limitative Suffix –*lla*

The *–lla* suffix has an essential meaning that can be compared with English words 'only,' 'just,' and 'very.' The appropriate interpretation depends on the contexts of its use. It is also a flexible suffix that can be added to different categories of words, including nouns, adjectives, adverbs, and verbs.

–Lla + Nouns

The limitative suffix is added to nouns before any case marking suffixes:

Aychallata mikuni. 'I eat only meat.'
Sawlillawan tarabani. 'I work only with a machete.'
Ñañallawan shamuni. 'I come just with my sister.'

–Lla + Adjectives

Although Quichua does not have a large class of adjectives, *–lla* combines easily with them:

Pay kushilla man. 'He/she is very happy.'
Napalla tukunimi. 'I've become very dirty.'
Ñawi pukalla man. '(My) face is just red.'

–Lla + Adverbs

–Lla is frequently used with adverbs:

Alilla tarabangichi. 'You-all work really well.'
Uktalla shamunawn. 'They come very quickly.'
Bagri tsapaklla urman. 'The catfish falls just *tsapak* (sound of hitting a surface).'

–Lla + Verbs

–Lla does not occur very often with verbs. Probably the most commonly occurring use of *–lla* with verbs is the first person future form used to announce a departure:

Ri-sha-lla, kumari. 'I will just go, *kumari*.'

Practice 3

For each of the following sentences, use the suffix –*lla* on one its words to change its meaning to 'just,' 'only,' or 'very.'

Example:

Pay kullkita shuwan > *Pay kullkillata shuwan*. 'He/she steals only money.'

1. *Wawa wakan.*
2. *Kan shamungi.*
3. *Pay shuwan.*
4. *Ñuka apa yaya taraban.*
5. *Leopoldo bagrita hapin.*
6. *Kanoa yakui shayarin.*
7. *Pay aychata mana kasanchu.*
8. *Ñuka turi pugllan.*
9. *Ñuka masha shamun.*
10. *Payba mikya paktamun.*

Practice 4

Make each of the following verbs an immediate imperative by adding any arguments listed below it. Then add the –*lla* suffix to give the command greater emphasis.

Example:

shamuna 'to come'/*ukta* 'fast' > *uktalla shamui!* 'Come really fast!'

1. *shamuna*

    ukta
    wayra shina
    kunan
    dzas

2. *mañachina* 'to loan' (+ –*wa*)

    llachapa
    kamba ali sawli
    paygunawa kullki
    ñuka masha yayawa hacha

3. *yuyana* 'to pay attention to, watch out for, be aware of'

    payba lomo
    ñukanchi yaku aycha

pita lala
puma

4. *apagrina* 'to go and get'

    wasima
    chagrama
    llaktama
    kuchama

5. *randigrina* 'to go and buy'

    ashka waska
    mushuk llachapa
    ali sawli
    aspirina

6. *pallana* 'to pick, gather, harvest'

    muyu
    panga
    sisa
    chunda

7. *rikuchina* (+ –*wa*)

    llulluku
    kamba chagra
    payba mushuk mukaha
    kamba mushuk kiru

8. *tandachina* 'to gather things or people together'

    aylluguna
    wawaguna
    llachapa

9. *tapuna* 'to ask'

    shuti
    gasta
    masha Cervantes
    apa mama

10. *puñuna*

    ukta
    chun
    wayra shina
    kunan

Culture Focus: Forest Resources: Fish Poisons

The verb *hambina* used in this chapter's opening narrative describes an important method for catching fish by means of plant substances. The leaves of the two plants pictured in the website supplement are grown in gardens. Their roots are pulled out of the ground and pounded until a milky white sap emerges. When rivers' levels are low during the dry season, people will often combine their efforts and 'treat' an entire expanse of a river by swishing their pounded barbasco roots into the water. This sap acts upon the fish by stunning them temporarily, causing them to rise to the surface, which then makes them easy to catch by scooping them up into a basket. *Barbasco* plants, in their strong and weak forms, are both significant for mythic thinking about masculine sexual energy, and also form the backdrop for an origin story about anacondas found at the following link:
http://andesandamazonfieldschool.com/Andes_and_Amazon_Field_School/Lonchocarpus_nicou.html

Part 2

SPACE AND TIME

We now begin a set of lessons which will teach basic structures for expressing temporal concepts such as past and future tense, as well as what linguists call 'aspect' distinctions having to do with the temporal unfolding of events, actions, and processes. You will learn how to talk about habitual, ongoing, and completed actions. You will also learn how to join clauses together to describe sequences of actions, and linkages between thoughts. You will learn how to express plans, desires, and emotions, and how cultural values require you to express the ideas of others through speech reports. You will learn about spatial suffixes that attach to nouns and verbs, and you will begin to understand the complex interconnections between time and space for Quichua-speaking people.

Lesson 11

Purpose, Directionality, Duration, Color

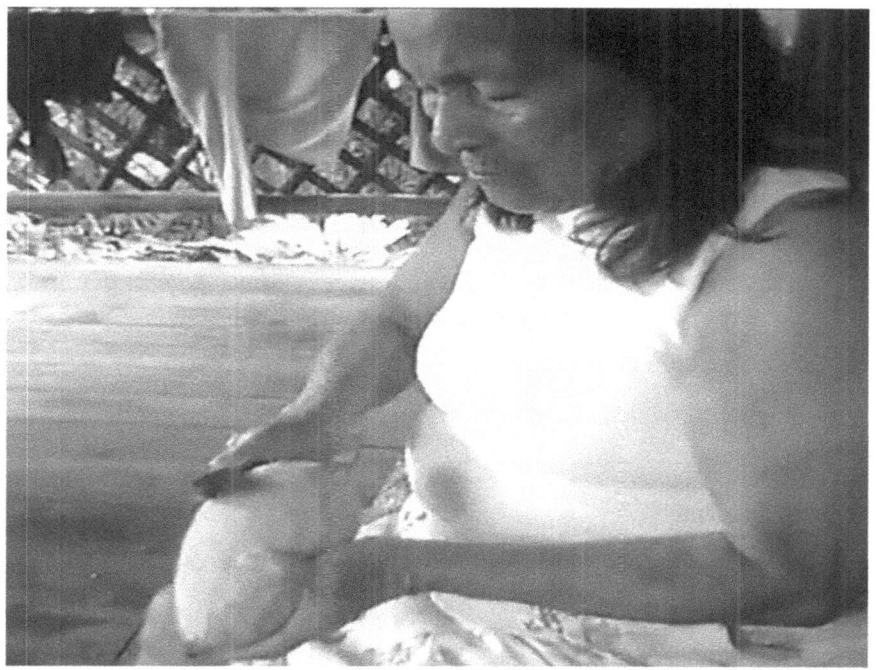

Pitun muyu 'the *piton* fruit'
JANIS NUCKOLLS

The Purposive –*ngawa*

Dialogue

1. Magdalena: *Mayta riungi, kumpari Miguel?* 'Where are you going, compadre Miguel?'

2. Miguel: *Pitunda pallangaw riuni. Kanga?* 'I'm going to harvest *pitun* fruits. And what about you?'

   pitun 'squash-like edible fruit'
   –ngaw 'in order to'

3. Magdalena: *Chundata kuchungaw riuni.* 'I'm going to chop down a *chunda* tree.'

   kuchuna 'chop, cut down a tree'

4. Miguel: *Kamba hacha mana valindzhu. Rikui ismuun. Shaka likiriun.* 'Your ax is no good. Look, it's rotting. It's splitting *shaka* (right in half).'

   hacha 'ax'
   valina 'to have value'
   ismuna 'to rot'
   shaka 'the lengthwise dimension of a split or tear' (Audiovisuals of the ideophone *shaka* may be observed at http://quechuarealwords.byu.edu/?ideophone=shaka)
   likirina 'to split, tear, lengthwise'
   –u [durative suffix]

5. Magdalena: *Ciertomi ningi. Kamba ali mushuk hachata mañachiwai.* 'You're right. Loan me your nice new ax.'

   mañachina 'to loan'

6. Miguel: *Wasii maun. Apagri.* 'It's in the house. Go and get it.'

   –gri [translocative suffix] 'to go and do something'

7. Magdalena: *Dyuspagarachu, kumpari.* 'Thank you, compadre.'

   dyuspagarachu 'thank you (literally: May God repay you)'

8. Miguel: *Ña! Yuyuta kachawangi.* 'Okay. (And) send me some heart of palm.'

   yuyu 'heart of palm'
   ña [discourse marker] 'Okay, then, now'

9. Magdalena: *Chunda aswata upik shamungi.* '(And) come and drink some *chunda aswa*.'

   –k [agentive suffix]

Quichua speakers often make use of a type of verb construction which expresses a purpose-driven, but not yet accomplished, action or process. By means of the suffix *–ngawa* 'in order to' (sometimes shortened to *–ngaw*), which is added to a verb root, speakers are able to express the motivation for a main verb's action. This is done for speakers of English with such sentences as the following: 'I'm going (in order) to buy food' or 'He's going (in order) to get some help.'

The main difference between such English language constructions and Quichua constructions is that in Quichua, the 'in order to verb' often comes before the main verb rather than after it. A Quichua speaker would therefore most likely say: '(in order) to buy food, I'm going' or '(in order) to get some help, he's going,' rather than 'I'm going (in order) to buy food' or 'He's going (in order) to get some help.' Please note that there are reports of NQ speakers in the Arajuno area using yet another variant of this construction, involving the suffixation of *–ngak* rather than *–ngawa* or *–ngaw*.

Although evidentials *–mi* and *–shi*, and also the interrogative *–chu*, may be suffixed to *–ngawa*, it is considered a terminal suffix because it cannot take tense suffixes, and because it replaces the infinitive *–na*:

randi-na 'to buy' > *randi-ngaw* 'in order to buy'
kuchu-na 'to cut, chop a tree' > *kuchu-ngaw* 'in order to cut/chop a tree'

Practice 1

Practice answering questions with purposive *–ngaw* forms. You may use any of the following expressions, all of which mean 'why?': *imamandata, ima rayguta*, or *imawata*.

Example:

Imamandata tarabangi? 'Why are you working?' Literally: 'What from are you working?'
Ñuka yaya/yanapana > Ñuka yayata yanapangaw tarabani.

1. *Imamandata aswangi?*

   runa/upichina
   ayllu/upichina
   masha/upichina
   baylakguna/machachina

2. *Imamandata chunda ruyata kuchungi?*

   chunda muyu/tandachina
   chunda aswa/aswana
   chunda muyu/mikuna

3. *Ima rayguta llaktama ringichi?*

   Mikuna/randina
   ali llachapa/randina
   mushuk hacha/randina
   suni waska/randina
   mushuk sawli/randina

4. *Ima rayguta ñambita rinawn?*

   wangana/maskana
   lomocha/hapina
   ali upina muyu/pallana
   runa/apanakuna

5. *Imawata kuchata hambingi?*

   yana bagri/hapina
   challuwa 'type of fish'/*mikuna*
   chulla shimi 'type of fish'/*aysana*
   tanlla 'type of fish'/*hapina*
   chambirima 'type of fish'/*mikuna*
   kungukshi 'type of fish'/*aysana*

6. *Imawata wasima tigran?*

   wawa/rikuna
   ashanga/maskana
   aswa/upina
   ñuka kari/upichina
   waska/maskana
   lomo/yanuna

7. *Ima rayguta ruyata kuchungichi?*

   muyu/pallana
   chagra/chagrana
   yuyu/mikuna
   muyu/upina
   panga/pitina

Practice 2

Construct mini-dialogues by answering the following questions in the affirmative. Then your instructor will ask you why you have something, and you will answer with a purposive construction.

Example:

Prompt: *Charingichu kayututa?*
Student: *Nda. Kayututa charinimi.*
Instructor: *Imawata charingi kayututa?*
Student: *Alita puñungaw.*

Choose your answers about why you are doing what you are doing from among the following sets of words.

sindzhita, tarabana
ruya, kuchuna
sachai, purina 'to trek in the forest'
Runa shimi, rimana
chagrama rina
lomo, pitina
aswa, upichina
alita, sirina
charapa aycha, mikuna
lomo, tarpuna
alita kawsana
aswa, aswana

1. *Charingichu chagrata?*
2. *Charingichu charapata?*
3. *Charingichu shimita?*
4. *Charingichu chakita?*
5. *Charingichu mukahata?*
6. *Charingichu hachata?*
7. *Charingichu hamangata?*
8. *Charingichu wasita?*
9. *Charingichu makita?*
10. *Charingichu sawlita?*
11. *Charingichu ñambita?*
12. *Charingichu lomota?*

The Ideophone *Shaka*

The ideophone *shaka* from the opening dialogue usually describes the lengthwise dimension of a split or tear. It may be used to describe the tearing of paper, fabric, or a long split in a piece of wood. Occasionally it may also be used to describe a linear marking on a surface that is made by painting or scoring that surface. Go to the following link:

http://quechuarealwords.byu.edu/?ideophone=shaka

Watch video 1 from a traditional story about two sisters who try to prevent two brothers from leaving them by running after them and grabbing their shirts, resulting in the tearing apart of their shirttails:

> *Shakaa shuk-bas shakaa-shi liki-shka-wna.* '(The first) one tore *shakaa* and then another *shakaa* had also apparently torn.'

These two sisters are the protagonists discussed in Lesson 8's Culture Focus on *wituk* and *manduru* (p. 92). The speaker uses *shaka* to describe the sisters' tearing actions. Watch how the speaker's gestures together with the ideophone *shaka* depict this. Notice the use of the evidential *–shi* suffix, discussed in Lesson 6, which indicates that the story is a traditional one and not being told from the perspective of the speaker herself. The use of 'apparently' in the translation is one way of translating this evidential. The *–bas* suffix, a variant of *–was* indicating inclusiveness, was discussed in Lesson 9. The *–shka* suffix, which is perfect, will be explained in Lesson 16.

The Durative Suffix *–u*

The durative suffix *–u* is used to describe an action that is continuous with respect to some other event. A Quichua verb suffixed with *–u* is similar to the English progressive construction "I am _____ -ing." Durative *–u* occurs after the last vowel of the root and before the tense suffix. When the last vowel of the root is *i*, then durative *–u* creates an extra syllable in a verb's form. For example:

> *rini* 'I go' > *riuni* 'I am going'
> *ringi* 'you go' > *riungi* 'you are going'
> *rin* 'he, she, it goes' > *riun* 'he, she, it is going'
> *ringichi* 'you-all go' > *riungichi* 'you-all are going'
> *rinawn* 'they go' > *riunguna* 'they are going'

When the last root vowel is *a*, then the vowel plus the *–u* are pronounced together as one diphthong, and there is no extra syllable in the durative form. For example:

> *apani* 'I take' > *apauni* 'I am taking'
> *apangi* 'you take' > *apaungi* 'you are taking'
> *apan* 'he, she, it takes' > *apaun* 'he, she, it is taking'

apanchi 'we take' > *apaunchi* 'we are taking'
apangichi 'you-all take' > *apaungichi* 'you-all are taking'
apanawn 'they take' > *apaunguna* 'they are taking'

When the last root vowel is also a *u* vowel, then the durative *–u* has the effect of lengthening that vowel. For example:

mikuni 'I eat' > *mikuuni* 'I am eating'
mikungi 'you eat' > *mikuungi* 'you are eating'
mikun 'he, she, it eats' > *mikuun* 'he, she, it is eating'
mikunchi 'they eat' > *mikuunchi* 'we are eating'
mikungichi 'you-all eat' > *mikuungichi* 'you-all are eating'
mikunawn 'they eat' > *mikuunguna* 'they are eating'

Practice 3

Answer the following questions, using a durative form for each verb.

Example:

Riungichu, kumari? 'Are you going, comadre?'
Nda. Riunimi, kumari. 'Yes. I'm going, comadre.'

1. *Wakaungichu?*
2. *Tarabaungichu?*
3. *Kasaungichu?*
4. *Tiyaungichu?*
5. *Apaungichu?*
6. *Waytaungichu?*
7. *Pitiungichu?*
8. *Upiungichichu?*
9. *Riungichichu?*
10. *Tiyariungichichu?*
11. *Llukshiungichichu?*
12. *Wasiungichichu?*
13. *Mikuunchu?*
14. *Wañuunchu?*
15. *Tigramuunchu?*
16. *Rikuunchu?*
17. *Muskuunchu?*
18. *Puñuunchu?*
19. *Shamuunchu?*
20. *Yanuunchu?*

Finally, notice that *–guna* is usually substituted for the third person plural suffix *–nawn* when durative *–u* is used. For example:

Payguna purinawn > payguna puriunguna, rather than **payguna puriunawn*

Practice 4

Practice making durative third person plural forms, using *–guna* with the verbs in each of the following sentences.

Example:

Pay shamun > Payguna shamuunguna.

1. *Wawa likcharin.*
2. *Hachi Venancio sachama purin.*
3. *Masha Ventura kuchamanda tigramun.*
4. *Pay ñukata riman.*
5. *Pani kayutui sirin.*
6. *Apa yaya ñambita apanakun.*
7. *Ñukanchi kanoa yakui shayarin.*
8. *Turi Cezar aychata munan.*
9. *Kan ñambita ñawpangi.*
10. *Kan kuchata puringi.*
11. *Pay pambai tiyarin.*
12. *Ñaña lomota yanun.*
13. *Kumpari Davis wanganata kasan.*
14. *Wawki wasimanda llukshin.*
15. *Pani pita lalata wañuchin.* (*pita lala* 'venomous snake')

Directionals *–ma* and *–manda*

The suffixes *–ma* and *–manda* are used to indicate directionality. The *–ma* suffix indicates action or movement directed toward a specific goal, such as a general or specific place. The suffix *–manda*, by contrast, indicates action or movement away from a specific location, person, or a general place, such as a village. An example of their typical use reveals a fundamentally important orienting principle for peoples' comings and goings. This orientation is provided by the flow of river systems which are described with *–ma* and *–manda* as either *hanak-ma* 'toward upriver' and *hanak-manda* 'from upriver' or *uray-ma* 'toward downriver' and *uray-manda* 'from downriver.'

A major river for PQ speakers is the Bobonaza River which flows into the larger Pastaza, which in turn flows into the Marañon, which flows into the largest river of all, the Amazon. The major river for Napo speakers is the Napo River. PQ speakers' memories almost always involve activities downriver, whether for trading, hunting, or organized conflict. Our older consultants recall hearing stories from their grandparents about expeditions of canoes that had to travel all the way to the Marañon River for the purpose of mining for salt, which was useful and necessary, not only for cooking but for drying meat. These expeditions became a kind of imaginative backdrop for a genre of legendary stories about encounters with giant, people-eating hawks, chain-saw anacondas, and other larger than life monsters.

Practice 5

Practice using *–manda* with each of the following noun/verb combinations, being sure to vary your use of person and number. Use the durative *–u* whenever possible.

Example:

wasi 'house'/*apamuna* 'to take'
Wasimanda aparmunchi. 'We're bringing (it) from the house.'

1. *chagra/paktamuna*
2. *kucha/hapina*
3. *ñambi/shamuna*
4. *sacha/llukshina*
5. *yaku/hapina*
6. *wasi/apana*
7. *chagra/pallana*
8. *kucha/aysana*
9. *uray/waytana*
10. *hanak/purira*

Practice 6

Practice using *–ma* with each of the following noun/verb combinations, using durative *–u* wherever possible.

Example:

wasi 'house'/*apana* 'to take'
Wasima apauni. 'I'm taking (it) to the house.'

1. kanoa/waytana
2. Quito/purina
3. sacha/rina
4. mama/kallpana
5. wasi/kallpana
6. chagra/rina
7. yaku/tuksina
8. allpa/kachana
9. yaya/purina
10. kaspi/waytana

Color Words and Their Extensions: *Puka* 'Red'

Words for colors can be difficult to translate from language to language. The Quichua color term *puka* is an example of this difficulty. In addition to its use for a focal red color, it is used to describe the orange-like flesh of the *pitun* fruit mentioned in this chapter's opening dialogue. *Puka* is also used to describe what in English would be labeled as 'pink' or 'rose-colored,' as the underside of the bark of an *amarun kaspi*, or 'anaconda stick,' tree discussed in Lesson 7. Furthermore, *puka* is also said to characterize the color of a deer, of reddish brown earth, or of the painted surfaces of pottery used for drinking bowls. Go to the website supplement for this chapter and observe the different colors that are all described by Quichua speakers as *puka* 'red.'

Advanced Translation Challenge: The Benefits of Tree Bark

Go to the following link:
https://www.youtube.com/watch?v=0BHdmoZZt6A

Listen to the transcribed excerpt, below, which occurs from 4 minutes until 4:33. The main speaker, using the Upper Napo dialect, is describing how to harvest bark from the *amarun kaspi*, or 'anaconda stick tree,' for medicinal purposes. She refers to the color of the interior surface bark as *puka* 'red,' and associates this color with a state of health, saying that if a person drinks broth from this processed bark, they will look healthy like the tree that it came from. Translate the transcriptions.

1. *Kasna ra-sha apina pay-wa kara-ra llushtina.*
2. *Gustu, puka pay-kwinta, ambi pay-wa yaku-ra upi-sha, pay-kwinta puka tukuna.*
3. *Mana tsalaaa-lla, mana sambaya-shka, mana ima-s rikuri-nga.*

4. *Pay-kwinta ursa-i, pay-kwinta shina gustu vivu, kolor kolor warmi, kolor kolor kari, tuku-nga, kay kara upina ni-nun.*

   1. _____
   2. _____
   3. _____
   4. _____

Helpful Hints

   Line 1: Translate the *–sha* suffix as meaning something like the *–ing* suffix in English. See Lesson 14 for more detailed information. This statement is a type of *kamachina* 'advising' construction covered in Lesson 9.
   Line 2: Can you find the Upper Napo variant of the direct object marker, discussed in Lesson 3?
   Line 3: Can you find the limitative suffix discussed in Lesson 10? The suffix *–shka* indicates that an action has been accomplished. This suffix is explained in Lesson 16. Did you notice the shortened form *–s* of the despitative *–was*, discussed in Lesson 9? The verb *rikuri-nga* has a form of the future tense, to be discussed in Lesson 17.
   Line 4: As there is no Quichua term for color in general, the Spanish term *color* 'color' is used here. You can translate this repeated occurrence as indicating 'very colored' or 'colorful.'

Lesson 12

Attribution, Location, Past Tense

Tinaha awak warmi 'woman making a tinaha'
JANIS NUCKOLLS

The Attributive –*k*

This lesson introduces a very important suffix. It is a bit like the *–er* suffix in words like 'do-er,' 'go-getter,' etc. However, it is used far more by Quichua speakers than the *–er* suffix is used in English. This suffix attributes a certain role, ability, activity, or characteristic trait to whatever agent is implied by the verb it is attached to. What is attributed by the use of *–k* does not have to be

134   *Lesson 12*

an essential or defining quality. When the attributive *–k* is suffixed to a verb root it can then function as a noun which is capable of taking any suffix that a noun would take, such as plural *–guna*. For example:

> *mandzhana* 'to fear' > *mandzhak* 'fear-er' > *mandzhak-guna* 'the fear-ers'
> *purina* 'to walk, to travel, to trek' > *purik* 'walk-er, treker-er' > *purikguna* 'the walkers'

The attributive *–k* may be present in one suffix already studied, the possessive *–yuk* suffix, which could be analyzed as *–yu-k*. When it is followed by voiced sounds, the final *–k* is pronounced like a *–g*. The following sentences illustrate some uses of this suffix.

> *Kawsa-k man!* 'It's alive!' (Literally: 'It's a live-er [about a snake lying belly up]')
> *Macha-k man.* 'He's drunk.' (Literally: 'He's an intoxicate-er')

Practice 1

Practice making attributive constructions using the following verb roots along with the verb *mana* 'to be' (*–mi* + *ana*):

Example:

> *ali/allmana* > *ali allmak man.* 'He/she is a good weeder.'

1. *ali/yanapana*
2. *sindzhi/wakana*
3. *yapa/pugllana*
4. *ali/tarabana*
5. *gustu/asina*
6. *yapa/mandzhana*
7. *sapalla/purina*
8. *hawa llakta shina/rikurina*
9. *taruga shina/purina*
10. *ali/karana*
11. *yapa/mitsana*
12. *sindzhi/waktana*
13. *sapalla/kawsana*
14. *wayra shina/ismuna*
15. *kungaylla/shamuna*

The attributive *–k* is also frequently used with imperative verbs. Consider the following construction:

Yanapak shamui! 'Come and help!' (Literally: 'as-a-helper, come!')

Practice 2

Practice constructions that use one attributive and one immediate imperative verb, using the following sets. Vary between the singular and plural immediate forms and be sure to add any case suffixes necessary for words other than verbs.

Example:

kantana/shamuna > kantak shamui! 'As a singer, come!'

Or:

kantak shamuichi! 'As singers, you-all come!'

1. *wawa/rikuna/shamuna*
2. *tarabana/shamuna*
3. *wawa/chuchuna/shamuna*
4. *bagri/aysana/shamuna*
5. *hambi/tuksina/shamuna*
6. *walo/kayana/shamuna*
7. *mishki yaku/upichina/shamuna*
8. *wawa/chuchuchina/shamuna*
9. *usa/rikuna/shamuna*
10. *manga/shayachina/shamuna*
11. *nina/hapichina/shamuna*
12. *tarapoto ruya/kuchuna/shamuna*
13. *hacha/mañachina (+ –wa)/shamuna*
14. *wawaguna/yuyana/shamuna*
15. *rimana (+ –wa)/shamuna*
16. *yanda/tsalina/shamuna*
17. *mukaha/awana/shamuna*

Written Exercise 1

Construct ten sentences, all using the attributive construction, to describe yourself. The way you describe yourself doesn't have to conform to your actual self or way of life. You can describe the kind of person you might be if, for example, you lived in a Quichua community. Try to make sentences that are more complicated than a basic attributive verb and main verb construction.

Example:

Ñuka aylluwan tarabak mani. 'I am one who works with my family.'

1. _____
2. _____
3. _____
4. _____
5. _____
6. _____
7. _____
8. _____
9. _____
10. _____

Ideophonic Adverbs and Attributive –k

Many of the examples shared in this chapter's discussion of attributive –k feature active verbs such as *shamuna* 'to come' and *waktana* 'to hit.' However, even verbs that describe relatively low animacy phenomena, such as design patterns or sounds, may occur with attributive –k. Go to following link: http://quechuarealwords.byu.edu/?ideophone=lyuw

Video 4 features a painted design that is said to be a depiction of a river which moves in a curved pattern on the interior surface of a drinking bowl. When describing this image, the speaker attaches the attributive –k to the verb *muyuna* 'to curve around,' effectively saying, it's a 'curver' along the pot's surface:

Kasna muyuk ara lluw ñambiga; chiwa rayguta kayga lluw muyuchishka wawata riki!
  'As for the path, this is how it's a curver, (going) *lluw*; look! That's why (the little lines) have been made to curve *lluw*.'

Locative Suffixes

The locative morphemes *–i/–bi* place an object, person, or some entity on, near, or in a specific location. Consider the following example:

> *Ñuka yayaguna, kallariga, Marañon-bi-shi kachita apak anawn.* 'My father and others, in the old days, would get salt (would be getters of salt) in Marañon (they say).'

It functions similarly to the English preposition 'in,' insofar as it is not only concerned with spatial location, but with blocks of time as well, as in the following example:

> *Kimsa killa-i-shi paktamuk anawn.* 'In three months, they come back.'

Speakers may vary between *–i* and *–bi*, which are dialect variants. These two variants have come to be used in two different environments. Generally, *–bi* is used for monosyllabic words and for words ending in a consonant, while *–i* is used elsewhere. Occasionally, speakers will use both of them together by combining them into one suffix *–ibi*. Go to the following link: https://www.youtube.com/watch?v=sIpkO3AGUmo

Listen to the first 15 seconds. Listen in particular for the word *sacha* 'forest.' Note how the speaker varies in his use of the locative suffix. Can you describe the two ways he uses the locative on this word by listening?

Written Exercise 2

Practice your use of *–i/–bi* by adding the appropriate suffix to the word in parentheses in the following sentences. Then translate each sentence.

Example:

> *Ñuka kawsak mani* _____ (*sacha*) > *Ñuka kawsak mani sachai.*
> Translation: 'I live in the forest.'

1. *Ñuka puñuk mani* _____ (*kayutu*).

2. *Ñuka hachi puñuk maun* _____ (*pamba*)

3. *Lagarto mana tiyanchu* _____ (*sacha*).

4. *Lomo kaspita astanchi* _____ (*kanoa*).

5. Ñukanchi rinchi ñuka mikyawa wasima; _____ (chay) upinchi aswata.

6. Hachi Loberto yapashi yanga sirik man _____ (hamanga).

7. Lomota yanuuni _____ (hatun manga).

8. Pumata rikurangichichu _____ (sacha ñambi)?

9. Yapami nanawan, ñuka _____ (changa).

10. Shuk _____ (killa) shamun yayaga Marañonmanda.

11. Ñuka aylluguna kawsanawn _____ (Tena).

12. (wasi) _____ tiyanawn aylluguna.

Written Exercise 3

In the next exercise, use either *–i/–bi*, *–ma*, or *–manda*, depending on which makes best sense. Translate your answer.

1. Wasi-_____ dzas llukshin, ukta wawata maskangawa.

2. Ñukanchi wasi-_____ tiyaunchi.

3. Chagra-_____ riunguna lomo kaspita tarpungaw.

4. Sacha ñambi tukurin. Chimanda llakta-_____ paktanawn.

5. Chay-_____ randigrichi mushuk llachapata!

6. Imata charingi kamba ashanga-_____?

7. Chagra-_____ paktamunawn.

8. Kanoa-_____ apagrinchi kachita.

9. Allkuguna tarapoto ruya-_____ pumata kallpachinawn.

10. Chundamuyuguna pukunawn. Chimanda urmanawn pamba-_____.

Interpretive Exercise

Astana 'to load'
JANIS NUCKOLLS

Imagine a story that could explain what is happening in this picture, or, alternatively, along with a classmate, construct a dialogue that could take place between the people in the picture. You could use verbs such as *astana* 'to load,' *apana* 'to take,' *shayarina* 'to stand,' *randichina* 'to sell,' as well as any others that occur to you. Be sure to use the durative suffix *–u* with at least some of your verbs, as well as the locative marker, to indicate anything that is inside of anything else. You might also consider using the suffix *–ndi* from Lesson 10, as well as the purposive suffix *–ngawa* from Lesson 11.

The Past Tense

The following is part of an interview between Janis Nuckolls and a speaker of PQ. The speaker is describing an otter's chasing of a catfish. PQ speakers refer to otters as *yaku lobo*, or 'water wolves.' Another term for them is *pishña*.

Narrative: "The Otter and the Catfish"

1. L: *Lobo hapiura bagrita yakui—kikin lobo.* 'An otter was chasing a catfish in the water—a real otter.'

–ra [past tense]
lobo literally: 'wolf,' but here refers to *yaku lobo* 'water wolf' which is an otter
kikin 'real, true, authentic'

2. *Hatun allku shina, ña lluw willmayuk man.* 'Like a big dog, it's shiny furred.'

   ña 'and, now'
   lluw 'ideophone describing a shiny surface of any chromatic value'

3. *Sida llachapa shina. Kan riksingichu chi lobota?* 'Like silk clothing. Are you familiar with that wolf?'

   sida 'silk' (cf Sp. *seda*)
   riksina 'to know, be familiar with'

4. N: *Mana chita riksinichu.* 'No. I'm not familiar with that one.'

5. L: *Chasna rikurin. Chima ñuka rikurani Tigri pungui.* 'That's how it looks. I saw it there at the entrance to the Tigri (river).'

   rikurina 'to appear'
   pungu 'door, entrance of river'

6. *Chitami "yaku allku" ninawn, runaguna.* 'That's what (some) people call a "water dog"'

   nina 'to call, name, refer to'

7. *"Rikuichi! Shamuichi! Lobomi hapiun bagrita" ninawn. Ñuka kallparani, rikungaw.* '"Look! Come! An otter is catching a catfish!" they say. I ran to look.'

   kallpana 'to run'

8. *Loboga apanakumuura muru bagrita.* 'The otter was following a speckled catfish.'

   muru 'speckled, splotched'

9. *Chi bagri yaku ukumanda dzas tsup^{h}oomi saltara.* 'That catfish leaped *dzas* from under the water (and fell back in) *tsup^{h}oo*.'

   dzas 'ideophone for any quickly accomplished action'
   saltana 'to leap'
   tsupo 'ideophone for sound of the moment of falling into water'

10. *Chimanda lobo polang rikura bagrita.* 'Then the otter (emerged) *polang* and looked at the catfish.'

polang 'ideophone for the moment of emerging from underwater'

For a revealing look at how ideophones are used, including several which occur in this narrative, visit the following links:

For *lluw*:
http://quechuarealwords.byu.edu/?ideophone=lyuw-2

For *dzas*:
http://quechuarealwords.byu.edu/?ideophone=dzas

For *tsupo*:
http://quechuarealwords.byu.edu/?ideophone=tsupo

For *polang*:
http://quechuarealwords.byu.edu/?ideophone=polang

For *chyuw* (Lesson 4):
http://quechuarealwords.byu.edu/?ideophone=chyuw

For *tak* (Lesson 7):
http://quechuarealwords.byu.edu/?ideophone=tak

The Past Tense Paradigm

The past tense morpheme *–ra* usually occurs before the person/number suffixes. The following paradigm represents its conjugations for PQ:

Ñuka ri-ra-ni 'I went'
Kan ri-ra-ngi 'You went'
Pay ri-ra 'He, she, it went'
Ñukanchi ri-ra-nchi 'We went'
Kanguna ri-ra-ngichi 'You-all went'
Payguna ri-naw-ra 'They went'

This paradigm illustrates the mostly regular past tense formation. The exceptional forms are the third person singular and plural. The expected third person singular form would be *riran. But the correct form is *rira*, because the third person singular *–n* is dropped. In the third person plural, the expected form would be *ri-ra-nawn. However, there is an inversion in the order of tense and person/number markers, so the actual form is *ri-naw-ra*.

The past tense conjugations for NQ work in the same way as for PQ. The past tense suffix is *–ka*, however:

Ñuka ri-ka-ni
Kan ri-ka-ngi
Pay ri-ka
Ñukanchi ri-ka-nchi
Kanguna ri-ka-ngichi
Payguna ri-nu-ka

Practice 3

Conjugate each of the following verbs into their past tense forms, along with their accompanying pronouns:

shamuna
puñuna
rimana
nina
urmana
shayarina
tiyarina
tupana
waktana
chagrana

Practice 4

Answer the following questions using words listed below each question.

Example:

Kaynaga, mayta rirangi?
  sacha > Sachama rirani.
  kucha > Kuchama rirani.

  1. *Kaynaga, imata rarangi?*

      ashanga/awana
      chagrai/tarabana
      llachapa/randina
      upina muyu/maskana
      payba ayllu/riksina

2. *Kaynaga, pita rikurangichi?*

> *payba ushushi*
> *kamba churi*
> *mikya Lolawa kari wawa*
> *kikin ali runa*

3. *Imata ninawra?*

> *aguha* 'needle'/*randigrina*
> *wawaguna/yuyana*
> *ali aycha/apamupana*
> *charapa lulun/kachana (+ –wa)*
> *wasi/sakirina, aychata rikungaw*

4. *Ima pundzhata hawa llaktama rirangichi?*

> *Martes*
> *Viernes*
> *Sábado*
> *Lunes*
> *Miércoles*
> *Jueves*
> *Domingo*

5. *Imata rikurira?*

> *muru bagri*
> *yana bagri*
> *payba singa*
> *payba chupa*
> *payba willma*
> *payba ñawi*
> *payba ñawi lulun*

Written Exercise 4

Fill in the following blanks with the correct past tense form of the verb in parentheses.

1. *Ñukanchi apa yaya* _____ *kayna* (*wañuna*).

2. *Ishkay sacha allku* _____ *yakui* (*urmana*).

3. *Kanguna, alillachu* _____ (*paktamuna*)?

4. *Ñuka mana* _____-*chu lomo kaspita* (*apamuna*).

5. Payguna _____ pawata kasangaw, sachai (*purina*).

6. Ñuka hachiguna sindzhi runa _____ (*mana*).

7. Kan _____-chu wanganata (*hapina*)?

8. Ima rayguta pay _____ allkuta (*watana*)?

9. Ñukanchi _____ palota, payta wañuchingaw (*waktana*).

10. Kayna tuta ñuka pachawan _____ (*puñuna*).

11. Kanguna mangata _____-chu (*randina*)?

12. Kunan pundzha ñukanchi chagrai _____; (*tarabana*) chimanda (*samana*).

Written Exercise 5

The following short section of a narrative is adapted from a traditional horror story called the *huri huri* story. The *huri huri* is a forest spirit which has the capacity to destroy humans. Briefly, the story relates how, when a group of men went hunting, a wife of one of the men was visited by mysterious strangers who, when offered *aswa* to drink, turned it down. The strangers wore green shirts and carried lances, which they used to poke the bundles of *aswa* pulp called *maytu*, which the woman had prepared. They then warn the woman about what will happen, and what she must do when the men return from their hunt. Translate the following introductory segment.

Huri Huri

Runaguna puringaw rinawra. Aychata hapingaw rinawra, win kariguna. Shuk warmishi sakirira wasii. Aswata aswaura. Karigunata chapaura. Chimanda ishkay virdi kamisayukshi paktamunawra. 'Imamandata kasna sapalla tiyaungi?' ninawrashi. Ñukanchiga histama shamunata munaranchi. 'Ña aychata hapingaw rinawra, winguna,' nirashi warmiga. Chasna nira warmiga. Chimanda aswata upichira. Mana munanawrachu. Ñawi kumulla manawra. Ñawita mana rikuchinawrachu, ishkandiguna. Chimanda payguna rikuuraguna aswa maytuta. Aswa maytuga tak montonarishka mawra. Chi ishkay virdi kamisayukguna lansayuk manawra. Chi lansawan shuk maytuta tsak, shuk maytuta tsak, shuk maytuta tsak tuksinawra. Chasna tuksinawrashi. Chimanda ninawra 'ama upichingichu kay aswa maytuta!' Ama upichingichu!' Hatun uktuta maskai! Hatun kumishinta maskai! 'Chawpi tuta huri huri huri uyaringa' nirashi: huri huri huri huri huri huri huri huri huri huri huri huri huri huri. Kamba yayata, kamba turita, kamba kusata hapi! Paygunata uktu ukui ling ling ling satingi. Kumishinwan tak tapangi, ninawrashi.

Lesson 13

Habituality, Movement Suffixes, Delimitation

Napo yaku 'Napo River'
TOD SWANSON

Habitual Aspect with Attributive –*k*

The following is a conversational narrative between two speakers of PQ, about grandparents' experiences navigating the Bobonaza, Pastaza, Marañon, and Wallaga River systems to mine for salt.

1. L: *Ñuka yayaguna kallariga Marañonbishi kachita apak anawra.* 'My father and others, in the old days used to get salt in Marañon.'

kallari 'beginning, beginning times, mythic times'
kallarina 'to begin'
Marañon 'large river in NW Peru flowing into Amazon River.'

2. J: *Ah ow! Wallagai, kikin Wallagai nik anawra.* 'Yup! In Wallaga, it was actually in Wallaga, they used to tell us.'

   kikin 'actual, real, authentic'

3. L: *Kimsa killaishi paktamuk anawra, chi Wallaga pungumanda, kay runaguna, tawna-lla-wan.* 'It would take three months for these people to arrive back (here) from the source of the Wallaga River, with only a steering pole!'

   killa 'moon, month'
   tawna 'long steering pole used to navigate a dugout canoe.'
   –lla emphatic suffix meaning 'only, just'
   pungu 'door, opening, entrance, source'

4. L: *Kaybi kachiga mana tiyak ara; Peruanomandalla kachiwan mikuk manawra; chuya shina, kamba kamisa shina ruyag kachi.* 'Here, there didn't use to be any salt; It was only with salt from Peru that they used to eat; It was clear-like, and it was salt that was white like your shirt.'

   chuya 'clear, empty'
   ruyag 'white'

5. L: *Ñuka yayaga nik ara mamata, "Kunanga haku, kachita apagrishun!" Wallaga pungui paktakpi, "kayta, kayta, kayta, pugrumi anawn," nik ara mamaga.*
   '(When it was time for a trip) my father used to say to my mother, "Let's go now, let's go and get some salt!" Upon arriving at the entrance to the Wallaga, "the pools of salt were here and here and here and here," my mother used to say.'

   haku 'let's go'
   pugru 'pool, well'

In Lesson 12 we introduced the attributive suffix *–k*, stating that it is used a lot more often by Quichua speakers than the somewhat equivalent *–er* suffix is used in English. This lesson introduces another compound verb construction that features attributive *–k*. In Lesson 12 we introduced *mikuk shamui!* 'As an eater come!' which combines two verb roots into one verb phrase. There are a number of other types of compound verb phrases used by Quichua speakers that any fluent speaker needs to be able to use.

The new type of compound verb construction introduced here is the habitual construction, which occurs in past and present tenses. The past tense forms follow:

PQ habitual past forms:

Ñuka upik arani 'I would/use to drink'
Kan upik arangi 'you would/use to drink'
Pay upik ara 'he/she would/use to drink'
Ñukanchi upik aranchi 'we would/use to drink'
Kanguna upik arangichi 'you-all would/use to drink'
Payguna upik anawra 'they would/use to drink'

NQ habitual past forms:

Ñuka upik akani 'I would/use to drink'
Kan upik akangi 'you would/use to drink'
Pay upik aka 'he/she would/use to drink'
Ñukanchi upik akanchi 'we would/use to drink'
Kanguna upik akangichi 'you-all would/use to drink'
Payguna upik anuka 'they would/use to drink'

Habitual constructions express a type of aspect distinction. To understand what aspect is, consider how it is independent from tense in the following examples featuring the progressive aspect in English:

Past tense/progressive aspect: 'I was going'
Present tense/progressive aspect: 'I am going'
Future tense/progressive aspect: 'I will be going'

Aspect is a grammatical distinction found in many languages. It encodes the temporal unfolding of actions, events, and processes with respect to their ongoingness or completiveness. Aspect has already been encountered in Quichua in the form of the durative *–u* suffix. The difference between aspect and tense is that tense relates an action, event, or process to the time of speaking, while aspect is about the ongoingness or completiveness of that action, event, or process aspect, tense (and mood as well) are complexly intermingled in languages and may at times converge within a single suffix. Do not be too concerned about trying to untangle them.

To illustrate the difference between aspect and tense in Quichua, consider the following examples. In example 1 below, the drinking of the *aswa* took place and, with respect to the time of speaking, is over. In example 2, the drinking of *aswa* is expressed as a habitual, ongoing activity that took place in the past.

1. *Aswata upirani.* 'I drank *aswa*.'
2. *Aswa upik arani.* 'I was an *aswa* drinker/I used to be an *aswa* drinker/I would drink *aswa*.'

In Quichua, a verb suffixed with attributive *–k*, when combined with the past tense, expresses a meaning that is comparable to the 'used to' or 'would do' construction in English. Whether a speaker used to do something and no longer does that activity or simply wants to express the idea that a certain activity took place on a regular basis will depend on context.

Practice 1

Construct sentences with each of the following sets of words, using the past habitual construction.

Example:

dzas/shamuna (instantly, quickly/to come)
Payguna dzas shamuk anawra.

1. *sindzhi/wakana* (strongly/to cry)
2. *yapa/pugllana* (a lot/to play)
3. *ali/tarabana* (well/to work)
4. *gustu/asina* (well, pleasantly/to laugh)
5. *yapa/mandzhana* (a lot/to fear)
6. *sapalla/purina* (alone/to walk)
7. *hawa llakta shina/rikurina* (like a highlander/to appear)
8. *alita/karana* (well/to give food)
9. *yapa/mitsana* (a lot/to be stingy)
10. *sindzhi/waktana* (strongly/to hit)
11. *sapalla/kawsana* (alone/to live)
12. *wayra shina/ismuna* (like the wind (quickly)/to rot)

Transcription and Translation Exercises: The Habitual Past Construction

1. Listen to the fifteen seconds from 22 through 37 seconds of a personal experience narrative at the following link:

https://www.youtube.com/watch?v=wOzfcM3ahTQ

There are three habitual past constructions occurring within this section of the narrative. Try to find the sentences in which they occur and then transcribe them below. Don't worry if you can't translate the entire sentence. Simply focus on translating the habitual constructions.

1. _____
2. _____
3. _____

2. Now listen from 4:52 until 5:08 at the following link:
https://www.youtube.com/watch?v=0BHdmoZZt6A

Listen to the words spoken by a woman who is explaining how roasted tree bark scrapings helped her children to be alert and get good grades in school. Try to transcribe and translate her sentences, while identifying the three habitual past constructions in this brief segment.

1. _____
   _____
2. _____
   _____
3. _____
   _____

The Cislocative Suffix *–mu*

The verbal suffix *–mu* indicates that an action is returning to its point of origin. A possible, but not necessary implication of this meaning is that it includes the idea of motion or action toward a speaker. As a specification of verbal motion, it may be thought of as a kind of spatially completed cycle for actions. Just as there is a temporal marking for what has been completed in the past, present, and future, there is also a cyclical returning to a spatial starting point.

Consider the following sentences from a narrative of personal experience. The speaker relates a frightening incident during a short trip she and others had taken, involving an encounter that her husband had with a deadly snake:

Taruga kachi-gama paktaranchi chishita. 'We arrived as far as Deer Salt in the afternoon.'
–gama 'as far as'

A bit later in the narrative, the speaker relates how her husband had, once they arrived, gone looking for something to eat, only to return to his original starting point, having encountered the deadly snake:

Kungaylla paktamura Tito. Tsala ñawiyuk ara. 'Suddenly Tito came back. His face was pale.'
kungaylla 'suddenly'
tsala 'pale'

The suffixation of *–mu* on *paktana* 'to arrive' encodes the idea of coming back to an original starting point. In this instance, Tito arrived back at the place where his wife and others waited for him

Other examples of how verbs' meanings change as a result of the suffixation of *–mu*:

shitana 'to throw' > *shitamuna* 'to throw back to a point of origin'
apana 'to take' > *apamuna* 'to bring'
hatarina 'to get up' > *hatarimuna* 'to get back up again (i.e., to lie or fall down and then get back up again)'
kungarina 'to forget' > *kungarimuna* 'to forget to bring something back home, e.g., to take something away with you and forget it there'
paktana 'to arrive at a destination' > *paktamuna* 'to come home; to arrive back at the starting point'
pushana 'to take a person or group of people to some destination' > *pushamuna* 'to bring a person or group of people back home or back to a starting point'
yaykuna 'to enter' > *yaykumuna* 'to come back in after going out'
katina 'to follow' > *katimuna* 'to follow a person back to their home or starting place'
rikuna 'to look' > *rikumuna* 'to turn and look back'
rikurina 'to appear' > *rikurimuna* 'to reappear, as the sun at sunrise'
tigrana 'to return' > *tigramuna* 'to return here to a starting place'
uyarina 'to be heard, to sound' > *uyarimuna* 'to sound in the direction of a listener, or speaker; said of the sound of airplanes or motorized canoes approaching'

The suffix *–mu* may also be used with verbs that express the cyclical movement of natural phenomena returning to a starting point:

tamya urma-mu-n 'rain falls'
indi llukshi-mu-n 'the sun comes up'

Verbs suffixed with *–mu* may be further suffixed with durative *–u* as long as the action is not accomplished quickly or instantaneously. The durative *–u* would occur right after the *–mu* suffix, as it does below, where an ongoing, rather than an accomplished arrival is encoded by the second example:

Canelosmanda paktamun. 'He/she has arrived from Canelos.'
Canelosmanda paktamu-u-n. 'He/she is (in the process of) arriving from Canelos.'

The Translocative Suffix *–gri*

The suffix *–gri* is used to refer to an action that is performed by transferring oneself to another location. It can be roughly understood as a 'to-go-and-do-something' suffix. Although *–mu* and *–gri* are not perfect semantic opposites, they can be contrasted in two ways. *–Gri* is usually used for actions that move away from a speaker, while *–mu* suffixed verbs often involve movement toward a speaker. They also contrast with respect to their grammatical aspect. Verbs suffixed with *–gri* typically refer to punctual, instantaneous actions and can therefore be modified by the ideophonic adverb *dzas*, as well as other adverbs that mean 'quickly' such as *ukta* and *wayra shina*.

For the same reason that *–gri*-suffixed verbs may be modified by *dzas*, *ukta*, or *wayra shina*, they may not be suffixed with the durative aspect marker *–u*, which would contradict the immediate meaning of adverbs having to do with sudden actions.

Practice 2

Make up sentences for each of the following verbs, adding the *–gri* suffix. Each of your sentences should make use of an appropriate adverb such as *dzas*, *wayra shina*, or *ukta*. Your sentences may make use of any type of verb that you have so far learned. A particularly appropriate verb for such a sentence would be an imperative, as in the following example:

Example:

maskana 'to search for'
Maytuna pangata ukta maskagrichi! ('You-all) go quickly and search for roasting leaves!'

1. *apana* 'to take'
2. *tiyarina* 'to sit down'
3. *pushana* 'to fetch'
4. *rikuna* 'to see'
5. *puñuna* 'to sleep'
6. *anchuchina* 'to remove, take off'
7. *llapina* 'to squeeze *aswa* pulp'
8. *kuchuna* 'to chop down a tree'
9. *allmana* 'to weed'
10. *taksana* 'to wash clothes'

Practice 3

Complete the following sentences by inflecting the verb for any person/number markers, and, considering the verb's meaning, add a durative *–u* if appropriate.

Example:

Ama motolo rukuta _____ (*wañuchigrina*)

An appropriate way to inflect this verb would be as follows, with no durative *–u*, since the verb is suffixed with *–gri*:

Ama motolo rukuta wañuchigrichu! 'Don't (you) go and kill that big pit viper!'

Once you have determined, based on the verb's meaning and context, whether it is appropriate or not to add durative *–u*, then, if the sentence does not already have an adverb, add any adverb that would be an appropriate modifier for each verb.

Example:

Ama motolo rukuta wañuchigrichu! > Ama ukta wañuchigrichu motolo rukuta!

1. *Urkuta* _____ (*sikagrina*)
2. *Urkumanda* _____ (*raykumuna* 'to descend')
3. *Sachamanda* _____ (*llukshigrina*)
4. *Motolo kiruta* _____ (*apamuna*)

5. Purun ñambii wawata _____ (ñawpagrina)
6. Sachai _____ (purigrina)
7. Alimanda _____ (llukamuna)
8. Dzas _____ (kallpagrina)
9. Tarugata _____ (kallpachigrina)
10. Ama _____-chu (urmagrina)
11. Ama tutai _____ (paktamuna)
12. Kunan _____ (tarabana)
13. Kunan _____ (tarabagrina) sachama
14. _____ (randigrina) kachita.
15. Uktumanda _____ (yaykumuna)
16. Ama ñuka mashata _____ (rimana)
17. Aswata _____ (llapigrina) ayllugunata upichingaw
18. Hatun chagrata _____ (kuchugrina)

The –*gama*, –*kta*, and –*ta*/–*ra* Adverbial Suffixes

The –*gama* and –*kta* suffixes both encode an idea of 'until.' The suffix –*gama* is the most unrestricted, as it may attach to any word class to indicate the idea that a spatial or temporal limit has been reached. In the first example below, a spatial limit is demarcated with –*gama* as the speaker relates how her father used to travel as far as the Marañon River in Peru.

–*Gama* for a Spatial Limit:

Ñuka yaya yapa purik mara Marañon-gama. 'My father used to travel as far as the Marañon River.'

In the next example, –*gama* specifies a temporal limit.

–*Gama* for a Temporal Limit:

Ñukanchi sakirinchi kayagama. 'We stay until tomorrow.'

The suffix –*kta* differs mainly from –*gama* insofar as it attaches to verbs for the purpose of turning them into adverbs. A verb suffixed with –*kta* has a completive sense insofar as the verb's action is now understood as having happened to the most complete extent possible. *–Gama*, by contrast, is affixable to nouns, and is more often used when a spatial limit has been reached. Consider how adding *–kta* to verb roots changes the meanings below:

illana 'to be lacking' > *illakta* 'until gone'
ismuna 'to rot' > *ismukta* 'until rotted'
sambayana 'to become tired' > *sambayakta* 'until tired out'
saksana 'to be full of food' > *saksakta* 'in a state of having eaten as much as one can'

Culture Focus: Forest Resources: Peach Palm Fruit

Morete palm trees grow clusters of maroon colored fruits, which can be viewed in the website supplement, that have been compared to hand grenades in terms of their shape. Between the large seed and hard scaly skin is an orange flesh with a squash-like consistency and a pungent sweet taste. *Moretes* are prized as a fruit by humans, birds, and animals. When they are ripe, the fruits drop to the ground. After being washed and softened in hot water the outer skin is peeled off and the meat consumed. *Moretes* bear fruit in December and January. In the wild, *moretes* flourish in swampy areas where they become groves called a *moretal* or a *morete cocha* (literally: '*morete* lake'). *Morete* trees are capable of actually growing in water for large parts of the year. Because the swamp limits access by hunters and the abundant fruit provides a wealth of food, *moretales* often become havens for mammals and birds such as macaws and other parrots. *Moretales* have an uncanny quality for many Amazonian people because they are identified as the home of anacondas with all their ambivalent religious significance.

Practice 4

Go to the following link:
https://www.youtube.com/watch?v=wN1NNJgJUXA&feature=youtu.be
 Listen and transcribe a brief section of a narrative, from 18 until 22 seconds, which features a *–kta* suffixed verb, from a traditional story about a human woman who becomes the wife of a tapir. The tapir manages to seduce the woman, in part, by giving her gifts of baskets full of *morete* fruit. In this segment, the narrator mentions how full these baskets of *morete* fruit were.

Transcription:

Written Exercise 1

Complete each of the following sentences with the best *–kta* adverb, choosing from *saksakta* 'full of food,' *sambayakta* 'completely tired,' *ismukta*, 'completely rotted,' and *illakta* 'until gone':

1. _____ *tarabarani.*
2. _____ *mikurani.*
3. *Kiwa* _____ *allmauranchi.*
4. *Chi amarun* _____ *wañura.*

The final suffix to be discussed, the adverbial *–ta* (PQ)/*–ra* (NQ), addresses yet another function for this suffix, which we have already met, in the form of the direct object marker *–ta/ra*, as well as the interrogative *–ta/ra* for information questions. The adverbial *–ta/–ra* suffix may be used to turn adjectives into adverbs:

ali 'good' > *alita* 'well'
sindzhi 'strong' > *sindzhita* 'strongly'
ñañu 'narrow' > *ñañuta* 'narrowly'
chulla 'uneven' > *chullata* 'unevenly'
chuya 'clear, empty, clean' > *chuyata* 'clearly, cleanly'
ichilla 'little' > *ichillata* 'slightly, incompletely'
iridza 'ugly > *iridazta* 'uglily, scarily, badly'

Written Exercise 2

Construct sentences using the following *–ta* or *–ra* suffixed adverbs together with a dialect-appropriate form of the verb in parentheses.

1. *iridzata* (*muskuna* 'to dream')
2. *alira* (*allmana* 'to weed')
3. *ichillata* (*kwintana* 'to speak')
4. *chuyara* (*sakirina* 'to remain)
5. *sindzhita* (*tarabana* 'to work')

Lesson 14

The Coreference Suffix –*sha*

Rayu sisa 'lightening flower'
TOD SWANSON

Anyone wanting to become fluent in Quichua will need to become comfortable with the use of adverbs and adverbial phrases. This may be difficult for speakers of English because the English language does not emphasize adverbs. Creative writers are told to avoid them. Formal approaches to grammar do not acknowledge adverbs as a significant word class. Some linguists consider adverbs to be a kind of residual category into which anything not identifiable as a noun, pronoun, adjective, or verb may be relegated.

158 *Lesson 14*

The reasons for all of this are complex, and probably have to do with the ways in which the English language tends to encode much information within a verb that in other languages is expressed by means of an adverb. Ideophones, which were introduced in Lesson 12, are one very important type of adverb for Quichua speakers. When verbs are suffixed with the attributive *–k* to form more complex verb phrases, as in *Mikuk shamui!* 'As an eater, come!' the attributive verb 'as an eater' may be regarded as adverbial in its function, since it modifies the main verb. Main verbs, or what linguists sometimes call 'finite verbs,' are verbs that have had some kind of person/tense marker added to them.

In Quichua, main verbs are quite often modified by some kind of adverb, which encodes manner of action or temporal dimensions of that action. The subject of this lesson is the *–sha* suffix, which may have adverb-like functions. It indicates that the action of the verb to which it is attached is performed by the same agent as the main verb. There is no comparable suffix in English. In the following traditional narrative about a man who tries to outsmart a forest spirit, but ends up, instead, being outsmarted by it, there are many *–sha* suffixed verbs used. Consider the importance of the *–sha* suffix in the following traditional tale meant to provoke laughter, about a mischievous forest spirit (*supay*) called the *Uchutika*.

Narrative: Uchutika Supay

1. *Mikunata maska-sha purik ara. Pukunata hapisha rira sachama.* 'Looking for food he would walk. Taking his blowgun (a man) went to the forest.'

    –sha coreference suffix
    pukuna 'blowgun' (noun), 'to blow with a blowgun' (verb)

2. *Sachama risha, sikwangata wañuschisha, tigramura.* 'Going to the forest, killing a toucan bird, he headed back.'

    sikwanga 'toucan bird'

3. *Yapashi ton ton ton ton ton ton ton takasha purik ara; washama y ñawpama; washama y ñawpamashi takasha purik ara.* '(Something) was hitting *ton ton ton ton ton ton ton*, a lot, as it walked; to the rear and to the front; to the rear and to the front (of the man) it hit as it walked.'

    washa 'behind, after'
    ñawpa 'in front of, before'
    takana 'to touch, hit' (also metaphorical of intercourse)

4. *"Imashi kasna takasha puriwan?" nira.* '"What on earth is hitting like that as it walks with me?" he said.'

5. *Win llatanasha, payba sikwangata warkura hawai.* 'Taking off everything, he hung his toucan above (on a tree branch).'

> *win* 'ideophone meaning all or every'
> *llatanana* 'to undress'
> *warkuna* 'to hang, suspend'
> *hawa* 'on top, above'

6. *Chasna rasha, payga kasna tay sirira; mana samashachu sirira. "Imashi shamunga?" nisha, chapara.* 'Having done that, he laid there *tay* (not moving) like this; he laid there not even breathing. Thinking "what in the world is going to come?" he waited.'

> *tay* 'ideophone for a complete lack of movement'
> *samana* 'to breathe'
> *chapana* 'to wait'

7. *Supayga wax wax wax wax wax wax wax waxshi uyarimura, ña runa shina uyarimura.* 'The spirit (came toward him) sounding *wax wax wax wax wax wax wax*, like a person it sounded.'

> *supay* 'spirit'

8. *Kay takasha purik supay ponzo umayuk shara.* 'This hitting-as-it-walks *supay* was a frizzy haired one.'

> *ponzo* 'frizzy haired'

9. *Runata rikusha, tukuytashi gustara. "Kaymandachu mikuk an? Kaymandachu samak an?" Chasna rimarisha gustaura runata.* 'Seeing the man, it marveled at every (part of his body). "Does he eat from here? Does he breathe from here?" Talking like that to himself, he admired the man.'

> *rimarina* 'to speak, talk to oneself'

–*Sha* Verbs: Varying Sequential Relations with Main Verbs

The coreference suffix –*sha* is suffixed to verb roots, and transforms them into adverb-like words. We consider them 'adverb-like' because adverbs are such a varied class of expressions, and are often a kind of 'last-resort' category used when no other word class would do. A –*sha* form can be translated with the English gerundial suffix –*ing*. The action of a –*sha* suffixed verb can take place at the same time as the action of the main verb, or independently of the action of the main verb. Despite the fact that tensed verbs are called 'main verbs,' –*sha* verbs can make major semantic contributions to a verb phrase. –*Sha* suffixed verbs may also have a variety of temporal relations with their main verbs.

In line 3 of the *Uchutika Supay* narrative, the action of the –*sha* verb *takasha* 'hitting' and that of the main verb *purina* 'to trek, walk,' take place simultaneously:

Yapashi ton ton ton ton ton ton ton takasha purik ara. '(Something) was hitting *ton ton ton ton ton ton ton* a lot, as it walked . . .'

By contrast, in line 2, the actions of the –*sha* verbs are independently performed actions, represented in an orderly sequence: the man first goes to the forest, then kills the toucan, then returns:

Sachama risha, sikwangata wañuschisha, tigramura. 'Going to the forest, killing a toucan bird, he headed back.'

In some instances, however, it may be difficult to decide whether actions are inextricably linked, or clearly separable. In the following example, the actions of tripping and falling seem difficult to separate conceptually:

Niktyasha urmara. 'Tripping, he/she/it fell.'

Another example of a –*sha* suffixed verb's action occurring simultaneously with a main verb can be heard at the following link:
http://quechuarealwords.byu.edu/?ideophone=shun
The speaker uses the ideophone *shun* to depict the snoring sound of an armadillo and then states, using a –*sha* suffixed verb: *Ronkasha puñun*! 'Snoring, it sleeps!'

–*Sha* Verbs: Facilitating Action of Main Verbs

A –*sha* verb can be linked with its main verb in a variety of ways. Sometimes a –*sha* verb indicates the reason or purpose for the action of the main verb. In the next two sentences, the –*sha* verb describes a way of thinking, or an action, which led to the action, or nonaction, of the verb in the main clause:

1. *Chita mandzhasha, payguna wagrata mana illapanawrachu.* 'Because they were afraid of it, they didn't shoot the tapir.'

2. *Ukuchata hapishaga churaranchi latai.* 'Grabbing a mouse we put it in the tin container.'

Another type of *–sha* linkage may be translated by an if/then or a 'when' construction in English:

3. *Animalguna pay raykashaga aysan maymandas.* 'If he's hungry/when he's hungry, he draws animals (toward himself) from wherever.'

Frequently, more than one *–sha* verb will be chained together to describe a rather lengthy set of interrelated actions. Consider the following description of a leaf cutter ant's attempts to pick up and carry off a manioc leaf stem:

4. *Lomo pangata pitin; chiwanga urmasha, hatarisha, shayarisha, mana ushashachu, rin.* '(First) he cuts the manioc leaf; (then) with that (leaf) falling, rising, standing, (but) not being able to do it, he goes.'

Practice 1

Practice making *–sha* verbs by creating sentences with the following word sets. Each sentence should have one *–sha* verb and one main (finite) verb.

Example:

(*paba* 'turkey,' *maskana* 'to search,' *purina* 'to walk, trek')
Pabata maskasha purinawn. 'Searching for turkeys, they trek.'

1. (*aswa* 'manioc beer,' *machana* 'become intoxicated,' *urmana* 'to fall,' *pamba* 'ground')
2. (*pishku* 'bird,' *rikuna* 'to see,' *illapana* 'shoot')
3. (*win* 'all,' *llatanana* 'undress,' *siririna* 'lie down')
4. (*ruya* 'tree,' *takana* 'hit,' *purina* 'walk/trek')
5. (*supay* 'spirit,' *rikuna* 'look at,' *mandzharina* 'be afraid')
6. (*urku* 'hill,' *sikana* 'climb up,' *paktamuna* 'arrive')
7. (*motolo kiru* 'motolo snake's teeth,' *apana* 'take,' *rina* 'to go')
8. (*pukuna* 'blow gun,' *apana* 'take,' *llukshigrina* 'go and leave')
9. (*sindzhita* 'strongly,' *tarabana* 'to work,' *ashka aswa* 'lots of aswa,' *upina* 'to drink')
10. (*ñawpa* 'front,' *uyarimuna* 'sound toward,' *purina* 'to walk, trek')
11. (*washa* 'back, behind,' *uyarimuna* 'sound toward,' *purina* 'to walk, trek')

Practice 2

Go to the following link, where an Upper Napo speaker describes how to harvest tree bark:
https://www.youtube.com/watch?v=0BHdmoZZt6A&t=75s

Begin listening at 56 seconds and stop at 1:14, while reading the transcribed words below. See if you can find and circle all of the suffixes in this very long sentence, which features several *–sha* suffixes. Notice how, when such lengthy sentences occur, speakers rely heavily on intonation to set apart the individual *–sha* marked actions within their verb phrases:

Payguna rimanawn kasna ambi karara sachama pallanga risha, yura siki paktasha, may challuwa kaspi, awa amarun kaspi, balsama yura shina paktasha, ñawpa punda shayarisha, payta kwintana nin, rimana.

Negating a *–sha* Verb

Speakers may negate a *–sha* suffixed verb to create a semantically more complex verb phrase which can communicate an idea of unexpectedness, or some kind of additional, perhaps surprising detail about the way in which the finite verb's action is carried out. In the example below, the negation surrounds *asina* 'to laugh':

Mana asisha-chu tarabanawn. 'Not laughing, they work.'

Such constructions often lead to inferences which are not overtly stated. If people are not laughing when they work, a possible inference is that they are behaving unnaturally, and may therefore be angry or sad, since good-natured laughter is the norm when engaging in many cooperative tasks.

Practice 3

Practice making negated *–sha* constructions by going through the following sets of verbs and make only the *–sha* verb negative. For each example state an inference that a speaker may want to suggest. Please note that if the *–sha* verb takes a direct object, it is not necessary to add a direct object marker to that object:

Example:

(*runa yanapana* 'to people-help (i.e., to help people),' *kawsana* 'to live')
Mana runa yanapashachu kawsanawn. 'Not helping people, they live.'
Likely inference: Speaker is being critical of people who don't help people

The Coreference Suffix –sha

1. (*asina* 'to laugh,' *baylana* 'to dance')
2. (*pugllana* 'to play,' *tarabana* 'to work')
3. (*ruya takana* 'to tree hit [i.e., to hit a tree],' *purina* 'to walk, trek')
4. (*uyarikta samana* 'to breathe audibly [literally: "to breathe until heard"],' *sirina* 'to lie')
5. (*rimana* 'to speak,' *tiyarina* 'to sit')
6. (*uyarimuna* 'to be heard,' *shamuna* 'to come')
7. (*rimarina* 'to talk to oneself,' *chapana* 'to wait')
8. (*rikuna* 'to see,' *pukuna* 'to blow with a blowgun')
9. (*supay* 'forest spirit,' *gustana* 'to enjoy, like,' *mandzharina* 'to be afraid')
10. (*amarun* 'anaconda, boa,' *rikuna* 'to see,' *waytana* 'to swim')

Written Exercise 1

Choose the most appropriate verb from the word bank below, to put in *–sha* form for each of the following sentences.

pukuna, tiyarina, wakana, purina,
muskuna, asina, aparina, llukana

1. Ñukanchi _____ puñunchi.
2. Wawa _____ sirin.
3. Payguna _____ tarabanawn.
4. Yaya pabata _____ paktamun.
5. Kanguna _____ chapangichi!
6. Pay alimanda _____ kasan.
7. Palo _____ purin.
8. Ñuka _____ kasani.

Written Exercise 2

Fill in the following blanks with a correct form of the verb in parentheses. Use either an adverbial *–ngawa*, *–sha*, or a finite verb.

1. Ñuka yayaga _____ (*kasana* 'to hunt') *rin, sachama*.
2. Kanguna _____ (*aswana* 'to make *aswa*') _____ (*chapana* 'to wait') *paygunata*.
3. Lomota _____ (*yanuna*) *aswanchi, paygunata* (*upichina* 'to give to drink') _____.

164　　　　　　　　　　　*Lesson 14*

4. *Ali aswata* _____ (*aswana* 'to make *aswa*'), *ñukanchi ali lomota* _____ (*yanuna* 'cook').

5. *Aswata* _____ (*tukuchina* 'to finish, run out'), *ñukanchi* _____ (*pingarina* 'become embarrassed').

Practice 4

For each of the sentences in written exercise 2 above, transform each finite verb into a past tense form. The point of this practice is to demonstrate how –*sha* suffixed verbs are independent of tense.

Questioning a –*sha* Verb

In addition to negating a –*sha* suffixed verb, speakers may also focus on the –*sha* verb to ask a yes/no question. If the –*sha* verb has its own direct object, then the question's scope will include that object:

Yaku hambishachu hapingi? 'Is treating water with venom (how) you catch (fish)?' (Literally: 'Water treating with venom do you catch?')

Possible response:

Nda. Yaku hambishami hapini. 'Yes. Treating water with venom is how I catch (fish).'

Practice 5

Answer the following questions in the affirmative.

Example:

Chunlla sirishachu puñungi? 'Quietly lying do you sleep?'
Nda. Chunlla sirishami puñuni.

1. *Kungaylla* 'suddenly' *mikushachu istudiangi?*
2. *Pukushachu kasangi?*
3. *Pambai llukashachu puringi?*
4. *Sindzhita kallpashachu puringi?*
5. *Aswa upishachu machangi?*
6. *Chunlla tiyarishachu istudiangi?*
7. *Sindzhita kantashachu istudiangi?*

Nina + –sha

When –*sha* is suffixed to the verb *nina* 'to say' it can have the effect of transforming its meaning from a verb which simply reports speech, or simply reports the act of speech, to a verb meaning 'wanting,' 'intending,' 'thinking,' or 'wondering.' For example, the following question is frequently used to ask someone what, in general, they might be up to: *Imata nisha puriungi?* 'What wanting, are you walking about?' Or simply: 'What are you doing walking about?' Or: 'What are you up to, walking about?'

Practice 6

Each of the following questions uses a –*sha* suffixed *nina* with another verb to ask a question. Answer the questions with the verb in parentheses.

Example:

Imata nisha shamurangi? (*yanapana* 'to help') 'What wanting, did you come?'
Yanapanata nisha shamurani. 'Wanting to help, I came.'

1. *Imata nisha dzas rirangi?* (*kasana* 'to hunt')
2. *Imata nisha sacha wagrata illapanrangichichu?* (*mikuna* 'to eat')
3. *Imata nisha mana dzas shamurangichi?* (*sakirina* 'to stay')
4. *Imata nisha nuspa shina muyuriungi sachai?* (*ala maskana* 'to search for mushrooms')
5. *Imata nisha chagrai chapangi?* (*aycha hapina* 'to catch meat')
6. *Imata nisha ruyata kuchungi?* (*chagrana* 'to make a *chagra*')

In addition to the expression of desires or plans to carry out an action, the verb *nisha* may express a bodily need or an emotional state. If the bodily or emotional process is not subject to a person's control, this construction may carry an inceptive 'about to' or a 'need to' meaning:

Piñarisha nin. 'He/she is about to get angry.'
Wakasha nin. 'She wants to cry.'
Puñusha nin. 'He/she wants to sleep.'
Imara upisha ningi? 'What do you want to drink?'
Kignasha nin! 'He/she wants to vomit.' Or 'He/she is about to throw up.'
Kay wawa ishpasha nin. 'This child needs to urinate.'
Kay wawa ismasha nin. 'This child needs to defecate.'

Language and Poetic Focus: –*sha* Suffix in Songs

Go to the following link: https://youtu.be/dfNxgrqzHUs
Listen to the song which occurs at 2:13 until 3:21. It is a song that causes tender feelings for the singer because it recounts memories of celebrations that took place during the Christian calendrical festivities of Christmas. According to the singer, children were instructed to gather and bring bundles of bright red *rayu sisa* flowers into a main central plaza, where people would eat, drink *aswa*, and dance together while men played flutes. Notice how important the –*sha* suffix is for conveying a general feeling of ongoingness that is evident in various activities. The song does not methodically describe the celebration as a series of discreet events. Instead, the singer evokes various images of ongoing activities that were salient for her as a child.

Practice 7

Listen again to the song from 2:13 to 3:21. See if you can find the verbs that have –*sha* suffixes. Underline them, and translate them.

> *Ñuka paktarikpiga hista paktarikpiga*
> *Sisatalla markasha sisatalla markarisha* (gestures closer to her body when she says *markarisha*)
> *Intirulla plazata tuta tukai puriunyari*
> *Ruku mama wawaguna markay markay puriunguna*
> *Sisatalla apasha*
> *kushi kushi shunguwan*
> *kushi kushi shunguwan*
> *ashka ashka tandarisha*
> *ashka ashka tandarisha*
> *muru muru mukahata*
> *upi upi riunchiyari*
> *chawpi polazabigaya kiwirisha baylasha*
> *ruku mamagunaga shaya shaya riunguna*
> *shaya shaya riungunaya*
> *ruku yayagunawa gustutalla baylaunguna*
> *aysashaya aysasha piwanota tukasha*
> *piwanota tukashaya*
> *Chasna kantak ara ñuka yaya piwanota tukak ara*

Lesson 15

The Switch Reference Suffix *–kpi*

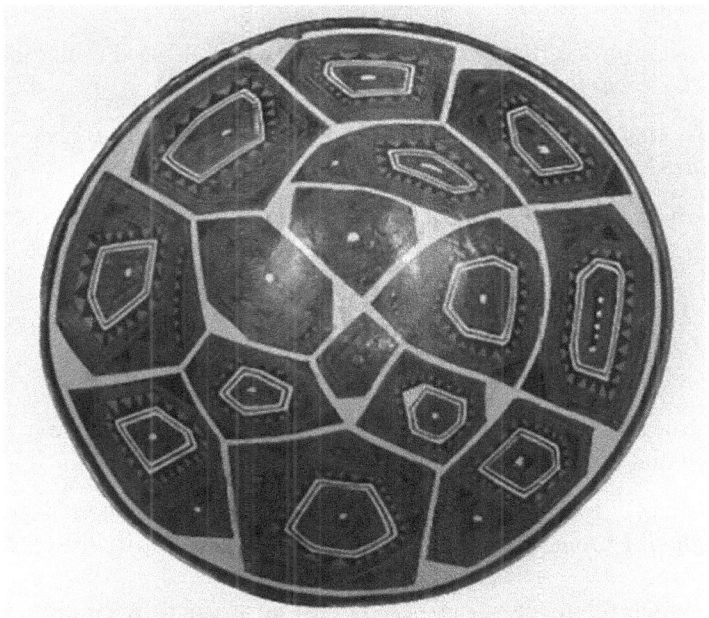

Interior view of *mukaha*
JANIS NUCKOLLS

Instructional narrative: "How we work with clay"

1. Q: *Ima shinata kawchungi manga allpata?* 'How do you roll clay?'

    kawchuna 'to roll or twist'

2. A: *Manga allpataga apagrirani manga allpa pugrui, Puka Yakumanda hanagma.* 'I went and got some clay in a clay pit, upriver from Puka Yaku.'

    pugru 'well, hole, pit'

167

3. *Chiimi tiyak man manga allpa.* 'That's where clay is.'

4. *Chita apamusha awakpi, tuvyara.* '(After) bringing that and (trying) to create (with it), it exploded.'

   tuvyana 'to explode'
   –kpi [switch reference suffix which establishes that the agent of its verb is distinctive from that of a following verb]

5. *Kosakpimi tuvyara.* '(When/while) (I/someone) fired it, it exploded.'

   kosana 'to roast, to fire'

6. *Chimanda apacharanta lluchugrirani.* 'Then I went and peeled some *apacharana* bark.'

   apacharana 'type of tree, the bark of which is used to fire clay'
   lluchuna 'to peel'

7. *Lluchugrisha, kutarani; kutasha, naranha pangai shushusha, chiwan karasha,*

   awarani mukahataga. '(After) peeling it, I ground it up; (after) grinding it, I filtered it through orange leaves, and after feeding (the clay) with that, I created a *mukaha*.'
   kutana 'to grind'
   shushuna 'to filter, sieve'
   karana 'to feed, fortify'

8. *Chiwanga, kosakpi, mana chari tuvangachu.* '(When) I fire it with that (ground up bark), it will not, perhaps, explode.'

9. *Kosakpi, kutillata tuvyakpiga, kutillata karani manga allpata.* 'If, (when) I fire it, it explodes again, (then) again I fortify the clay.'

The switch reference suffix *–kpi* is best understood by contrast with the coreference suffix *–sha* because their meanings are opposite and they would never co-occur in the same verb. Just as coreference *–sha* establishes that two actions are performed by the same subject, *–kpi* establishes that the action of the *–kpi* verb and that of a finite verb are performed by different subjects. A nice way of metaphorically conceiving of the function of *–kpi* is to imagine that it acts as a spotlight which highlights a different player in a dramatic performance. It is always suffixed behind the last vowel of a root:

llukshina 'to emerge' > *llukshi-* + *–kpi* 'someone (other than the subject of the finite verb) emerges'

A verb root suffixed with *–kpi* is not marked for person (the 'I,' 'you,' 'he/she/it' etc., suffixes), tense, or number (singular vs. plural). Speakers will sometimes use a subject, where ordinarily they wouldn't, in order to be specific about who is doing what, but it's not required by this kind of construction. Notice that lines 4, 5, 8, and 9 of the narrative all use switch reference suffixes, but none of the subjects of the switch reference verbs is specified. Context plays an important role in identifying subjects of switch reference verbs.

To understand the nature of the relationships between actions linked by a *–kpi* suffix, it is useful to think of them as either causally linked or temporally contiguous, as is also the case for the *–sha* suffixed verbs described in Lesson 14. Such linkages may be translated with a variety of different phrases, none of which occurs in Quichua, such as "if *x* happens, then *y* will happen"; "because *x* happened, *y* happened"; "when *x* happens or happened, *y* happens or happened." In some instances, more than one of these interpretations may be equally plausible.

If/Then *–kpi* Constructions

If the finite verb linked with a *–kpi* verb does not specify that an action is in the past, then the *–kpi* verb and the finite verb may be linked by an if/then relationship. An example of an if/then-like relationship between verbs linked by *–kpi* is found in example 9 of the instructional narrative:

> *Kosakpi, kutillata tuvyakpiga, kutillata karani manga allpata.* 'If, (when) I fire it, it explodes again, (then) again I fortify the clay.'

Another example of such a linkage is found in the following:

> *Mana tamyakpi, sachama purini.* '(If, when, because) it doesn't rain, I walk to the forest.'

Temporal Linkages Formed by *–kpi* Constructions

Another type of conceptual linkage between a *–kpi* suffixed verb and a main verb is temporal. This type of relationship is most evident when the finite verb is in the past tense. In such examples, the two actions may happen simultaneously with each other (when/while *x* happened, *y* happened), or one action may precede another (after *x* happened, *y* happened). In such cases, there is no necessary causal relationship between the two actions, but rather a temporal or sequential relationship. Example 5 from the narrative illustrates the simultaneous relationship between two actions:

Kosakpimi tuvyara. '(When/while) (I/someone) fired it, it exploded.'

A similar kind of sequential relationship is found in example 4, where one action precedes another:

Chita apamusha, awakpi, tuvyara. '(After) bringing that and (trying) to create with that clay, it exploded.'

Practice 1

Practice switch reference constructions by making sentences with the following sets of words. Then provide a translation of the sentence you constructed.

Example:

(*ñuka ñañawa wawa, wañuna/ñuka, wakana*)
Ñuka ñañawa wawa wañukpimi, ñuka wakarani. 'When/because my sister's baby died, I cried.'

1. (*wawaguna, killachina/ñuka, rina*)
2. (*kanguna, ashka pangaguna, pallana/mama, alita, kosana*)
3. (*Hachi Fernando, raykaywan wañuna/ñuka, pay, karana*)
4. (*Mikya Lola, shamuna/ñuka, aswa, pay, upichina*)
5. (*indi pundzha, ana/yaya, paktamuna*)
6. (*apa yaya, mushuk hacha, kuna/ñuka, wangana aycha, kasana*)
7. (*puma, ñuka, apanakuna/sindzhita, kallpana*)
8. (*ñukanchi, alita, allpa, allmana/paloguna, shamuna* [neg])
9. (*lomo, chayana/payguna, mikuna*)
10. (*sacha supay, wawa, hapina/kutillata rikurina* [neg])
11. (*supay, pay, nitina/pay, asinayana*)
12. (*payba mushuk hacha, shuwana/pay, muskuchina*)
13. (*runa, likcharina/supay, kallpana*)
14. (*runa, puñuna/supay, pay, rikuna*)
15. (*washamanda, ruya, takana/runa, pay, maskana*)

Sequencing of –*sha* and –*kpi*

The designated name of –*kpi* as a "switch reference" suffix is an accurate indication of its function. Every time you see or hear a –*kpi*, you should expect the very next finite verb to "switch" to a different agent (or subject). In line 4 of the narrative, the *–sha* verb which precedes the *–kpi* verb can be understood to refer to the same agent or actor as the *–kpi* verb:

Chita apamusha awakpi, tuvyara. '(After) bringing that and (trying) to create (with it), it exploded.'

In this line, the first verb *apamusha* 'bringing' has the same subject as its immediately following verb *awakpi* 'someone creates.' However, since this second verb is suffixed with *–kpi*, the very next verb has to refer to a different agent or actor than that of the preceding *–kpi* verb. And in fact it does, since the exploding clay is distinctive from the person referred to by *awakpi*, who shaped the clay.

Consider, again, line 9 from the narrative:

Kosakpi, kutillata tuvyakpiga, kutillata karani manga allpata. 'If, (when) I fire it, it explodes again, (then) again I fortify the clay.'

In this example, there are two switch reference verbs which occur right next to each other. The first verb *kosakpi* from *kosana* 'to fire, roast,' refers to the action of firing by the narrator. The next verb *tuvyakpi* refers to a different event, that of the exploding of the pottery. The fact that this verb, too, is suffixed with *–kpi* means that the very next verb has to refer to yet another distinctive agent, which it does. Remember that even though the agent of the final verb and of the first verb of the sentence are the same, the first verb has to be suffixed with *–kpi* to keep it distinguished from its immediately following verb. Syntax, then, is an important part of the proper usage and interpretation of the *–kpi* and also *–sha* suffixes.

Written Exercise 1

Practice using *–kpi* and *–sha* by completing the following sentences with the correct form of the verb in parentheses. You will either use *–kpi*, *–sha*, or a finite verb. Then provide a possible translation

Example:

_____ *(tamyana), payguna mana paktamunawrachu.* > *Tamyakpi, payguna mana paktamunawrachu.* 'Because/since it rained/is raining, they didn't arrive.'

1. _____ *(shamuna)* _____ *(tiyarina), payta upichirani aswawan.*

_____.

2. *Pay tukuyta* _____ *(llatanana) payta* _____ *(rikuna) supayga.*

   _____.

3. *Supay* _____ *(uyarimuna), ñukanchi* _____ *(mandzharina).*

   _____.

4. *Runagunaga mana* _____*-chu (samana)* _____ *(sirina).*

   _____.

5. *Pay ñukata* _____ *(nitina)* _____ *(asina).*

   _____.

6. *Pay ton ton ton* _____ *(takana)* _____ *(purina) payta uyarani.*

   _____.

7. *Chunda* _____ *(pukuna) payguna* _____ *(pallana).*

   _____.

8. *Pumata* _____ *(rikuna), ñukanchi* _____ *(kallpana).*

   _____.

9. _____ *(tamyana) ñukaga* _____ *(likcharina* [neg]*).*

   _____.

10. *Kumari Faviola* _____ *(hatarina), aswata* _____ *(upina), chagrama* _____ *(rina).*

    _____.

11. *Ñukata* _____ *(upinayana), aswa* _____ *(tiyana), payguna ñukata* _____ *(upichina).*

    _____.

Practice 2

Construct switch reference sentences with the following sets of words.

Example:

(*upinayana/upichina*) > *Kanda upinayakpiga, ñuka kanda upichini.*

1. (*puñunayana/rina*)
2. (*ñuka, llakina/payguna, aycha, karana*)
3. (*puma, sindzhita, kallpana/ñukanchi, sindzhita, apanakuna*)
4. (*pay, wawa, markanakan, ashanga, aparina*)
5. (*wawaguna, killachina/pay, llukshina, wasi*)
6. (*indi pundzha, ana/chagra, ñukanchi, tarabana*)
7. (*palo, wasigama, llukana/wawaguna, mandzhana*)
8. (*amarun, ñukanchi, rikuna/ñukanchi, kallpana*)
9. (*kari, shuk warmi, munana/warmi, llakirina*)
10. (*puma, urku, sikana/payguna, pay, rikuna* [neg])
11. (*kan, ñuka, tapuna/kan, tukuy, rimana*)
12. *manga allpa, tuvyana/mukaha, awana* [neg])

Written Exercise 2

Decide on a *–kpi* verb or a coreference *–sha* verb, or a tensed finite verb for each of the following sentences.

Shuk apa mama tiyaura. Chi apa mama ishkay churiyuk mara. Kay ishkay churiwan _____ (kawsana) tiyaura. Chagrama _____ (rina), lomota _____ (tarpuna) palandatawas _____ (tarpuna) kawsara. Payba churiguna aychata hapingaw _____ (purina). _____ (aswana) chapara apa mamaga.

Payguna aycha illak _____ (paktamuna) apa mama _____ (piñana) mana paygunata upichirachu.

Kayandi, aychata _____ (hapina) pukunawan _____ (markana), wasii _____ (paktamuna), apa mama _____ (kushiyana) upichira paygunata.

Practice 3

Go to the supplement site for this lesson and make up three sentences that tell a short story about each image. Make sure that at least one sentence uses a switch reference construction. A possible verb to use is given for each.

A. *awana* 'to make'

1. _____
2. _____
3. _____

B. *chunda aswana* 'to make *aswa* with *chunda*'

1. _____
2. _____
3. _____

C. *asina* 'to laugh'

1. _____
2. _____
3. _____

D. *chapana* 'to wait'

1. _____
2. _____
3. _____

Lesson 16

The Present Perfect –*shka*

Apasha rin, ñukanchi llakiushkata 'It goes, taking away our sadness'
TOD SWANSON

The following narrative relates one woman's personal experience of learning about a small plane that had crashed.

Narrative: 'A plane crash'

1. *Rikungi. Chagrai ñuka riurani, lomota apangaw.* 'Look. I was going along in the *chagra*, to get manioc.'

2. *Chiga, avionga, kasna wamburisha riura, riki!* 'Then the plane, it was gliding like this, as it was going, look! (gestures)'

   avion 'airplane'
   wamburina 'to float, glide, fly'

3. *Mana kasnaga rirachu; ña kasnamallaga, chupami allpama; pay singaga hawai chupaga allpama. Mana kuskata, mana usharachu.* 'It wasn't going like this (gestures); now just like this, the tail (was) lowered; its nose (was) upward. It wasn't able (to go) straight.'

4. *Ña chiga yapa kargashkawna: kimsa tanque gasolina; ishkay saco arroz; shuk azucar; chimanda anawra runagunaga.* 'Now, they've loaded it a lot: three tanks of gasoline; two sacks of rice; one of sugar; and then there were the people.'

   kargana 'to load'
   tanque (Sp.) 'tank'
   saco (Sp.) 'sack'
   azucar (Sp.) 'sugar'

5. *Ñuka shuk ushushillawan maurani chagrai, ichilla wawagunawan. "Wawaguna rikuichi avionda!" nini; "Mana kuskata rindzhu; siki urmanga raun!" nirani.* 'I was with only one daughter, and some little ones, in the *chagra*. "Children look at the plane!" I say; "It's not going straight; its rear is going to fall" I said.'

6. *Chiga ña mayta taco tuvyashkata shina uyarani, ñuka, chagramanda!* 'Then somewhere I heard (what was) like exploded dynamite, from the *chagra*.'

   mayta 'somewhere, wherever'

7. *Chiga "Huuuuuuuuuuu huu huumi" chagra ñambimanda kaparimunawn.* 'Then "*Huuuuuuuuuu huu huu*" from the *chagra* path they shout toward me.'

   kaparina 'to shout'

8. *"Imatashi kaparinawn?" nishami, uyasha shamuni.* 'Listening and wondering "what (on earth) are they shouting (about)?" I come.'

9. *"Wañuuuuuuushka! Wañuuushka!" ninawn. "Winshi rupashkawna," ninawra.* '"Died! They've died!" they say. "All of them have burned," they said.'

   rupana 'to burn, be hot'

The Present Perfect –shka

The present prefect *–shka* expresses the present relevance of an already accomplished action which may or may not have been witnessed. It's most comparable to the English present perfect construction 'I have gone.' The present prefect paradigm is reproduced below:

Ñuka rishkani 'I've gone'
Kan rishkangi 'You've gone'
Pay rishka 'He/she/it's gone'
Ñukanchi rishkanchi 'We've gone'
Kanguna rishkangichi 'You-all have gone'
Payguna rishkawna 'They've gone'

Practice 1

Add the complete set of perfect suffixes to the following verbs:

churarina
gustana
hambina
hapina
hapichina
ichuna
kallpana
kamana
kanina
hapichina

Written Exercise 1

Complete the following sentences with a *–shka* verb, deciding which verb of the pair is most appropriate. You may want to review Lesson 8 on the semantics of the *–ri* suffix.

1. (*tukuna, tukurina*)

    Aswa charak mana _____ *chan.*

    Imata _____ *kamba mamaga?*

2. (*hapina, hapirina*)

    Kunan ñuka ushushi _____ *man.*

    Kunan nina _____ *man.*

3. (wiñana, wiñarina)

　　Payba ushushi ＿＿＿＿＿＿＿ man.

　　Ñukanchi papagunaga ＿＿＿＿＿＿＿ man.

4. (allsana, allsarina)

　　Payba chakita ＿＿＿＿＿＿＿ turumanda.

　　Mushuk killa ＿＿＿＿＿＿＿ maura Sara Yakuma.

Written Exercise 2

Fill in the following blank spaces with a correct –*shka* form of the verb in parentheses.

1. *Chita uyasha, payguna dzas* ＿＿＿＿＿＿＿ *(llukshina + –gri) wasimanda.*

2. *Kanguna yapami* ＿＿＿＿＿＿＿ *(kargana) ashangata pallashkagunawan.*

3. *Kan mukahata* ＿＿＿＿＿＿＿ *(awana) tayllayashka manga allpawan?*

4. *Ñukanchi mana* ＿＿＿＿＿＿＿ *-chu (rikuna) ali mushuk llachapawan churarishkagunata.*

5. *Ñuka makita* ＿＿＿＿＿＿＿ *(rupana) mangata shayachisha ninai.*

6. *Ñuka ñaña* ＿＿＿＿＿＿＿ *(hapina) man Lobertowa churiwan.*

Narrative Past –shka

The forms included in the present perfect paradigm outlined in part 1 have another kind of function in narrative. However, this function is restricted to third person singular and plural forms. When people tell stories they frequently use the third person present perfect verb form instead of the ordinary past tense. *–shka* suffixed verbs are not always used throughout the course of a narrative. Speakers will sometimes begin a narrative with *–shka* verbs, and then switch to the ordinary past tense forms. The *–shka* suffixed verb may therefore be considered a genre marker for *kallari timpu* or 'beginning times' stories. Such stories often concern mythic, magical, or other-worldly events that are said to have happened too long ago to be remembered by contemporary people.

Practice 1

Practice your command of *–shka* forms by reading the following narrative, and transforming all of the third person singular and plural past tense verbs (excluding the prologue) into *–shka* verbs. The story concerns a legend about how people came to grow old and die. According to this legend, when people would become old, they could bathe themselves with a plant called *wiwilan*. Doing this would cause a person to shed their old age the way a tree sheds bark. After an old woman did this one day, however, she encountered her grown son who then mistook her for an attractive and available young woman. He raped her, with the result that renewing oneself was no longer possible.

Example:

Chiga apa shara mamaga. > *Chiga apa shashka mamaga.* 'So once upon a time there was an old woman.'

Narrative: 'How people didn't used to get old'

Prologue

Kallariga, ñukanchi rukayasha, wiwilanda allaranchi. Wiwilan tiyan sachai. Wiwilan nishkata, mana riksirangichu? Shuk angu man. Chiga, allpai, payba, wiñarishka anguga rin. Ichilla panga wawayuk man; ukuimi aparin shuk anguta. Chigama, chigama, chigama, sunigunata aparin. Chitami allasha, wiwilanda takasharni armak anawn, runaguna, hasta kunangama armanawn. Jabon shina puskuyan. Napata win anchuchisha armak anawn.

Story

1. *Chiga apa shara mamaga.* 2. *Chiga churiga: "puñugrishalla mama; kanga tiyaungi" nishashi sakira mamata.* 3. *"Ari ... muskuk puñugri, ñuka tiyausha."* 4. *Wiwilanda allara.* 5. *Kunanga armagrishalla, ismu llachapata llatanagrishalla, nisha ushushita, wasimanda llukshira.* 6. *Semanata, manashi rikurira.* 7. *Maytashi mama rin?* 8. *Churi paktamura.* 9. *Chiga, mamaga, chita rira.* 10. *Charak mana rikurindzhu.* 11. *Imanasha chari?* 12. *Chagrai wiwilanda allara.* 13. *Ñuka yuyaibi "chi ismushka llachapata anchuchingaw, chari, rira" nirami.* 14. *"Ñuka pushagrishalla mamata" nira chi waglichina runa.* 15. *Chasna nishaga churiga kallpasha rira.* 16. *Rikukpi, kaywan pariulla akchayuk shara pay, sultira shina.* 17. *Ali warmi shara.* 18. *Ña mamaga chikan rikurik warmi shara.* 19. *Chasnashi ña win wiwilanda armashaga, apangura lluchurishkata rikuk changi? 20. *Ña win, llullu shinalla, ima munay rikurik warmi shamura!* 21. *Chiga, payba churita rikusha, "Shamurangichu churi?"* 22. *"Atsatsay! Kanga mana ñuka mama changi!"* *nirashi.* 23. *"Munasha, rikugri ñuka ismushka llachapata, ñuka llatanash-*

kata," nirashi mamaga. 24. Mana uyarachu churiga. 25. Sira shinashi kipirira mamata, "mana ñuka mama changi kanga," nirashi. 26. "Mana churi, kamba mama mani ñuka; ñuka ismushka llachapatami llatanasha shamuni" nirashi. 27. "Imawata kasna kipiriwai?" 28. Puñuy kallarira. 29. Churi chasna rausha mandzharira. 30. Chimanda, "ñukama hapishkangi, ñukama hapishkangi" nisha, payta aysasha rira. 31. "Mana churi, ñuka mani kamba mama. 32. "Sakiwai," nirashi. 33. "Ñuka ismu llachapata rikugri yakuma," nirashi. 34. Mamaga yaku shinalla wakasha, wasii paktamura. 35. "Shamungichu mama?" nirashi ushushiga. 36. "Kanga ñuka mama kasna ñawpa rikurik arangi, sultira asha." 37. "Mana ñuka wawa shinachu rawan," nirashi mamaga. 38. "Kunanga yakuma riunimi" nisha, rira. 39. Ushushi payta apanakura. 40. Rikukpimi, mamaga barawan kumurishashi shamura. 41. Kunan apa mama shina rikurik shara. 42. "Kunan imaynata rukuyasha wañuni? Chasnallata kangunawas wañungichi. 43. Mana llatanangichichu. Kunan ñuka wawa kasna rasha waglichin kayta. 44. Mana llatananata ushangachu raungichi. 45. Piwas mana llatanangachu. 46. Barata hapirisha, chi aychallanmi wañungichi, nishashi rimasha wakara." 47. Chimanda apa wañura.

Grammatical Characteristics of –shka

Although the –shka suffix is most at home on verb roots, it may be further suffixed to function in various grammatical capacities. As stated earlier, it is suffixed to a verb root, replacing the infinitive –na:

tukuri-na 'to finish up, end' > *tukuri-shka* 'finished'

However, a –shka suffixed verb can itself be further suffixed, depending on its grammatical function within a sentence. –shka is semantically similar to the past tense –ed suffix in English, which can be used in a variety of grammatical constructions:

–ed suffix for verb: 'He toasted his bread.'
–ed suffix as adjective: 'The toasted food became dried out.'
–ed suffix as a predicate adjective: 'The bread was toasted.'

In PQ:

–shka for verb: *Pay mikunata yanushka.* 'He cooked the food.'
–shka for adjective: *Yanushka mikuna tiyan.* 'There is cooked food.'
–shka for predicate adjective: *Mikuna yanushka man.* 'The food is cooked.'

–*Shka* suffixed roots may take a variety of other suffixes, such as plural –*guna*/–*una*, direct object –*ta*/–*ra*, and others to be discussed later.

Written Exercise 1

Fill in the following blank spaces with a –*shka* suffixed form of the verb from the word bank that is most appropriate:

sambayana, chayana, ismuna, chunllayana, puchuna machana, kushparina, llakirina, witayana, kumurina

1. *Ñuka mana tarabashka chagra _____ tukun.*
2. *Wawagunaga mikushka washa _____ tukunawn.*
3. *Hapishka bagriga _____ kanoai.*
4. *Pundzha chishakta tarabasha chagrai _____ tukuni ñuka.*
5. *Paygunawa wawa wañukpi _____ tukuranchi.*
6. *Ña _____ man, lomo.*
7. *Ñuka _____ apa mama alimanda purik man.*
8. *_____ -ta muktingichu?*
9. *Kay _____ -ta wakaichingi!*
10. *_____ -guna yapa baylanawn tuta pagarikta.*

Culture Focus: Forest Resources: *Pitun*

The *pitun* flower (*Lecythidaceae Grias neuberthii*) is believed to help influence the taste buds of a woman's mouth so that she will be able to make flavorful *aswa*, which requires the mastication of cooked manioc tubers, a task traditionally done by women. When the pale yellow *pitun* flowers appear, they might be given to a little girl to hold in her mouth, so that her saliva can acquire the habitual taste of the flower, which will then be imparted to the *aswa* when the manioc is chewed. The assumption here is that the girl's mouth doesn't just borrow the perfume of the flower momentarily, but actually learns to produce this scent. In other words, the mouth becomes *yacharishka* 'accustomed to' this scent which then becomes part of the girl's own bodily knowledge. Interestingly, the *pitun* flower's taste is slightly bitter.

182   *Lesson 16*

Another traditional practice that makes use of the *pitun* tree is believed to enhance beauty, and involves the long leaves of this tree, which are compared to flowing human hair. Moreover, people have observed that this tree does not shed many of its leaves. The long leaves therefore evoke the desirable characteristic of thick, flowing hair that does not easily shed. For this reason, Runa women have traditionally bathed their own hair in pounded leaves from the *pitun* tree.

Promises, Threats, and Other Expressions with *–shka*

Besides its function as an adjective, predicate adjective, subject, or direct object of a sentence, a verb suffixed with *–shka* is also used in a number of idiosyncratic expressions. It is often used with evidentially suffixed *alimi* 'good (according to speaker),' and *ana* 'to be,' to express a compliment:

Ali mashka! 'It's good/nice!'

The following are just a few contexts where this use has been documented:

1. After hearing a good story
2. While eating or drinking something tasty
3. Upon seeing that something broken has been repaired
4. Upon seeing a Swiss army knife completely unfolded

Notice that although *–shka* was defined earlier as referring to events or processes that are complete, the above usages are not so restricted. Example 2 above uses a *–shka* verb to talk about the ongoing experience of enjoying food or drink.

> *–Shka* also forms part of an exclamation used to express amazement, surprise, or awe, particularly when looking at something very nice, such as well-made, finely painted pottery:
> *Ushashka!* < *ushana* 'to be able'

This expression is not easy to translate. English exclamatives like 'wow!' come close. It is also interesting to point out that there is a semantics of 'unpreparedness' that goes along with this expression, and has been reported by linguists as a function of perfect grammatical markers in other languages.

Yet another type of *–shka* usage is found when speakers want to make promises or threats. In such usages, a speaker is saying to someone that something is so certain to happen or not to happen to or for then that it is as good as accomplished. This is expressed by taking the *–shka* suffixed verb root and adding *angi* 'you are' or *angichi* 'you all are.' In the narrative 'How people didn't use to get old,' this construction occurs in line 30, reproduced below:

30. *Chimanda, "ñukama hapishkangi, ñukama hapishkangi" nisha, payta aysasha rira.* 'And then "You are mine, you are mine! (literally: to me you are caught)," saying, pulling her, he went.'

For another example, again from a narrative context, consider the following threat that someone once made to someone else:

wañuchi 'kill' + *–shka* = *wañuchishka* 'killed' + *angi* = *wañuchishkangi* 'you are killed'

This sentence does not mean that the speaker is addressing a corpse. It means, rather, that the speaker is making a prediction, which in this case is interpretable as a threat. A typical way to say this in English would be: 'you are as good as dead.'

–Shkangi constructions are not only used for threats. In the following example, it is used to tell someone that they will receive harvested fruit from the speaker:

Chunda muyuta pallakpiga ashkata kushkangi. 'If/when (someone) harvests a lot of *chunda* fruit, you are given a lot of them.'

And, the following warning by a mother to a young child as they were about to go to their *chagra* was overheard:

Masnata wakakpiwas, mana aparishkangichu. 'No matter how much (you) cry, you are not going to be carried.'

Listening Exercise: The Promise/Threat –shkangi and the Surprise –shka

Examples of both a promise or threat *–shkangi* construction as well as a surprising observation with *–shka* are found in the following video clip featuring a speaker describing a practice used to determine a baby's gender. This is accomplished with a flower called the *papangu sisa*. The speaker repeatedly taps the flower against her abdomen while asking which of the two names she has picked for either a boy or a girl will end up being used. She then stops tapping, and says that she's going to cut it open. To communicate the clean break she will make by cutting the flower open, she uses the ideophone *chyuw*. After seeing what is inside she exclaims, 'It's a girl!' Watch the following link, from 12 seconds until 25 seconds, to see both constructions: https://www.youtube.com/watch?v=YVqqwvUdPJM&t=8s

Warmi mashka! 'It's a girl!'
TOD SWANSON

> *Kunan amo rimarimun: "kungata chyuw pitishkangi."* 'Now the owner (of the flower) speaks (to herself): "Your neck is going to be cut apart *chyuw*!"' (opens flower)
> *Warmi mashka!* 'It's a girl!'

Practice 2

Fill in the following blank spaces with a correct *–shka* form of the verb in parentheses.

Example:

> *Aswata upichichik shamui! Mana _____ (tukurina)-chu an.* >
> *Aswata upichik shamui! Mana tukurishkachu an.*

1. Ñuka _____ (wañuna) mikya Theresa mana ali tarabak chara.
2. Mikuk changi paygunawa _____ (pallana).
3. Kay mana ali _____ (yacharina) gringo, turuyasha purik man.
4. Chi ali _____ (churarina + plural + acc) rikurangichichu?
5. Ñukata aychata apamukpiga _____ (llakina).
6. Paparaw aswa pukukpiga, wayra shina _____ (upichina).
7. Kan, kay llaktamanda rikpiwas, mana _____ (kungarina).
8. Kan ñukata kayakpiwas mana _____ (yanapana).
9. Supay _____ (uyarimuna) kanda kwintauni.
10. Ñuka ali, mana _____ (ismuna) hachata aparirani, ruyata kuchungawa.
11. Chi _____ (turuyana) runata rikuranchi _____ sacha ñambii.

Culture Focus: The Healing Power of River Foam

Lesson 11 mentioned the importance of rivers in Runa lives, for basic spatial orientation. In Lesson 12, we saw the shape of a river's movements painted on the inside of a drinking bowl. In the following brief narrative, a man explains how the foam from river water is believed to have curative powers for lovesickness.

Go to the following link and listen to a man named Luis briefly explain to another man named Pedro, as well as to Tod Swanson, about the curative power of foam from large rivers, which is said to be helpful when a person is saddened because of love. Listen to the section that begins at 34 seconds, until the video ends:
https://youtu.be/UDEHzLOTtcE

Grammar Awareness Prompt

Notice how the speaker uses the –*shka* suffix. Which of the functions of –*shka* do you see being used below?

Ima rasha apan llakira? 'How does it take the sadness?'

1. *Chi pusku, no cie(rto), yaku kayta rin kakurishka washa.* 'That foam, right?, the water goes this way, after it was rubbed.'
2. *Yakui armana, chiwan kakurisha, yakui arman pichasha, pusku ña rin urayta (uray)llata.* 'One has to bathe in the water, and with that (foam) rubbing, in the water one bathes sweeping (it), and the foam then goes downriver, just downriver.'
3. *Chay apasha rin payga ña ñukanchi llakiushkata.* 'That's how it goes then, taking what has made us sad.'
4. *Chaybi ñukanchita ña llaki kalmarin ña pasarin.* 'And then the sadness passes us, it calms down.'
5. *Ña kuti llakiushas, chasna chasna kimsa kutin chasna armana. Chibi ña pasarin llaki.* 'Again becoming sad, like that, like that, three (more) times one is to bathe. With this the sadness passes.'

Lesson 17

Talking about the Future

Mana raykay wañushunchu sachai. 'We will not die of hunger in the forest!'
TOD SWANSON

Narrative: 'Uncertainties'

1. Sylvia: *Mama! Raykaywan wañuuni!* 'Mother! I'm dying of hunger!'

    raykay 'hunger'

2. Theresa: *Imata rashun? Aycha illanmi. Lomo illanmi. Palandawas illanmi. Imata mikushun?* 'What will we do? There is no meat. There is no manioc. And there aren't even plantains. What will we eat?'

    –shun [first person pl future]

3. Theresa: *Kaya chari mana tamyangachu. Kaya risha chagrama.* 'Tomorrow perhaps, it won't rain. Tomorrow I'll go to the *chagra*.'

   –sha [first person sg future]

4. Sylvia: *Ima urasta tigramunga yayaga?* 'When will father come back?'

   uras 'general time frame, hour'
   –nga [third person sg future]

5. Theresa: *Indi pundzha shamungami. Kaya chari paktamunga.* 'He'll come on a sunny day. Tomorrow perhaps he'll arrive.'

   indi 'sun'

6. Sylvia: *Ñañagaya? Ima urasta shamungawna?* 'And what about my sisters? When will they come?'

   –ngawna [third person pl future]
   –gaya emphatic topicalizer

7. Theresa: *Kan yapa killachiwaungi, kasna tapusha. Ima urasta shamungawna, payguna? Ima shinata yachasha, ñuka, ña?* 'You are bothering me a lot, asking like that. When will they come? How will I know now?'

   killachina 'to bother, disturb'

8. Sylvia: *Ringami rauni, paygunata maskangaw!* 'I'm going to go and look for them.'

   –nga + rana [compound future construction]

9. Theresa: *Ama richu! Sakiri! Hapiy tukungami raungi supay!* 'Don't go! Stay here! You're going to be caught by a *supay*!'

This chapter introduces the future tense. It is used, as in English, to refer to actions which are projected to take place *after* the time at which the speech event takes place. However, an important cultural observation is that Runa are very cautious about stating predictions concerning action that is a year or more in the future because the future is considered so uncertain.

Making predictions about actions in the distant future, like 'counting chickens before they hatch,' is considered arrogant and precipitous. It tempts fate and is therefore considered bad luck. Although the grammar allows one to express future action, it is generally used to express immediately pending action. For example, someone might use the future to say, 'I am going to the river to bathe, so if it rains bring the clothes in.'

By contrast it is rare to hear a person say something like, 'three years from now my daughter will graduate from high school.' Generally, statements of the long range future are avoided altogether. If statements of long range planning are made by traditional Runa, they are prefaced by something like this: 'Only God knows if we live or die, perhaps if we live (X will happen, or I will do Y).' A short hand for expressing this sentiment is the verb *kawsasha* which means 'being alive, (I, you, he, she, it, we, or they) will . . .' The word *kawsasha* is generally placed at the beginning of any sentence expressing action a year or more in the future:

Kawsasha, shamuk wata shamunga. 'Being alive (or: if he/she lives), he/she will come next year (literally: the year that comes).'

The actual future tense paradigms follow. The differences between the two dialects are only obvious in the third person plural.

1. Future construction in Upper Napo Quichua:

   ñuka shamu-sha
   kan shamu-ngi
   pay shamu-nga
   ñukanchi shamu-shun
   kanguna shamu-ngichi
   payguna shamu-nunga

2. Future construction in Pastaza Quichua:

   ñuka shamu-sha
   kan shamu-ngi
   pay shamu-nga
   ñukanchi shamu-shun
   kanguna shamu-ngichi
   payguna shamu-ngawna/-nguna

One complication regarding the future tense in PQ is that its third person plural form changes when the vowel immediately preceding the *–ngawna* is [*aw*], as happens also when the durative aspect is used. In such an environment, the future suffix is the same as the plural marker *–guna* that is used for nouns. For example:

**Payguna raungawna* > *Payguna raunguna*

Written Exercise 1

Fill in the following blanks by choosing either a past or future form of the verb in parentheses. For some sentences, both may be possible.

1. *Kaya ñuka mukahata* _____ *(awana).*
2. *Ima urasta* _____ *(apamuna) payguna, kanoata?*
3. *Pay* _____ *(chapana) chari, payba ayllugunata.*
4. _____ *-chu (rina) kanwas, sachata puringaw?*
5. *Ñukanchi wagrata rikusha* _____ *(wañuchina)!*
6. *Kanguna supayta uyasha, chunlla* _____ *(shayarina).*
7. *Wawaguna pambai* _____ *(llukana), purina urasgama.*
8. *Pay mana kutillata* _____ *(paktamuna); rira hawa llaktama.*
9. *Kayna yapa ñukata* _____ *(killachina) kasna tapusha.*
10. *Kayna tuta, piguna* _____ *(shamuna)?*

Culture Focus: Forest Resources: Cane

The opening image for this chapter features *Gynerium sagittatum*, called *pindu* or *pindo*, which is the distinctive cane that grows along river banks. In some regions *pindo* so dominates the vegetation of islands and riverbanks that at least two rivers in the Ecuadorian Amazon are named after it. One of them is a tributary of the Puyo which in turn flows into the Pastaza. *Pindo* cane can grow four meters high, which is over 13 feet. It is the most preferred material for the long poles used to maneuver canoes in whitewater areas where paddles are less useful. *Pindo* is also used for chicken coops, for framing temporary shelters when camping on islands, or for making *garabatus*, which have hooks on the ends of long *pindo* poles for harvesting fruits growing high in the trees. Before the 1960s when agrarian reform and the establishment of schools imposed a more settled life, many Quichua and Shuar families migrated seasonally to *"purina chagras"* or hunting camps located several days' or even weeks' journey up or down the rivers. To avoid enemies, families generally camped on the *pindo*-dominated islands sleeping in temporary shelters constructed out of this plant. While the men journeyed inland to hunt during the day, the children, particularly the girls, hunted for bird eggs in the vegetation of the islands. Thus the sight of *pindo* often evokes memories of this riverine life.

Practice 1

Go to the following link:
https://www.youtube.com/watch?v=XaDuzJKcTOc

Listen from 30 seconds until 2:14, beginning with the question *pukushka chan?* 'Is it ripe?' Using a large knife, the speaker is meticulously peeling *pitun*, which is comparable to a butternut squash, as it has a very firm flesh. Watch how she skillfully peels it with no cutting board, using only her hands. At about 2 minutes, she proudly proclaims that being a Runa person for her means that she has expert knowledge of the forest and its resources. Listen carefully as she uses a future tense verb to say that she will not die in the forest. She states this because of her detailed knowledge of the forest's resources. The other speaker, Nuckolls, is asking informal questions. Some of the dialogue is transcribed below. Listen and fill in the blanks with what has not been transcribed. With your instructor's help, translate what the narrator says:

N: *Pukushka chan?*

C: *Pukushka! Mana pukushkaga, _____!*

N: *Kay sani shina –*

C: *Kay puka, puka pukushka! Ayyy! _____.*

N: *Imata?*

C: *Kay pitunda Kaaasna _____ tiyan.*

N: *Chuba pitun shuk sami?*

C: *Shuk sami! Muyu wawa kaylla muyu! _____! Chita risha chibi tiyak, Awka chari anawn, Chiribogai _____. Kanoai pachaga! Imata shina _____ astarinawn! Astarishaga tinahai, ismu tinahai _____. Y payguna undachisha _____, ña chayakpi, chayan _____ chayan chili muyu shina! Chili muyuta _____?*

N: *Riksinimi.*

C: *Eso! Chi shina _____.*

N: *Ima ali aswa?*

C: *Ima ali aswa!*

N: *Ña hurti chan?*

C: *Ndaya ima munayta ranawn!* _____*! Ñukanchi runaga?*

N: *Chi? Mana raykay wañushunchu sachai!*

The Compound Future Construction

The compound future construction which was used in line 8 of the dialogue can best be translated by the English 'I'm going to do X,' where X stands for some verb. The verb expressing the main idea of the action that will take place is suffixed with the third person singular *–ngawa*, which is often shortened to *–nga*. This construction describes an action which will happen in the fairly near future, and in fact, may already be starting to happen. Unlike the 'going to do' suffix *–gri*, there is no change of location implied by this construction. It is also used far more often than the future tense. It is always used with a durative form of the verb *rana* 'to do, make.' Furthermore, speakers usually add the evidential suffix *–mi* to the *–nga* verb. The following examples illustrate the compound future and ordinary future constructions:

tiyarina > tiyarisha 'I'll sit down.'
tiyarina > tiyaringami rauni 'I'm going to sit down.'

Practice 2

Practice the compound future by constructing sentences that use the following sets of words.

Example:

(*hawa llaktai/kawsana*) > *Kawsangami rauni hawa llaktai.*

1. (*pay/yanapana*)
2. (*upina/aswa*)
3. (*puñuna/kay wasii*)
4. (*kasana/sachai*)
5. (*hatun lagarto/wañuchina/kunan pundzha*)
6. (*mushuk hacha/maskana*)
7. (*maskana/ali tuku*)
8. (*turu llachapa/taksana*)
9. (*apa yayagunata/chapana*)
10. (*hatun ruya/kuchuna*)

Practice 3

Revisit the examples of practice 1 and transform each of the preceding sentences by combining a compound future form of *rina* 'to go' with the main verb in an 'in order to' adverbial form.

Example:

Kawsangami rauni hawa llaktai > Ringami rauni hawa llaktai kawsangaw.

1. _____
2. _____
3. _____
4. _____
5. _____
6. _____
7. _____
8. _____
9. _____
10. _____

Questioning with the Compound Future

The verb that is the most important semantically of the compound future construction is the verb suffixed with *–nga*. Evidence for its importance is found in the construction of yes/no questions. Speakers frequently ask yes/no questions about a compound verb's action by suffixing *–chu* onto the *–ngaw* verb rather than onto the finite verb:

Ringachu raungi kachun? 'Are you going to go, sister-in-law?'
Ari! Ringami rauni. 'Yes! I'm going to go.'

Practice 4

Practice asking yes/no questions about compound future actions by transforming the following statements into questions.

Example:

Ringami rauni Quitoma. 'I'm going to go to Quito.'
Ringachu raungi Quitoma? 'Are you going to go to Quito?'

1. *Paktamungami rauni kaya.*
2. *Aparingami rauni papachinata.*
3. *Tarpungami rauni lomota.*
4. *Pallangami raun pangata.*
5. *Kasangami raunguna aychata.*
6. *Kuchungami rauni ruyata.*
7. *Llukshingami raun ruyamanda.*
8. *Likcharingami raun kunan.*

Exhortative Future Constructions
"Should I?" "Should We?" and "Let's"

The questions expressed in English such as "should I?"' "should we?" and "let's" are constructed in Quichua as follows:

Baylashachu? 'Should I dance?'
= *bayla-* + *–sha* (first person singular future marker) + *–chu* (yes/no question marker).
Aswata upishunchu? 'Should we drink *aswa*?'
= *upi-* + *–shun* (first person plural future marker) + *–chu*
Baylashun! 'Let's dance'
= *bayla* + *–shun* (first person plural future marker)

Practice 5

Translate the following into English.

The 'should I' construction:

1. *Luzda sindishachu?* _____

2. *Luzda wañchishachu?* _____

3. *Punguta paskashachu?* _____

4. *Punguta tapashachu?* _____

5. *Kaybi tiyarishachu?* _____

The 'should we' construction:

6. *Luzda sindishunchu?* _____
7. *Luzda wañuchishunchu?* _____
8. *Punguta paskashunchu?* _____
9. *Punguta tapashunchu?* _____
10. *Kaybi tiarishunchu?* _____

The 'let's' construction:

11. *Luzda sindishun.* _____
12. *Luzda wañuchishun.* _____
13. *Punguta paskashun.* _____
14. *Punguta tapashun.* _____
15. *Kaybi tiyarishun.* _____

Written Exercise 2

Runa shimima pasachi. 'Translate to Quichua.'

1. I will go. _____
2. You will cook. _____
3. They will drink. _____
4. S/he will come to eat. _____
5. He/she/it will come tomorrow. _____
6. We will eat in the house _____
7. Next week we will go to Quito. _____
8. In one year I will return. _____

Useful Expressions for Talking about Temporality

There are a number of temporal expressions that function as adverbs which establish a temporal frame for the accomplishment of an action, event, or process. One interesting difference between the way Quichua speakers and

English speakers talk about the past is in how it is metaphorically conceptualized. We talk about the past as being metaphorically 'behind' us as we move 'forward' in time. For Quichua speakers, by contrast, the future is metaphorically 'behind' because what is in the future is unseen. This is evident in the expression *kaya washa* 'the day after tomorrow,' which literally translated is 'the day behind tomorrow.' Some of the most widely used temporal expressions are listed below:

ñalla 'soon, almost'
kaya 'tomorrow'
pasak 'last, previous'
shamuk 'coming, next'
shamuk semana 'next week'
shamuk killa 'next month'
shamuk wata 'next year'
washa shamuk watauna 'distant future'
mindzha 'day after tomorrow' (NQ)
kaya washa 'day after tomorrow' (PQ)

Written Exercise 3

Check the following sentences to see if the temporal expressions match the tense used for the sentence. If the sentence doesn't work, correct it with an acceptable sentence.

Example:

Kayna waytangami rauni. 'Yesterday I am going to swim.' (not acceptable)

Acceptable sentences:

Kayna waytarani. 'Yesterday I swam.'
Kaya waytangami rauni. 'Tomorrow I am going to swim.'

1. *Kaya ñuka kamba wasima shamusha.*
2. *Kaya pundzha llaktama rikani.*
3. *Kayna palandara mikukani.*
4. *Mindzha Ecuadorma shamushami.*
5. *Shamuk wata ashkara pasiyanga rauni.*
6. *Shamuk killa ñuka llaktai tiasha.*
7. *Shamuk semanauna Quitoi tiyanga rawni.*
8. *Kaya sachama rikani.*
9. *Kayna sachamanda paktamukani.*

10. *Kaya Napo yakui waytanga raunchi.*
11. *Kunan llachapara taksanga rauni.*
12. *Kaya wawaunawan pukllanga raunchi.*
13. *Ñalla Tenama ringa raunchi.*
14. *Ñalla sachamanda shamukani.*
15. *Kaya chagrai tarabakani.*
16. *Shamuk killa ñuka llaktama ringa rauni.*
17. *Kaya Tenama risha.*
18. *Shamuk wata Sudamericama puringawa risha.*

Culture Focus: Forest Resources as Aesthetic Expression

The importance of *Banisteriopsis caapi* for the western Amazon cannot be overestimated. Along with *yuca*, it is among the most important plants that is associated with Amazonian cultural identity. It gives a distinctive shape to visual art, such as the pottery design pictured in this lesson's supplement, as well as to music and medicine. Most importantly, perhaps, it shapes relationships between communities as well as between humans and other species.

According to Runa thinking, drinking *ayawaska* allows people to communicate with plants, animals, and also to understand aspects of human interrelations that may be masked by the daily rituals of life. People say that certain kinds of social problems, especially disruptions in social relationships, can be better understood while under the influence of *ayawaska*.

According to chemists *ayawaska* is essentially a vehicle for delivering dimethyltryptamine, or DMT, in a form that can be more easily remembered and reflected upon. There are two forms of DMT. One form is produced by the pituitary gland during deep rapid eye movement sleep, as well as at the transitional moment of death. This form of DMT produces the ordinary dreams that all people have at night as well as the visions associated with near death experiences. The problem is that very little can be retrieved from these processes because most dreams are almost immediately forgotten or are remembered in a very vague or hazy form.

The *ayawaska* drink, however, allows the inducement of visions to take place unhindered, and over a period of time because the DMT, along with other chemicals in this plant, produce a sort of 'waking dream' that can be reflected upon and remembered.

Significantly, Runa do not use fortune tellers. When a *yachak*, i.e., shaman (literally: 'knower'), or any ordinary person drinks *ayawaska*, he or she discerns what has happened in the past or what is happening in the present, but drinkers generally refrain from making predictions.

Practice 6

For each of the following sentences, transform it from a past to a future tense sentence.

Example:

Kayna pundzha Napo yakui waytakanchi. 'Yesterday we swam in the Napo River.'
Kaya pundzha Napo yakui waytanga rawnchi. 'Tomorrow we're going to swim in the Napo River.'

Or:

Kaya pundzha Napo yakui waytashun. 'Tomorrow we will swim in the Napo River.'

1. *Kayna tuta lumura yanukani.*
2. *Kayna pundzha wawaunawan wasii pukllakangichu?*
3. *Kayna pundzha sachama rikani.*
4. *Unay Quitoy sakirikangichi.*
5. *Pasak killa chagrai tarabakani.*
6. *Pasak wata ñuka llaktama paktamukani.*
7. *Mario kayna punzha Tenama rika.*
8. *Kayna wawaunawan pasianga rikanchi.*
9. *Pasak wata ashka yachakunara riksikanchi.*

The Attributive Future

The future tense can be used in compound constructions, such as those formed with attributive suffix –*k*, discussed in Lesson 13. Consider the following example:

Yanapak shamusha. 'I'll come and help.' (Literally: 'as a helper, I'll come.')

Practice 7

Practice the attributive future construction by responding to each of the following sentences with a future tensed attributive sentence using the verbs in parentheses. Vary your use of person and number.

Example:

Kamba hachi yandata munan. (*apana/rina*) 'Your uncle wants some wood.'
Ñuka apak risha. 'I'll go and take some.' (Literally: 'as a taker I will go.')

Or:

Kan apak ringi. 'As a taker you will go.'

1. *Payba pani raykaywan wañuun. (aycha/karana/purigrina)*
2. *Ñukanchi ñaña kayutui sirin. (hambina/rina)*
3. *Ñukanchi hacha shaka likirira. (ali hacha/mañana/tapugrina)*
4. *Kanguna yapa mandzharirangichi supayta. (sachai/kasana/rina* [neg])
5. *Ñuka churita upinayan. (aswa/llapina/upichina)*
6. *Ñuka yaya yapa nanaywan purin. (pay/pukuna* 'to cure by blowing smoke'*/shamuna)*
7. *Mana ima mikunatawas charinchichu. (maskana/rina)*
8. *Lomo illakpi, pay mana ima aswatawas charinchu. (lomo/apana/shamuna)*

Practice 8

Review the difference between *–kpi* and *–sha* by using one or the other in the following sets of words. If the word sets call for the switch reference *–kpi*, make the following clause in the future (either the simple or compound).

Example:

pay, shamuna/ñuka, upichina > pay shamukpiga, ñuka upichisha 'If he/she comes, I will give *aswa* to drink'

1. (*manga allpa, tuvyana/ñuka, karana*)
2. (*tamya, kallarina/payguna, chagra, rina* [neg])
3. (*wawaguna, yapa, wakana/kallpana, wasi*)
4. (*ñuka, mushuk llachapa, randina/ñuka, dzas, churarina*)
5. (*maki riru, ñuka, nanana/ñuka, doktor, rina*)
6. (*chi señora, illapata, randichina/ñuka, paba, kasana*)
7. (*ñuka, lomo kaspi, tarpuna/lomocha, chagra, shamuna*)
8. (*pay, ñuka, tapuna/ñuka, pay, kuna*)
9. (*payguna, yapa, ñuka, upichina/ñuka, saksakta, tukuna*)
10. (*yayaguna, unayana, sacha/ñukanchi, dzas, tigrana* [neg])

Practice 9

People drink *aswa* in many kinds of situations, including when traveling away from their homes. It is often more practical to drink from small aluminum bowls which can't break easily rather than from beautiful but fragile *mukahas*. Imagine a possible story involving these two men. Describe, using future tense statements, what will happen next. You might want to describe where they will go, what they will do, who they will see, etc. Be sure to use

200   *Lesson 17*

Aswa upina 'to drink *aswa*'
TOD SWANSON

a variety of future expressions learned in this lesson, including simple future, compound future, and attributive future constructions.

1. _____
2. _____
3. _____
4. _____
5. _____
6. _____
7. _____

Lesson 18

Varieties of Compound Verbs

Sikwanga amarun 'toucan boa'
TOD SWANSON

Narrative: 'Chased by a *motelo*'

1. *Ñukanchi chagrangaw riranchi, ñuka, Tito, Kumpari Galves, Taruga kachigama.* 'We went to make a *chagra*, myself, Tito, and Compadre Galves, all the way to Deer Salt.'

    taruga 'deer'
    kachi 'salt'

2. *Taruga kachii paktaranchi chishita.* 'We arrived at Deer Salt in the afternoon.'

    chishita (adv) 'afternoon'

3. *Kariguna ruyata kuchunawra hachawan; tsuping kuchunawra.* 'The men chopped down trees with axes; *tsuping* (clearing everything) they chopped them.'

   tsuping 'ideophone for a complete stripping or clearing away'

4. *Ñuka yanapak arani ismu hachawan.* 'I was a helper with my rotted ax.'

   ismu (adj) 'rotted'

5. *Chimanda kanoata rirani aswata llapingaw.* 'Then I went to the canoe to squeeze some *aswa*.'

   llapina 'to squeeze, usually said of squeezing cooked, fermented *aswa* pulp in water'

6. *Aswata llapiurani, paygunata upichingaw. Kungaylla paktamura Tito. Tsala nawiyuk ara.* 'I was squeezing *aswa* to give them to drink. Suddenly Tito arrived. His face was pale.'

   tsala 'white, pale, usually said of skin'

7. *"Kumpari Galves kazi wañui tukura!" niwan.* '"Compadre Galves almost ended up dead," he tells me.'

   tukuna 'to become'
   kazi 'almost' (cf. Sp. *casi*)

8. *"Imata pasara?" nini.* '"What happened?" I ask.'

9. *Hatun motolo ruku payta kallpachira. Tarapoto ruyai tiyaun kunan. Ama rikugrichu!* 'A great big *motolo* chased him. He's up in a *tarapoto* tree now. Don't go and look!'

   motolo 'type of pit viper'
   kallpachina 'to make run; to chase'
   tarapoto 'name of a tall palm tree'

Nominalizing Verbs with –y Suffix

It is possible for Quichua speakers to turn verbs into nouns by deleting the infinitive *–na* and adding a *–y* suffix, which then becomes part of a compound verb construction. The *–y* nominalizing suffix is also found in other Quechua dialects outside of Ecuador (Adelaar and Muysken 2004, 226–227). Compound verbs formed with a *y*-suffixed verb are quite common in PQ and NQ.

The 'Become' Construction: –*y* Verb + *tukuna*

The verb *tukuna* 'to become, turn into' may be used with a –*y* suffixed verb root to indicate that a process is happening with little volitional control on the part of a person, or other, typically sentient being. For example, *wañuy tukuna* may be used and translated 'to become dead, end up dead,' as it is in Line 7 of the opening narrative:

> *Kumpari Galves kazi wañuy tukura.* 'Compadre Galves almost ended up dead.'

Note that this nominalized –*y* suffix is pronounced the same as the singular immediate imperative –*i*. We use a –*y* suffix for nominalized verbs both because it has been the preferred way to represent nominalizations in other varieties of Quechua, and also to distinguish it from imperative –*i* verbs. *Wañuy* is considered a nominalized form because it can function as a noun-like word meaning 'death.'

In combination with the verb *tukuna* 'to become,' however, the nominalized verb may be conveniently thought of as having the same meaning as a past participle. The construction *wañuy tukuna* can be literally translated 'to become dead, to end up in death, or more simply, to end up dead.' *Tukuna* forms compounds with many different verbs.

Practice 1

Say the correct form of the verb in parentheses for each of the following sentences.

Example:

> Ñukanchi _____ tukuranchi ismushka aycha. (*kwinana* 'to be nauseous, to vomit')
> Ñukanchi kwinay tukuranchi ismushka aycha. 'We became nauseous from the (smell of the) rotten meat'

1. Ñukanchi _____ tukuranchi Ulpiano wasii. (*karana*)
2. Pay _____ tukura payba kachunmanda. (*upichina*)

3. *Tarabashka washa* _____ *tukurangichichu?* (*pagana*)
4. *Bagri* _____ *tukura ñuka likai* (*lika* 'fishing net'). (*hapichina*)
5. _____ *tukushun puma o amarun.* (*mikuna*)
6. *Ñukanchi mana* _____ *tukuranchichu mingangaw.* (*kayana*)
7. *Puma* _____ *tukunawra sachai.* (*apanakuna*)
8. *Motolo* _____ *tukura Kumpari Galves.* (*kallpachina*)
9. *Ñuka pani* _____ *tukun kari.* (*ichuna*)
10. *Ñuka* _____ *tukurani Anna Maria.* (*llullana*)

Culture Focus: Forest Resources: *Lumu*

Manihot esculenta, the species name for what is commonly known in Quichua as *lumu*, or by non-Quichua speakers as manioc, yuca, or cassava, is a major source of carbohydrate energy for residents of Amazonian Ecuador. For Quichua-speaking Runa, it is a garden staple that is mostly used to make *aswa*, a lightly fermented drink which is a major source of carbohydrate energy, consumed by all. It is an intrinsic part of hospitality rituals as well as major celebrations. The preparation of *aswa* is traditionally done by women who boil the manioc tubers and then mash them together in a large wooden vat. The traditional method of making *aswa* also involves taking a small portion of the cooked, mashed manioc and letting it sit inside one's mouth for a few minutes. This process of mastication introduces enzymes from saliva which catalyze fermentation.

Manioc gardens are significant spaces for working and socializing. Although many other crops are grown along with it, manioc is the most intensively cultivated. Women may spend hours every week weeding, cultivating, harvesting, and protecting their gardens from pests. They nurture their manioc tubers and may even think of them metaphorically as their children. Not surprisingly, the significance of gardens often involves beliefs about the sacredness of such spaces and the reverence that should be accorded to them. According to one woman, one should announce oneself by lightly rapping on trees when entering one's own *chagra* so that the spirits of the garden are alerted to your presence. Attempting to quietly enter someone else's garden will result in illness, because the spirits of the garden will quickly detect your presence and realize that you are an intruder, and likely a thief as well, and, in a vampire-like way, they will suck your blood!

Translation Challenge

Go to the following link:
https://www.youtube.com/watch?v=hWub9fPll-4

Listen to the first minute and twelve seconds which has been transcribed and partly translated, featuring a speaker's description of proper etiquette when entering one's agricultural field, as well as a warning about not entering other peoples' agricultural fields. The suffix *–chun* in line 4 will be discussed in Lesson 20. It is similar in meaning to the suffix *–nga* 'in order to.' Try to translate the untranslated sentences below:

1. *Chitaga ñukanchita ñukanchi yayaga nik ara: "shukba chagraiga mana yaykuna chan."* 'This is what our father used to say to us: "Into another person's *chagra*, one is not to enter."'

2. *"Amowa chagraibi ruyata kasna taw taw taw taw taw, taw taw taw taw taw waktasha yaykuna nik an."*
   " _____ "

3. *"Dinuga shukba chagraibiga mashti amo kantasha, sakishka manga," nik ara.* '"Otherwise, into another person's *chagra*, the owner, singing (magical songs) will have left (the *chagra*)" he used to say.'

4. *Ñukanchi yawarta win upichun nisha!* 'In order that they (the garden's spirits), wanting to, will drink all of our blood.'

5. *Mana shukba chagraiga mana yaykuna nik ara.*
   ' _____ '

6. *"Kanguna yaykukpiga, kanguna yawarta upikpiga tsalaaa tukungichi," nik ara.*
   " _____ "

"Chiga lomo mamaga win! amo, lomo amoga upi tukungichi yawarta" nikga. '"And so the mother (spirit) of the manioc, all of it! You-all will end up (having all of) your blood drunk by the manioc's owner spirit" he would say.'

Mana yaykuna chan shukba chagraibiga.
' _____ '

Amowa chagraibi, mashti, ruyai waktasha yaykuna an nisha nira.
' _____ '

"Mashti, yumingasha sakishka dinuga, kangunataga, mashti, upi tukungichimi yawarta" nik ara. '"Um, having left it, hexing it, and so, you-all, um, will end up with your blood drunk," he would say.'

Chiwa raygu mana yaykuna chan shukba chagrai nisha ñukanchita wawamandata kunasha (kunana 'to advise') ñukanchita wibai tukuk aranchi.

'_____

_____,'

Practice 2

Answer the following questions by making use of the words in parentheses.

Example:

Imata tukushun? (*mikuna, puma*) 'What will become of us?'
Mikuy tukushun puma. 'We'll end up being eaten by a jaguar.'

1. *Imata tukunga?* (*kanina, palo*)
2. *Imata tukusha?* (*hapichina, amarun*)
3. *Imata tukungi?* (*mikuna, amarun*)
4. *Imata tukungawna?* (*llullana, kachun*)
5. *Imata tukushun?* (*ichuna, kari*)
6. *Imata tukungichi?* (*kallpachina, motolo*)
7. *Imata tukungichi?* (*kayana, kumpari Galves*)

Completive *–y* Verb + *Pasana* Constructions

In addition to the compound construction just discussed, featuring a nominalized verb and an inflected form of *tukuna*, there is the possibility of using the verb *pasana* 'to pass, finish' with a nominalized verb to express completive meanings. We have discussed the use of *–shka* as a perfect aspect marker that is also used as a kind of genre marker for beginning times stories, and in expressions linked with surprise.

We now introduce a more 'everyday' construction for expressing completive meaning. This construction is formed by suffixing a verb root with *–y*, which is then used together with an inflected form of the verb *pasana* 'to finish, pass.' The resulting construction expresses the idea that something is completed and its completion is relevant to the time of speaking. This construction is therefore comparable to a present perfect construction in English:

Mikuy pasangichu? 'Have you finished eating?'
Ña riy pasan 'He/she/it has already gone.'
Armay pasanawn 'They have finished bathing.'

Practice 3

Practice expressing the completive construction by responding to the following direct imperatives. Remember that the imperative *–i* and the *–y* sound are pronounced the same.

Example:

Mikui! 'Eat!'
Ña mikuy pasanimi! 'Well I've (already) eaten!'

1. *Upichi!*
2. *Tarabai!*
3. *Chagrata allmaichi!*
4. *Ayllugunata upichi!*
5. *Kosasgunata alichi!*
6. *Maytuna pangata pallaichi!*
7. *Mukahata pintai!*
8. *Wasita pichai!*
9. *Aychata chakichi!*
10. *Kallari timputa kwintai!*

Review Question: *–shka* Suffix

Go to the following link:
http://quechuarealwords.byu.edu/?ideophone=kushning

Listen to video 1, featuring a speaker using the construction we have just practiced, using the verb *rina* 'to go' suffixed with *–y*, along with *pasana*. The speaker is describing a personal experience of expecting to find her mother by searching for her in her garden, and then realizing that she had already gone.

In this example, however, the speaker is using the *–shka* suffix, rather than an ordinary past tense suffix, saying *ri pasashka* rather than *ri pasara*. Can you explain why?

Mama chagrai paktaranchi. Rikukpi mama kiwata allmanga shamukga kushning! Ña ri pasashka mara mama! 'We arrived at mom's *chagra*. Upon looking (we realized that), mom, having come to weed, (all that was left was a bit of) smoke (from her campfire)! She had already gone, mom had!'

Inceptive –*y* Verb + *Kallarina* Constructions

The verb *kallarina* 'to begin' can be used in a type of compound verb phrase which is semantically similar to the English 'begin to do something' construction. Furthermore, it is formed according to the same principles as the other compound constructions already discussed in this lesson: the verb + *tukuna* and verb + *pasana* constructions. Consider the first example below:

Wawaga waka-y kallarira. 'The baby began to cry.'

In this sentence, the nominalizing –*y* turns the verb root *wakana* into an infinitive-like form, translatable as 'to cry.'

Practice 4

Practice this construction by transforming the following verbs into inceptive constructions, using the past tense for the main verb.

Example:

(*ñuka, pay, apanakuna*)
Ñuka payta apanakuy kallarirani. 'I began to follow him/her/it.'

1. (*pay, chagrana*)
2. (*pay, ñuka, chapana*)
3. (*ñukanchi, paba, wañuchina*)
4. (*turiguna, taruga, kallpachina*)
5. (*kanguna, ñuka, killachina*)
6. (*payguna, ruya, kuchuna*)
7. (*payguna, baylana*)
8. (*yachak, takina*)
9. (*wawaguna, pugllana*)
10. (*ñukanchi, upichina*)

Review Question: –*shka* Suffix

Go to the following link:
http://quechuarealwords.byu.edu/?ideophone=kushning
  Listen to video 3, featuring a speaker using the construction we have just practiced, using the verb *sindina* 'to burn' suffixed with –*y*, along with *kallarina*. By way of background, the speaker is describing events from long ago, which he has heard about from others, when intertribal warfare was common. In this particular description, he explains how houses would begin to burn after being set on fire by aggressors. Can you explain why he says *sindi kallarishka* rather than *sindi kallarira*?

Chiga ña wing wasi sindi kallrishka, hapirishka wasi kushning. 'And so then, the entire house began to burn, being caught (by fire) it (went up in) smoke.'

General Principles of Sentence Construction: Subject Deletion

Quichua belongs to a typological category of languages which arrange their meaningful elements in a subject/object/verb order. This means that a sentence which actually has a subject, direct object, and a verb will most likely feature these constituents in an SOV (subject, object, verb) pattern when a speaker is attempting to present information as unambiguously as possible. However, word order is subject to tremendous variation and there are several permutations of this general, ideal model. One important variable is the presence of a subject. As you have probably already noticed, subjects are frequently omitted.

Practice 5

Identify the subjects of the following sentences, and remove them, repeating whatever remains of the sentence.

Example:

Ñuka apa yaya kunan shamun. > *Kunan shamun.*

1. *Ñukanchi ukta shamuranchi, paygunata yanapangaw.*
2. *Kan imata munangi?*
3. *Payguna yandata tsalisha tarabanawn.*
4. *Kan ama ñukata tapuwangichu!*
5. *Ñuka hachi Cervantes ñawpa ali kantak mara.*
6. *Payga ñañawanshi purik ara.*
7. *Kanguna tragota upi pasarangichichu?*
8. *Ñuka wawa yakui pugllasha armak an.*
9. *Puka yakumanda warmiguna gustuta baylauragunami.*
10. *Shuwak runaga wasimanda kungaylla llukshira.*

General Principles of Sentence Construction: Subject Transposition

When a speaker wants to emphasize the action or event described by a sentence, if a subject is in fact mentioned, then that subject may be moved into the sentence's word-final position. Consider by way of illustration the following sentence:

Pundzhanshi rikurinawra, estelleresga. 'Brightly (they) appeared, those stars.'

The speaker of this sentence shifted the subject so that it was last, in order to emphasize the brightness of the stars. However, it is difficult to translate this into English, because we don't usually construct sentences with adverbs in initial position.

Practice 6

Move subjects to sentence final position to emphasize the action or event referred to in the sentence. Note that example sentences 1 through 6 use ordinary nouns such as *pundzha* 'day,' *wasi* 'house,' *uma* 'head,' *yana* 'black,' and *ruya* 'white' in a special adverb-like way with the suffix –*n*, which is probably a shortened form of the instrumental –*wan*.

First pronounce each sentence as it is and then recombine its elements.

Example:

Estelleresga pundzhanshi rikurira. 'The stars, brightly they appeared.' > *Pundzhanshi rikurira, estelleresga.* 'Brightly appeared the stars.'

1. *Tangu pundzhan pundzhanshi rikurik man.* 'The beetle brightly appeared.'
2. *Talmu kuru* (type of worm) *lomo kaspiwan wikan wikanshi purik man.* 'The *talmu* worm with a manioc stick, pointing up, pointing up, was a walker.'
3. *Armadillu tazin wasinshi rikurin.* 'The armadillo nest, house-like, it appears.'
4. *Amarunga yaku hawai uman rikuriura.* 'The anaconda on top of the water with its head it appeared.'
5. *Siluga kungaylla yananmi tutayara.* 'The sky suddenly black-like it became night.'
6. *Siluga ruyanmi pundzhayara.* 'The sky white-like, it became day.'
7. *Ñukaga mana tukuta mikunichu.*
8. *Kikin lobo yakui bagrita hapiura.*
9. *Bagriga yaku ukumanda dzas saltara.*
10. *Ñukaga lomo kaspita mana apamuranichu.*
11. *Ñuka ñañawa churi yapa shuwak man.*
12. *Payba llullu wawa mundo wakaysiki* (crybaby, literally: 'cry-butt') *man.*
13. *Payga ñawi lulunwan mana rikunata ushandzhu.*

Lesson 19

Conditionality, Ordering, and Connecting Ideas

Indillama 'sloth'
TOD SWANSON

The Present Conditional *–ma*

The present conditional is a mood that expresses possibility. However, Quichua speakers do not have separate words for auxiliary verbs such as 'would,' 'might,' 'should,' and 'could.' One suffix *–ma* may be used for any of these meanings. For simplicity, we will refer to all of the semantic moods of this suffix as 'conditional.' The conditional is formed by adding the *–ma* suffix to a verb after the present tense suffixes have been added. This is a fairly regular process. Only the first person conditional is irregular. It is formed by the same process as that used for immediate imperatives:

Shamui-ma (instead of *shamuni-ma) 'I would/might/should/could come'

The remaining paradigm is regular:

shamungima 'You would/might/should/could come.'
shamunma 'S/he would/might/should/could come.'
shamunchima 'We would/might/should/could come.'
shamungichima 'You (pl) would/might/should/could come.'
shamununma (NQ) 'They would/might/should/could come.'
shamunawnma (PQ) 'They would/might/should/could come.'

The *–ma* conditional suffix is identical to the directional *–ma* suffix which expresses the idea of motion toward a goal. The main difference is in their distribution. The directional *–ma* is suffixed to nouns, while conditional *–ma* occurs on verbs. It is possible that conditionality evolved out of directional *–ma*'s meaning.

The conditional *–ma* may itself be further affixed with evidentials *–mi*, *–shi*, and the negation/question suffix *–chu*. The following examples illustrate such constructions:

Sachai purimami 'I (assert) that I might walk in the forest.'
Tukuta mikungimachu 'Might you eat grubs?'
Payguna mana paktamunawnmachu 'They might not arrive.'

Written Exercise 1

Translate the following conditional statements.

1. *Rupay tukusha, yakuimi armanchima.* 'Becoming hot (feverish) we might bathe in water.'

    _____

2. *Palandara tarpungimachu?*

    _____

3. *Ushasha rimanma.*

   _____

4. *Baylak shamunawnma.*

   _____

5. *Pita lalata wañuchima.*

   _____

6. *Mana riksishka sachaimi pandanawnma.*

   _____

7. *Mana piñasha ñukata kipirinma.*

   _____

8. *Yuyangi! Kamba makita rikuchikpi pay kaninma!*

   _____

9. *Kan sambayasha sakiringima kaybi.*

   _____

10. *Kamba llachapa turuyakpi taksangima.*

    _____

Practice 1

Go to the following link:
https://www.youtube.com/watch?v=wOzfcM3ahTQ

Listen from 37 until 57 seconds to part of a personal experience narrative told from a woman's childhood memory, involving a trek through the forest with her father. In the final sentences you will hear the conditional *–ma* to describe what her father said might happen if she doesn't follow his advice. Fill in the words that are missing below and then translate the sentences.

1. *Chi pay* _____ _____ _____ *Runas illashka sachai! Nukata*

2. _____ *yaya: kushillu ismata, wira ismata* _____ *purik man pumaga!*

3. *Rikusha* _____! _____ _____! *ni-wara ñuka yaya.*

Translation:

_____

_____

_____

The Relative Order of Meaningful Elements

In Lesson 18, we began to learn about the syntax of Quichua utterances. The principles of subject-object-verb word order and subject deletion and transposition were explained. Besides the frequent deletions and transpositions undergone by grammatical subjects, there are several other principles to keep in mind. Although it is usually true that direct objects precede their verbs, they may also occur immediately after their verbs. What is most important is that a direct object is closer to its verb than instrumental *–wan* or locative *–i* forms, called obliques. For example, consider the following two sentences. The first is completely acceptable because the direct object is closer to the verb than the oblique phrase *sachay* 'in the forest':

Sachai pawata wañuchira. 'In the forest the turkey he killed.'

The second, however, would be much less likely:

**Pawata illapawan wañuchira.* 'The turkey with a rifle he killed.'

The preceding sentence is unlikely to be heard because it places the oblique instrumental argument *illapawan* 'with a rifle' closer to the verb than its direct object. The reason that direct objects occur in close proximity to their verbs has to do with the fact that they are typically most affected by the verb's action. There is a greater semantic relatedness between a verb and its object, and this is reflected by its placement close to the verb, whether immediately before it, or immediately following it. The relative order of these forms may be diagrammed as followed:

1. oblique—2. direct object—3. verb

Common oblique suffixes are:

locative *–i*
instrumental *–wan*

direction toward –*ma*
direction from –*manda*
distance/temporal suffix –*gama*

What is important to emphasize, again, is that direct object forms most commonly precede verbs, but may also occur after their verbs. Recall the following example, from line 1 of Lesson 9, where the direct object is placed right after the verb, and is followed by a locative form:

Lobo hapiura bagrita yakui. 'A wolf was catching a catfish in the water.'

The relative order of these forms may be diagrammed as followed:

3. verb—2. direct object—1. oblique

Whatever their position, direct objects will almost always be in closer proximity to their verbs than a locative, instrumental, or directional form. This means that either of the following two sequences may occur: 1 2 3 or: 3 2 1. The following two examples illustrate both of these possibilities:

1 2 3: *Hachawan pita lalata pitira.* 'With an ax, he cut the *pita lala.*'
3 2 1: *Pitira pita lalata hachawan.* 'He cut the *pita lala* with an ax.'

Although both of these examples are possible, the overwhelming majority of sentences will use the 1 2 3 principle of word order.

Practice 2

Practice forming constructions with the following sets of words, using instrumental, locative, or direct object markers. Assume that subjects have been deleted. First go through each example, inflecting its verb for present tense, and use the 1 2 3 principle of syntax. Then turn that sentence into a present conditional form, using the 1 2 3 word order.

Example:

masha Alberto/upichina/aswa
Aswawan masha Albertota upichin. (1 2 3)
Aswawan masha Albertota upichinma (1 2 3, present conditional)

1. *ñambi/linterna/purina*
2. *mushuk llachapa/randina/kullki*
3. *rina/hawa llakta/kanoa*
4. *yanuna/manga/lomo*

5. *tsalina/hacha/yanda*
6. *shayachina/nina/manga*
7. *puñuna/pacha/kama*
8. *sawli/waktana/palo*
9. *allpa/mukaha/awana*
10. *wawa/wasi/apagrina*

Practice 3

Now construct sentences, again following the 1 2 3 or 3 2 1 order, using the following word sets, and also use *–gama* or *–manda* suffixes wherever possible. Assume that subjects have been deleted, and use the 'going-to-do' compound future construction in any person/number.

Example:

chaki/chagra/rina
Chakiwan chagrama ringa rawnguna. 'They are going to go to the *chagra* on foot.'

1. *trago/upichina/tukurina*
2. *llakta/saplla/purina*
3. *tukurina/aswa/upichina*
4. *Kwankiri yaku/sindzhita/waytana*
5. *payba tambu/wayra shina/rina*
6. *mikyawa wasi/kusa/katina* 'to follow'
7. *wiki llukshina/ñuka/asina*
8. *chayana/lomo/yanuna*
9. *maki/waska/watana*
10. *shimi/bagri/hapina*
11. *linterna/maskana/wawa*
12. *wasi/ñambi/apanakuna*
13. *llakta/purina/alimanda*

When Order Is Not Strictly Regulated

When a sentence consists of two or more forms belonging to one slot, their relative order is not as strictly prescribed. Speakers often take two constituents belonging to the same slot and place one in front of the verb and the other after the verb. This helps to distribute the sentence's semantic weight a little more evenly. For example, either of the following two sentences could occur, because both of the case marked constituents have slot 1 suffixes:

Hanagma rira kanoawan. 'Upriver went (he/she) by canoe.'

Or:

Kanoawan rira hanagma. 'By canoe went (he/she) upriver.'

The semantic differences between these equally possible sentences will largely be a result of the speaker's intentions for meaning. Generally, the constituent mentioned first has a certain priority for the sentence's overall meaning. However, intonation can be at least as important for communicating semantic significance.

If ever in doubt about where to place the elements of a sentence, a good rule of thumb is to place any words or phrases referring to animate objects, agents, etc., in closer proximity to the verb than words referring to inanimate objects, entities, etc.

One final point needs to be made. The rule stating that words suffixed with slot 2 forms must occur before the verb can be circumvented by placing one word before the verb and another after the verb. For example:

1 3 2: *Alita karanawra wawata.* 'Nicely (they) fed the child.'

Or:

2 3 1: *Wawata karanawra alita.* 'The child (they) fed nicely.'

Both of these sentences are technically consistent with the rules previously outlined because they place the direct object *wawata* 'the child' immediately adjacent to the verb.

Practice 4

Construct sentences with the following word sets, using suffixes from slots 1 and 2. Arrange your constituents in any order, as long as you place the direct object close to its verb.

Example:

ruya/mana valik hacha/kuchuna
Ruyata kuchurani mana valik hachawan. 'I chopped the tree with a no good (literally: a not valued) ax.'

1. *hawa llakta/kanoa/tigrana*
2. *mandzhana/yaku/yaykuna* [neg]

3. *llakta/sapalla/purina*
4. *kungaylla/chupa/rikuchina*
5. *wawaguna/yapa/unayana*
6. *kari/alita/kawsana*
7. *turu/allpa/urmana*
8. *kungaylla/maki/rikuchina*
9. *payba warmi/yanga/llullana*
10. *Irmilinda/chari/rina*
11. *ashanga/charapa lulun/maskana*
12. *shaka/sapi/likirina*
13. *kaya/hanag/rina*
14. *lomo kaspi/chagra/apagrina*
15. *yaku hawa/polang/rikurina*
16. *uma/hapina/akcha*

Culture Focus: Forest Resources: Sloths and Bromeliads

The three-toed sloth is commonly encountered in the Ecuadorian Amazon. Known for its extremely slow movements and its habit of sleeping most of the day, it is often made fun of or pitied. Ideas vary on whether its meat is appropriate for humans to eat. Some Runa profess to never eat sloth meat because of this animal's extremely vulnerable and pathetic nature. Others will, nevertheless, kill sloths for meat.

Also common are plants called bromeliads. There are thousands of species of bromeliads, many of which are found in the Ecuadorian Amazon. Many have a structure that allows them to hold rainwater, which is drunk by hundreds of species of organisms. Besides their ability to hold rainwater, their leaves are also food for sloths. In the following video, women find bromeliad leaves that have been partially eaten by sloths. This finding inspires one woman to think about sloths and some of their endearing behavior. She then explains how pathetic they are and asserts that she would never eat them, despite knowing that some people do.

While explaining her empathy for the sloth, the narrator also relates how the sloth is like a person who has a *chagra*. Just as people live from certain plants grown in their gardens, the sloth is also said to have its own garden high in the canopies of trees where bromeliads are found. When it has eaten all of the bromeliads in a particular place, it is said to climb down from its perch very slowly, over the course of an entire day.

Conditionality, Ordering, and Connecting Ideas 219

Written Exercise 2

Go to the following link:
https://www.youtube.com/watch?v=JLO2tie3SJw&feature=youtu.be

Watch the video, first in English, then in Quichua, about a sloth, perceived by the narrator to be rather pathetic.

Next, try to imagine yourself as a poor sloth in search of food high in the canopy. Write five sentences in Quichua below that would capture a sloth's perspective as it climbs slowly. Use varied sentence structures, including coreference verbs modifying main verbs, switch reference verbs, future tense verbs, habitual constructions, and conditional verbs. Each sentence should have at least five words.

1. _____
2. _____
3. _____
4. _____
5. _____

Tools for Connecting Ideas

Quichua does not have conjunctions to connect clauses. English words such as 'but,' 'and,' 'or,' and 'if' have no translational equivalents for Quichua speakers. Much of what creates cohesion between different clauses depends on intonation which, together with function words and comparative terms, may help create links between sets of ideas. Two such terms that are often used together are *imayna*, a contracted form of *ima shina* 'how like' and *chasnalla* 'just like that.' To illustrate this, consider the following example from a traditional story about a man who was considered repulsive until a forest spirit helped him become irresistibly attractive to all women.

In the following example, the forest spirit addresses the man and tells him what is about to happen, using a set of comparative terms to introduce two different thoughts:

> *Imaynata kan ñukata maskaurangi? Chasnallatami warmiguna kanda munasha maskanga raunguna!* 'In the way that you were searching for me? In just that way, women (who are) wanting you, are going to search for you.'

The first sentence is articulated with a rising question intonation which is followed by a second sentence that falls assertively with its intonation.

Practice 5

Construct two sentences that establish a comparison, using *imayna* and *chasnalla*, with appropriate intonation. Also, be certain to use a future tense, a compound future construction, or a conditional verb in the *chasnalla* sentence.

Example:

Kan, sindzhita, tarabana/pay, sindzhita, tarabana
Imaynata kan sindzhita tarabarangi? Chasnallata paymi tarabanga raun! '(You know how) you worked so hard? In just that way, she is going to work!'

1. *kan, aswa, upichina/ñuka aswa, upichina*
2. *payguna, wawa, maskana/ñukanchi, wawa, maskana*
3. *kanguna, aycha, hapina/ñuka, aycha, hapina*
4. *wawaguna, sambayasha puñuna/apa mamaguna, sambayasha puñuna*
5. *ichilla wawa, wakay kallarina/indillama, wakay kallarina*
6. *kan, ichuy tukurina/ñuka ñaña, ichuy tukuna*
7. *kanguna, mikuy pasana/ñukanchi, mikuy pasana*
8. *payguna, motolo, tupana/kan, motolo, tupana*
9. *kan, tiyarik shamuna/ñuka tiyarik shamuna*
10. *payguna, raykaywan, kawsana/ñukanchi, raykaywan, kawsana*

Lesson 20

Evidentiality, Speech Reports, Inchoative –*Ya*, and Purposive –*Chun*

Sacha wagra 'tapir'
GREG MAULDIN

Evidential –*cha* and *Chari*

We turn now to a third member of the evidential set of suffixes that Quichua speakers may employ to specify an unknown perspective. This third evidential marker *does* imply a lack of certainty, and may therefore be considered conjectural. When a speaker states something that is not grounded either in that speaker's or anyone else's perspective, the evidential –*cha* is used. It is possibly a shortened form of the adverb *chari* 'maybe, perhaps.' –*Cha* is used more by Upper Napo speakers, while the adverb *chari* is most often used by Pastaza Quichua speakers.

To understand the importance of *–cha* and *chari*, it is important to emphasize the desirability of open-endedness in peoples' assertion making habits. Speakers are careful to clarify the sources of their statements, *not* because they wish to be empirically accountable to objective facts that are verified by means of evidence. Rather, they exercise such care because there is a cultural preference for contextualizing statements within a perspective. Although being empirically objective and carefully framing a statement's perspective may at times seem to converge with the same end result, namely, a statement that is careful about making any claims at all, the underlying motivations are different.

Speakers wishing to be careful about making only empirically based claims would have to be concerned with an abstract, de-contextualized notion of truth. In Amazonian Quichua culture, by contrast, there is a moral and aesthetic preference for articulating the perspective from which a statement is made. This perspectivism is not only part of human communication. It is part of Quichua peoples' animistic cosmology, which allows for the possibility that all life is capable of articulating a perspective.

However, there doesn't seem to be much interest on the part of Quichua speakers in articulating a synthesis of multiple perspectives to arrive at a final, coherent picture. Instead, people are anxious to avoid a kind of moral presumptuousness, which is how speaking about others' actions and words, without properly contextualized knowledge, is interpreted. Perspectivism for Quichua speakers, then, seems motivated, in part, by a kind of negative politeness, in that speakers do not wish to impose on others by presuming to speak for them.

The concept of negative politeness does not fully explain things, however, since it is based in an individualized notion of selfhood. The Quichua self is more of a relational self than an individualistic one. A relational self is one that is situated in one's family group or *ayllu*. There is a professed ideal for speaking well, *ali rimana*, which involves speaking relationally, and which, for Quichua speakers, means speaking perspectivally. Someone who does not speak from an acknowledged perspective is a *killa* 'useless,' a *lulla* 'liar,' or a *lala* 'exaggerator.' Because strength is relational and relational speech is perspectival, speaking perspectivally is a key quality of being a *sindzhi runa* 'strong man' or *sindzhi warmi* 'strong woman.' Speaking relationally is considered empowering because it forges bonds of interconnectedness with others.

Being uncertain and being careful about not saying more than one is sure about are therefore acceptable ways of speaking. When *–cha* is used, it behaves like the evidential enclitics *–mi* and *–shi*, attaching to any class of word after other suffixes have been added. However, it is the least used enclitic, and may be falling into disuse. Speakers are more likely to use the conjectural adverbial *chari* to express uncertainty than they are *–cha*. It is not clear whether *–cha* is simply a shortened form of the adverb *chari*, or was once a more actively used enclitic suffix that is on its way to becoming obsolete. Their semantics are fairly interchangeable in Pastaza Quichua:

Payba mikya Lolacha shamura. 'His/her Aunt Lola perhaps came.'

Or:

Payba mikya Lola chari shamura. 'His/her Aunt Lola perhaps came.'

Napo Quichua speakers will often use *–cha* instead of *–chu* when asking a yes/no question. This is an alternative way of asking a question without being so direct. For example: *Kariyukcha an?* 'Is she married (i.e., Is she perhaps a husband-possessor)?' This might be a sensitive topic and so could be translated as 'Is she maybe/perhaps married?'

In Napo, questions with *–cha* are often used to elicit a confirmative response from interlocutors which sometimes simply serves, like the English 'uh-huh,' to keep the conversation going. If the speaker would like to assert that something is emphatically the case, he or she will often answer with *–da/–ra*, which could be translated as 'It sure is the case that . . .' Consider the following examples:

Paywa pani shamundzha? 'So his sister (perhaps) has come?'
Shamundá. 'She sure has come.'
Tamiandzha? 'Is it (perhaps) raining?'
Tamiandá. 'It sure is raining.'

Or with the future:

Paywa pani cirtu shamungachá? 'Is his sister really, perhaps, coming?'
Shamungará. 'She is coming all right.'

In Napo, speakers may also use *chuy* 'really, for real?' to imply that someone is skeptical of something. For example:

Pay kariyukchuy? 'Is she really married?'
Pay shamuundzhuy? 'Is he really coming?'

Written Exercise 1

Translate the following English sentences into Quichua:

Example:

Does she really have a child?
Pay wawayukchuy?

1. Does he really have a wife?

2. Did you-all perhaps drink *aswa*?

3. Have you perhaps come to help (literally: as a helper perhaps, have you come)?

4. When you arrived, were they perhaps home?

5. Might we perhaps go to the forest today?

6. Will he perhaps go to the forest in order to hunt for meat?

7. Did they really see a *pita lala*?

8. Did the *aswa* perhaps run out? (*tukurina*)

9. Has Uncle Fausto really come?

10. Your child has perhaps lied.

---

11. We perhaps are going to go to sleep.

Speech Reports

Having shown how the grammar of Quichua encodes perspective, which is highly valued over decontextualized certainty, we turn now to a discussion of discourse practices which also encourage speakers to attend to perspective by representing what others say. An important difference between Quichua and a standard average European language like English is that Quichua has very few illocutionary verbs. Verbs such as 'to warn,' 'to announce,' 'to proclaim,' 'to threaten,' 'to reassure,' 'to insist,' and 'to explain' are just a sample of the many illocutionary verbs, also known as 'speech act verbs,' that populate everyday English language discourse. All of them have in common their encoding of an act of speaking that is accomplished in a certain manner or mood, or for a certain purpose.

By contrast, Quichua verbs that encode speaking constitute an extremely small group. They include: *nina* 'to say,' which is often used to frame quoted speech; *rimana* 'to speak, tell,' which simply states that speaking took place, but not necessarily anything about the content of what was spoken; *kaparina* 'to shout'; *kamina* 'to insult'; and *llullana* 'to lie.' Another difference is that Quichua speakers do not typically comment on what people say without reporting the words that were spoken. To illustrate this point, consider the following sentence, which would be typical for a speaker of English:

'The Peruvians explained how to grab (it).'

A Quichua speaker, instead, would report the words that explained, rather than stating that explaining took place:

"*Kasna rasha kapingi,*' *ninawnshi peruanoguna.* '"This is how, doing, you grab (it)" say the Peruvians (according to someone)'

Another important difference between represented discourse in Quichua and in English is that Quichua speakers do not make a distinction between direct and indirect speech. Unlike languages such as English, there is no way to give an indirect report, such as the following:

'He said he would go.'

In Quichua, by contrast, the words that served as the announcement for the person's departure would be represented in a speech report as follows:

"Riunimi," nishashi nira pay. '"I'm going," saying (according to someone), he/she said.'

Although it sounds redundant, the formula *nisha nira* 'saying he/she said' is commonly employed. It is used to frame discourse as a speech report by representing actual words that someone would or did say.

Written Exercise 2

Translate the following Quichua sentences into English.

Example:

"Bagrita mikushun," nishami ninawra payguna.
'"Let's eat catfish," saying (I-as-speaker assert) they said.'

1. *"Tiyarik shamui aswata upingawa," nishami nin pay.*

2. *"Ñukaga mana warmiyuk chani," nishashi nin.*

3. *"Ñukanchiga pugllanakuuranchi," nishashi ninawra.*

4. *"Ñukanchi rinchima," nishashi ninawra.*

5. *"Runagunata upichingawa aswasha," nishami nin payga.*

6. *"Ringami rauni sachama,"* nishashi nin Hachi Albertoga.

   _____

7. *"Wañuchi tukungami raunchi puma,"* nishami niranchi.

   _____

8. *"Kandzhu rikuk arangi indillamata,"* tapusha niwan pay.

   _____

9. *"Ña mikuy pasanchimi,"* nishashi niwanawn.

   _____

10. *"Ama sapalla sakiringichi ichushka wasibi!"* nishami nin.

    _____

Culture Focus: Forest Resources: Tapirs and the Foods They Eat

The Amazonian tapir is a large mammal that eats many kinds of plants, including fruits from palm trees, which it helps to propagate through the cycle of eating and defecating the fruits' seeds as it travels through the forest. People often attempt to hunt tapirs by anticipating where they will most likely feed, based on knowledge of fruits' seasonal maturation and decay. Two palm tree fruits enjoyed by people, the *chunda* (discussed in Lesson 2) and the *morete* (dicussed in Lesson 13), are also enjoyed by tapirs. The following traditional story reflects tapirs' enjoyment of *morete* insofar as it features a mythic tapir man who initiates a relationship with a human woman by giving her gifts of large baskets full of *morete* fruits.

Translation Challenge

Go to the following link:
https://www.youtube.com/watch?v=wN1NNJgJUXA&feature=youtu.be

Listen to the first 2 minutes and 12 seconds of the narrative about a woman who marries a tapir and eventually becomes one herself. Notice how many examples of speech reports there are. See if you can transcribe and translate the speech reports that are missing below:

1. *Shuk warmishi sapalla tiyak ara ushushillawan.* 'A woman (they say) lived alone with just her daughter.'

2. *Y tiyashkayshi "_____," nishashi ashangata aparisharin.* 'And being there (they say) "_____," saying (they say) taking the basket, she (the daughter) goes.'

3. *Chiga churuwawaguna, imawawagunatashi, lluchunawawagunatashi hapisha apamusha karak ashka.* 'And so little snails, whatever little things (they say), little crayfish (they say) taking, bringing back, she would give (her mother) to eat.'

4. *Chasna raushashi shamura pay.* 'Doing like that (they say), she came.'

5. *Ashangai hundakta moretetashi aparimura.* 'She brought *morete* in a basket completely filled.'

6. *Shuk pundzhatas chingarira.* 'On another day also she disappeared.'

7. *Ali mama maskauuurashi.* 'Her good mother was lookiiiing all over for her.'

8. *Chiga tak aparisha shamusha "_____," nishkashi, "sachai,"* 'And then carrying a completely filled (basket), in the forest, coming, (the daughter) (apparently) said' "_____."

9. *"Chimi kasna moreteta pallasha kuwan ñukata! _____!" nishkashi.* '"That's who, harvesting, gave this many *morete* to me. _____" (they say) she said.'

10. *"_____!" nishka mama. "_____!"* said the mother.'

11. *Chiga warmiga "_____!" nisha kayashka. Chi kallari urasga runa shara kay wagra.* 'And so then the woman, saying "_____!" called him. In beginning times, this tapir was a person.'

12. *Chiga shamushka, Ima rigra rukuyuk shashka!* 'And so that one came, and what a huge (set of) arms he possessed!'

13. *Mama ali rikusha "_____," nishkashi, "_____," nirashi mama.* 'The mother, looking carefully, "_____," she apparently said, "_____," apparently said the mother.'

14. *"Hm hm. Shinawangachu?" nishkashi. Pay waktakpi ñukawasmi randi apasha garotiwan!*
"Hm hm. Is that what will happen to me?" she apparently said. "If he hits (me), I will be the one, instead, to take (and beat him) with a club."

15. "_____," *nishkashi*, "_____," *nishka*. "*Ñukaga*— _____," *shamushka kari shamusha tiyawshka*. "_____," she apparently said, "_____," she said. "As for me— _____," (her) husband who had come, coming (to the mother and daughter) he was there.'

16. "_____. _____," *nishka*.
  "'_____. _____," he said.'

17. *"Shinasha ña pay munashkama. Piru rikusha puriwangichi," nishkashi mamaga.* "'Like that being, then it's what she might want, but come and visit me," apparently said the mother.'

18. *"Ari," nishka. Nisha apasha rishka.* "'Okay,' he said. Saying, and taking (her) he went.'

19. *Apasha rik, rishka warmiga ña, apasha rik, ña rik, semanai shamushka.* 'Taking (her) and going, the woman she went, then, as he was taking (her) and going, So then going, in another week, she came.'

20. *Kuti moreteta apamushka.* "_____." 'Again she brought *morete*. "_____"'

21. "_____?" "'_____?"'

22. *"Ima aychaschu illan?" nirashi.* "'Is there no meat whatsoever for you?" she apparently said.'

23. *"Shinashaga kutiga aychatami apanga rauni" nishkashi.*
  "'_____," she apparently said.'

24. *Chiga turigunaga tandarishkawna.* "_____, _____! *Maybishi sirtu atun wasi kawsan?*" 'So then the brothers gathered together (and said) "_____, _____! Where on earth is this actual house where he lives?"'

25. *Apanakusha rishkawna.* 'Following along they went.'

26. *Rishkay rikukpiga, kasna shashka atun angu*! 'Having gone, and looking around, there was this big buttress root!'
27. *Chitashi payba wasi ashka.* 'That, apparently, is where his house is.'
28. *Mayta angu shashka, chi shashka payba wasi.* 'Wherever there's a buttress root, that, apparently is his house.'

Culture Focus: Forest Resources: Buttress Roots as Homes

The term '*angu*' has a number of meanings, including vine, vein, and buttress root. Buttress roots are large structures that grow around trees as supports, typically, for trees with shallow root systems. In Amazonian Ecuador, buttress roots are considered to be the dwelling places for animals of all kinds.

The Inchoative Suffix –*ya*

The inchoative suffix –*ya* describes a change of state. It can be translated by the English "to become X." In the overwhelming majority of cases, the change of state described by –*ya* is a perceptible change. This is a very productive suffix. It often transforms a noun, adjective, or adverb into a verb. For example, one derived –*ya* verb which should already be familiar to you is *pundzhayana* 'to become day.' A few of the more commonly derived –*ya* verbs follow:

tuta 'night' > *tutayana* 'to become night'
puka 'red' > *pukayana* 'to become red'
wira 'fat' > *wirayana* 'to become fat'
kuska 'straight' > *kuskayana* 'to become straight"
chuya 'clear' > *chuyayana* 'to become clear'
wiksa 'stomach' > *wiksayana* 'to become pregnant'
wawa 'baby' > *wawayana* 'to give birth'
allu 'mold' > *alluyana* 'to become moldy'
kaspi 'stick' > *kaspiyana* 'to become rigid'
kuru 'short' > *kuruyana* 'to become short'
witu 'weed' > *wituyana* 'to become weedy'
chulla 'uneven' > *chullayana* 'to become uneven'
wistu 'crooked' > *wistuyana* 'become crooked'
ichilla 'little' > *ichillayana* 'to become little'
kushi 'happy' > *kushiyana* 'to become happy'

Written Exercise 3

Construct ten sentences using any of the inchoative verbs from the above list.

Example:

kushiyana 'to become happy'
Payba wawa mikushka washa, kushiyaun. 'His/her baby after having eaten, is becoming happy.'

1. _____
2. _____
3. _____
4. _____
5. _____
6. _____
7. _____
8. _____
9. _____
10. _____

Transcription and Translation Challenge 1

Go to the following link:
https://www.youtube.com/watch?v=0BHdmoZZt6A

Listen from 5:10 to 5:18 to the exchange where women assert that a tree will not die after its bark is harvested. Transcribe and translate what she says. Note her use of the inchoative suffix –*ya*.

Transcription:

_____
_____
_____
_____

_____

_____

_____

_____

The Purposive Suffix –*chun*

The suffix –*chun* is similar to the purposive –*ngawa* learned in Lesson 11. The main difference is that –*chun* is used in an 'in order to' sense that encodes a different agent or entity than that of the main verb. The example below illustrates the appropriateness of the purposive –*ngaw* used to describe an action performed by the same agent as that of the main verb:

> Ñuka riunimi wasima, aswata upingaw. 'I (assert that I) am going home in order to drink *aswa*.'

When a purposive clause expresses the idea that a different agent will accomplish an action or process, then –*chun* is used instead, as in the following example:

> Ñuka riunimi wasima pay aswata upichun nisha. 'I (assert that I) am going home in order that (i.e., wanting that) he/she drink *aswa*.'

The second example sentence would be appropriate if it was necessary for the person heading home to be there in order for someone else to drink *aswa*. This might be the case if, for example, there was no *aswa* at home, and the person heading there was bringing it.

As is true for the example above, the verb *nisha* 'wanting,' which modifies the main verb, often follows the –*chun* suffixed verb form as a way of indicating that the verb's action or process is subordinated to the will, desire, or intention of the main verb's agent. Unlike many main clauses in Quichua, which have an optional subject or subject pronoun, the clause which contains the –*chun* verb often has an explicit subject, expressed as a definite individual or as a pronoun.

If a –*chun* clause encodes a third person plural verb, then the verb takes its regular third person plural ending with –*chun* added last:

Ñuka riunimi wasima, payguna aswata upinawchun nisha. 'I (assert that I) am going home in order that (i.e., wanting that) they drink *aswa*.'

An additional property of *–chun* clauses is that they can be and often are negated. Someone can do something in order for something else *not* to happen. In such instances, the negation form *ama* occurs before the *–chun*-suffixed verb:

pay wañuchun nisha 'wanting that it die' > *ama pay wañuchun nisha* 'wanting that it not die'

Practice 1

Practice negating *–chun* clauses.

Example:

Pay riksichun nisha 'wanting that he/she become acquainted > *Ama pay riksichun nisha* 'not wanting that he/she become acquainted'

1. *payguna mikunawchun nisha.*

2. *pay upichun nisha.*

3. *payguna pandanawchun nisha.*

4. *pay wañurichun nisha.*

5. *pay sambayachun nisha*

6. *payguna makanakuchun nisha.*

7. *pay raykaywan wañuchun nisha.*

   _____

8. *pay sambayachun nisha.*

   _____

9. *payguna hapi tukunawchun nisha.*

   _____

Practice 2

Practice your command of *–chun* by constructing sentences with the following sets of words.

Example:

Ñuka/pallana/palanda; wawaguna/mikuna
Ñuka palandata pallanga rauni, wawaguna mikunawchun nisha. 'I'm going to harvest plaintains in order that the children eat.'

1. *Kan/ukta/purina*; (negate) *payguna/chapana*
2. *kan/sindzhita/allmana*; (negate) *kiwa wiñana*
3. (imperative) *kanguna/sindzhita/kawina*; (negate) *payguna/hapi/tukuna/amarun*
4. *ñuka lomo kaspi/tarpuna*; *lomo/wiñana*
5. *ñuka/pay/kantana*; *pay/ñuka/llakina*

Culture Focus: Forest Resources for Beautification

Quichua peoples' ideas of beauty are closely linked with nature. When people attempt to express beauty, it often involves responding to what is appealing, vital, and salient in nonhuman species by attempting to imitate those qualities, thereby becoming more like them. For example, when a Quichua woman was asked by Tod Swanson for a special word to describe a particular shade of purple in the berries of an *anthurium*, she responded not by describing the berry's color, but by expressing her feelings about its beauty, saying, in effect, "How I would like to look like that fruit!" Looking like the land does not mean simply imitating its designs, however. It means adapting the body to the land through habitual patterns of aesthetic response, like dancing adapts bodily movements to a partner. Thus a person comes to look like the land much like a husband or wife comes to resemble their partner, sharing mannerisms and so on, after decades of living together.

Examples of how people bring about this process of resembling nature are the many ritual songs through which women take on the attractive qualities of sweet-smelling or sweet-tasting plants. However, everyday practices of beautification also reveal attempts to emulate nature. In Lesson 16, the value of applying the *pitun* tree's pounded leaves to one's hair to ensure against excessive shedding was discussed. We now mention two other plants said to be beneficial for hair.

Transcribe and Translate

Go to the following link:
https://www.youtube.com/watch?v=q3UsLVsohTs

Transcribe and translate the brief description of what people from a village called *Sara Yaku* are said to do to make their hair grow better and thicker. Listen for the speaker's use of the purposive *–chun* form of the verb *wiñana* 'to grow.'

Transcription:

_____

_____

_____

Transcription:

_____

_____

_____

An example of a plant said to be beneficial for making hair shiny is found in video 2 at the following link, where the speaker uses the ideophone *lluw* to describe the shininess that will result from bathing one's hair with this plant's leaves:
http://quechuarealwords.byu.edu/?ideophone=lyuw-2

Vocabulary

A

achachaw 'expression of feeling heat'
achachay 'expression of cold'
agllana 'to choose; to elect'
aguha 'needle'
akcha 'hair' (on the human head) (contrasts to *wilma/ibma* which is body hair; the fur of an animal or the feathers of a bird)
akchayana 'to grow hair'
aku 'let's go' (addressed to one other person and assumes that only one other person will go) (see also Sierra Kichwa *haku*)
akwichi 'let's go' (addressed to more than one other person and assumes that three or more people will go)
ala purama (NQ) 'backward (clothes)'
ali 'good'
alichina 'to fix; to heal; to make right'
ali maki 'right hand'
ali pacha 'certainly, for sure'; also *ali pacha rikuna* 'to stare'
alilla 'well' (also *alita*)
alimanda 'slowly'
allana 'to dig'
allku 'dog'
allmana 'to weed, i.e., remove weeds from'
allpa 'dirt, earth'
allsana 'to pull, drag, stretch something out' (see also *aysana*)
allu 'mold'
alluyana 'become moldy'
amarun 'anaconda, boa'

amarun kaspi 'plant species: *Cespedesia Spathulata*. Family: *Ochnaceae*'
amay (NQ) 'expression of fear (often used with children) or surprise'
amaylla 'frighteningly'
ambichina 'to feel a stinging sensation; to heal' (syn.: *laurana* 'to cause a burning sensation')
ambirina 'to heal'
amichina 'to make one bored; to cause one to have had enough' (overlaps with *saksana* 'to be satiated,' but *saksana* has a more positive connotation of having eaten to satisfaction)
amsa (PQ) 'a little, few'; also (NQ) *ansa*
amulana 'to sharpen (e.g., a machete, a knife or an axe)'; also 'to polish a *mukaha* or other ceramic vessel with a smooth stone after the slip has dried but before firing'
amulana rumi 'smooth stone for polishing a ceramic vessel before firing'
amulina 'to put, hold in the mouth, as when masticating cooked manioc to make *aswa*'
ana 'to be'
anchuchina 'to remove something; to take away'
anchurina 'to remove oneself from a place; to withdraw'
ang 'a mouth wide open'
anga 'hawk; owl'
angu 'tendon; vein; buttress root' (see also *sapi*)
ansawalla 'just a little bit; indicates a small quantity (of food, not for spatial proximity)'
anzhuchina (NQ) 'to take away; to clear away'
anzhurina (NQ) 'to get out of the way; to retreat'
anzelo 'fish hook'
anzi 'the pulpy dregs left over when mixing *aswa*'
apa (PQ) 'old, elderly person'; also (NQ) 'relative, family relation'
apa mama (PQ) 'grandmother'
apa yaya (PQ) 'grandfather'
apamuna 'to bring'
apana 'to take'
apanakuna 'to follow'
apangura 'Amazonian river crab'
aparina 'to carry on one's back; to carry a baby in a carrying cloth; to bear fruit'
apichina 'to light a fire; to turn on a motor'
apina 'to grasp; to catch; to pick; to take in marriage'
apirina 'to catch on fire; to ignite'
ari 'yes; kay'

armachina 'to have something or someone bathed'
armana 'to bathe something, someone'
armarina 'to bathe oneself'
ashanga 'woven basket'
ashka 'many'
ashkata 'a lot'
asichina 'to cause to laugh; joke'
asina 'to laugh'
asiwag 'funny'
asna añangu 'tiny reddish brown ant that smells a little like canela when crushed'
asnana 'to give off a fragrance or odor'
aspina 'to scratch; to write; sign'
asta pacha (NQ) 'at least'
astana 'to transport'
astawn 'more'
aswa 'beverage made from boiled and mildly fermented manioc'
aswana 'to make *aswa*'
ata (NQ) 'poor, poverty-stricken'
atalla 'chicken'
atarina 'to get up'
atashaylla! (NQ) 'interjection expressing delight or approval of an act of skill such as kicking an extraordinarily difficult goal in soccer or making a difficult shot with a rifle or shotgun'
atipana 'to be aware' (see also *riparana*)
atsatsai 'exclamation conveying disbelief or skepticism'
atyun (NQ) 'next' (used for sequencing numbers, e.g., 10 *atyun*, 11 *atyun*, etc.)
aviu 'a fruit called "kaimitu" in Spanish; or the tree that bears the fruit'
awa 'high'
awa llakta 'the Sierra; someone from the Sierra'
awa pacha 'heaven'
awana 'to make a clay pot; to weave a basket; to make a hammock'
awano 'type of hardwood tree'
awarina 'to tangle'
awas 'anything which causes itching' (i.e., *awas kuru* 'caterpillars which irritate the skin causing itching')
awing 'to completely open, uncover, or expose a space'
awirina 'to paint oneself with cosmetics or dyes from plants'
awlla 'a distant member of an affinal *ayllu*'
ay! 'expression of unwillingness or laziness,' i.e., *Ay! killanay!*

ay ay ay 'expression of pain'
aya 'ghost; spirit; dead body'
aya punzha 'Day of the Dead'
aya tullu 'skeleton'; also a species of mushroom (lit.: 'ghost bone')
ayag 'bitter; hot, as in hot peppers'
ayawaska 'an hallucinogenic plant: *banisteriopsis*' (lit.: 'ghost vine')
aycha 'meat; the body in general as in English "the flesh"; the flesh of an edible fruit called *piton*; the bark of a tree'; also *sacha aycha* 'game, wild meat'; *yaku aycha* 'fish'
aycha yaya 'term of respect for a man who is a great hunter'
aychawa (NQ) 'fish'
aychayuk 'corpulent'
ayllu 'family'
aysana 'to pull, drag, stretch something out' (see also *allsana*); 'to catch a fish with fish hooks, pulling it in'
aysarina 'to recede (said of liquids such as a flooded river or a swelling in the body, i.e., *yaku aysarin* 'the flood water recedes'); to stretch; to go down'
aytana 'to step, or walk on'

B

ba 'to spread something out along a surface, such as spreading a blanket on a bed'
bagri 'catfish'
balig 'valuable' (cf. Sp. *valer*)
bara 'stick, cane staff' (cf. Sp. *vara* 'cane, staff')
baratu 'common, cheap, plentiful' (cf. Sp. *barato*)
baylana 'to dance'
bhux 'a bursting forth out of water, especially by a freshwater dolphin called *bugyu*'
biruti 'dart used with blowguns'; also 'spirit dart' shot by a *yachag*
bola 'to shape something into a ball or move like a ball'
bruho/buruhu 'shaman or *yachag*' (but with possible negative semantic prosody, especially when accusing someone of causing sickness through their magic. Shamans in good standing [grandparents, etc.] are usually called "*yachag*-s" rather than "*buruhu*-s," even if the speakers are evangelicos who disapprove of drinking *ayawasca*. Often times both terms are politely avoided and the term "*ruku*" is used. Weddings are performed by a *padrino* who is customarily a *yachag*. Here the *padrino* is often referred to as "*buruhu*" when the bride's family are explaining that they agreed to the marriage out of fear of reprisal. "*Buruhu*" might be used in a neutral context when the alleged power of a shaman is being emphasized)

bugyu 'freshwater dolphin'
bullukuku 'a type of hawk; also the characteristic sound it is said to make'
bura/buda 'the Quichua wedding ceremony'
burla shuti 'the new name given to the groom in a Napo Kichwa wedding'

Ch

chagra 'agricultural field'
chagrana 'to make a *chagra*'
chaki 'foot'; also *auto chaki* 'tire'
chaki kara 'shoes'
chaki muku 'ankle'
chaki pamba 'sole of foot'
chaki riru 'toe' (lit.: 'foot finger')
chakichina 'to dry something, or to do something that causes it to dry, e.g., placing in the sun'
chakirina 'to dry up, dry out, e.g., a river, clothes, skin, etc.'
challwa 'type of fish'
chambirima 'type of fish'
champi champi 'describes someone who walks like a toddler'
changa 'leg'
chapana 'to wait; to lie in wait in an ambush; a hunting blind'
charag 'yet, still, as of now'
charapa 'turtle'
chari 'maybe, perhaps' (often: *ima chari?* indicating uncertainty or possibility)
charig 'a wealthy person, with lots of possessions'
charina 'to have'
chaskina 'to receive'
chasna (PQ) 'like that, in that way'
chawpi 'half; in the middle of'
chawpi shungu 'the center, the middle, halfway between'
chawpichina 'to divide; to divide in half'
chay 'over there; also said about that which is unexpected or in an unknown or faraway place'
chayana 'to cook to the point of doneness, e.g., meat, vegetables'
chayashka 'cooked'
chi 'this; that which has already been mentioned, or is already known, or is going to be relevant for what is about to be said'
chi raygu 'that's why'
chichu 'pregnant' (syn.: *iksayuk*)
chikan 'different; separated; belonging to a different person or unit'
chikanyachina 'to divide or separate'

chikanyashka 'divorced; separated'
chikichina 'to tickle'
chikiyana 'to become accustomed'
chikta (NQ) 'a small side branch of a river'; (PQ) *challas*
chilla 'that is it, no more, it is finished'
chillchi muyu 'marakas, baby rattle'
chillpina 'to tear into pieces, e.g., meat, cloth, paper'
chimanda 'then; because of that'
chimba 'across; on the other side'
chimbachina 'to take someone across a river; to pass a sickness to another person'
chimbana 'to cross over; to infect someone with illness'
chimbilaku 'bat'
chinda 'brush pile' (usually refers to a driftwood pile in a river or to branch piles made while clearing a field. In the Amazon, long narrow *chindas* mark the boundaries between *chagras* or manioc fields)
chingachina 'to lose or cause to disappear'
chingarina 'to become lost; to disappear'
chiri 'cold'
chiri puyu 'mist'
chirichina 'to make something cold' (often used with an impersonal subject to indicate the effects of weather, i.e., *ñukata chiriwanmi* 'it causes me to be cold')
chishakta 'throughout the afternoon, day'
chishi 'afternoon'
chiwilla 'pineapple'
chuchawasa 'medicinal tree bark'
chuchu 'breast'
chuchu punda 'nipple'
chuchu wasi 'brassiere'
chuchu yaku 'milk'
chuchuchina 'to nurse a baby'
chuchuna 'to nurse'
chugrichina 'to wound or cut someone'
chugrina 'to be wounded or cut'
chukana 'to choke or drown'
chukchuchina 'to make something shake'
chukchuna 'to shake'
chukchurina 'to tremble; to have a seizure'
chulla 'uneven'
chulla shimi 'type of fish with uneven mouth'

chullana 'to become uneven'
chunda 'palm fruit tree' (cf. Sp. *chontadura*)
chunki (NQ) 'crooked'
chunlla 'quietly'
chupa 'tail'
churachina 'to dress someone'
churana 'to put, place; to impregnate'
churarina 'to get dressed'
churi 'son'
chushag 'hollow, empty'
chutarina 'to stretch'
chuya 'clear; empty; clean'
chuyayana 'to become clear, empty, clean'
chyu 'a complete cutting or severing'
chyu (NQ) 'clean, transparent'
chyuxlla 'clean, clear, transparent'

D

dawa 'type of bird'
dibi 'debt, debtor'; also *dibi tukun* 'to become a debtor; to go into debt'
dundu 'name of a tree which bears fruit preferred by bats'
durana 'to last'
duzi 'noon; the zenith'
dwiño 'the owner; the very person' (i.e., *dwiño mamara tapungui* 'Ask [the child's] own mother herself')
dyuspagarachu 'thank you' (cf. Sp. *Dios paga* 'May God repay')
dzas 'to do something quickly, punctually'
dzaw 'a centripetally oriented, pluractional movement, such as the swarming of insects around a source of food'
dzhing 'sound of cicadas buzzing'
dzir 'a frictional sliding movement'

G

ganana 'to win' (cf. Sp. *ganar*)
ganas (NQ) 'tranquil, relaxed'
ganas kawsana 'peace'
garabatu 'stick about three feet long with a forked branch left on and used to hook and pull away grass or brush while clearing an area with a machete; also used for any hook on a pole used to pull fruit from a high tree'
garganta 'throat'
garoti 'stick or pole used as a club'

gasta 'surname'
gernillas 'passion fruit' (cf. Sp. *granadilla*)
gurún, gurún, gurún 'sound of an angry armadillo' (from Carolyn Orr)
gustana 'to like, enjoy, prefer'
gustu 'good; beautiful; good tasting; good smelling; enjoyable'
gyú, gyú, gyú 'a cutting action'

H
habon 'soap'
hacha 'ax'
hachi 'uncle'
haku 'let's go' (see also *aku*)
hamanga 'hammock'
hambi 'medicine'
hambina 'to treat water with venom; to give medicine of any kind to a person'
hambirina 'to heal; subside'
hanakta 'upriver'
hapichina 'to cause to catch; to light a fire'
hapina 'to catch an animal; to attract someone to oneself for romantic purposes'
hatun 'big'
hawa 'on top of; above'
hayambi 'lizard'
hista 'celebration'
huku 'wet'
hundachina 'to have someone fill something'
hundana 'to fill something'

I
ichana 'to scatter (seed in a field)'
icharina 'to drop fruit (said of trees); or caterpillars dropping from trees'
ichay (NQ) 'up river' (the primary direction in most Andean/Amazonian roads or towns is described in local Spanish as *para arriba* or *para abajo*; *ichayma* is used very similarly to the local Spanish *para arriba*)
ichilla 'little'
ichillata 'little bit-ly'
ichuna 'to throw away; abandon; divorce; abort'
iksa (NQ) 'stomach, belly'
iksayuk 'pregnant' (syn.: *chichu*)
ikuchina (NQ) 'to make someone or something enter'
ikuna (NQ) 'to enter'

illana 'to be lacking; to be absent; to not exist' (frequently occurs in the third person singular *illan*; opposite of *tiyana* 'to exist; to be present')

illapa 'rifle; a muzzle loading shotgun; any kind of gun' (In colonial and pre-contact Andean Quechua *illapa* meant thunder. Because of the similarity of sound and destructive power, the word was later applied to firearms. When the Winchester .44 rifle appeared during the rubber boom of the 1880s the word *carabina* came to be used to distinguish rifles from the *illapa* which now meant shotgun. Later the word *retrocarga* was introduced to refer to the new breach loading shotguns leaving *illapa* to refer to the cheaper old fashioned muzzle loaders. In a generic sense the word continues to refer loosely to long barreled firearms as a whole)

ilma (NQ) 'fur of an animal; human body hair; feathers'

ima raygu 'why; what reason?'

imamanda 'what from?'

indi 'sun'

indi chaki 'the afterglow of the sunset on the clouds'

indi pagarina 'sunrise'

indi tamya 'rain that occurs while the sun is shining'

indiglla asna 'to smell sweaty' (lit.: to smell like one has been in the sun)

indillama 'sloth'

indina 'to shine' (of the sun)

indipurama 'sunwise, i.e., in the direction of the sun'

ing 'a fissure or split'

inta 'dark; burned; dark skinned'

intayana 'to become tanned'

inzhi 'peanut'

irguna (NQ) 'to descend (in the spatial rather than genealogical sense); to go downward'

iridza 'ugly'; also *irus*

irina (PQ) 'to fry' (from *wira* 'fat or grease')

iritanana (NQ) 'to fry' (from *wira* 'fat or grease')

ishkana (NQ) 'to close' (syn.: *tapana*)

ishkarina (NQ) 'to close oneself in'

ishkay 'two'

ishkuna 'to shell corn'

ishpana 'to urinate'

ishpingo 'type of cinnamon: *Ocotea quixos*' (Sp. *canela*)

isma 'feces'; also *rinri isma* 'ear wax'

ismana 'to defecate'

ismu 'rot, rotted'

ismuna 'to rot'
istudiyana 'to study'
itsingama (NQ) 'face up'
iyachina (NQ) 'to make someone think or remember; to remind'
iyana (NQ) 'to think'
iyarina (NQ) 'to remember'
iyashalla (NQ) 'thoughtfully; carefully'
iyay (NQ) 'idea; thought'
iyayug (NQ) 'intelligent'
iyu 'tiny reddish ant'

K

kacha 'once and for all, at one time, in one blow'; also *shuk kachay*
kachana 'to send'
kachun 'sister-in-law'
kaha 'box; casket; drum'
kahana 'to beat a drum'
kakuna 'to rub'
kakurina 'to rub oneself'
kalapa 'wood chips' (contrasts with *shapa* 'sliver' and *walis* 'small branches for kindling')
kallari 'beginning'
kallari timpo 'beginning times'
kallarina 'to begin'
kallpachina 'to chase'
kallpana 'to run'
kallu 'tongue'
kaltuna 'to gulp soup in a hurry'
kama 'bed'
kamachina (NQ) 'to preach'
kamana 'to test, try out'
kan 'you'
kanba 'your'
kanchis 'seven'
kanguna 'you-all'
kangunawa 'your-all's'
kanina 'to bite'
kanisto (NQ) 'tight narrow space'
kanoa 'canoe'
kanoana 'to make a canoe'
kantana 'to sing'

kanzhama 'outside'
kanzhana 'to roast'
kanzhashka 'roasted'
kapag 'thick' (said of liquids)
kaparina 'to shout'
kara 'skin; peeling bark'
karana 'to give food; to fortify clay'
kargana 'to load'
kari 'man'
kariyachina (NQ) 'to encourage; to motivate; to inspire'
kariyana (PQ) 'to dress up'
kasana 'to hunt'
kasha 'thorn'
kasna 'like this'
kaspi 'stick; tree'; also 'slender' (syn.: *irki*)
kaspiyana 'to become thin, stick-like'
katichina 'to copy'
katikachana 'to follow like a shadow; to stick to following someone'
katimuna 'to follow back to a point of origin or starting point'
katina 'to follow; to continue'
katuna (NQ) 'to sell'
kaw 'sound of crunching crisp food, or stepping on dried vegetation'
kawchu 'rubber'
kawchuna 'to roll or twist (especially clay)'
kawsag 'alive, living'
kawsana 'to live, be well'
kawsarina 'to revive'
kawsay 'life' (Frequently used to refer to something people habitually depend on and enjoy "as if their lives depended on it." Most commonly it is used in a positive sense to refer to *aswa* as a favorite drink. To say jokingly that *aswa* is '*paywa kawsay*' means to say that a person couldn't live without it. In a negative sense it is also used of trago or rum when referring to an alcoholic. Some *yachags* use the term as an indirect way of referring to *ayawaska*. It may also be used in a derivative sense to refer to spirit helpers)
kay 'this; here'
kaya 'tomorrow'
kayana 'to call or summon'
kayna 'yesterday'
kayutu 'bed'
kazi 'almost' (cf. Sp. *casi*)
kazi 'quiet, still, calm' (i.e., *kazi tiay!* 'Settle down!' or 'Sit still!')

kazuna (NQ) 'to obey; to take to heart; to pay attention to' (cf. Sp. *hacer caso*)
kignana (NQ) 'to vomit'
kikin 'real, true'
kila 'breadfruit'
killa 'lazy'; also 'month; moon'
killachina 'to bother, annoy; flirt'
killana 'to be lazy'
killkana 'to write'
killpundu 'small red bird with large beak'
kilpana (NQ) 'to cover; to make love' (syn.: *tultuna* 'to cover completely')
kimirina 'to lean against; to lean on'
kimsa 'three'
kingray 'diagonally or off center from some locus
kingu 'bend, zig zag pattern'; also *yaku kingu* 'the bends in a river; a decoration pattern on *mukahas*'
kinguchina 'to use nonsense syllables to catch or complete the rhythm pattern of a song'
kingurina 'to turn in a dance pattern'
kipa 'younger (of a sibling)'
kipi 'a pile, a bundle' (i.e., *llachapa kipi* 'a pile of clothes'; *ayaspa kipi* 'a group of wasps piled up')
kipina 'to make a bundle of something'; also 'to hug' (syn.: *ugllana*)
kipinlla 'in a piled up way' (i.e., *avispa kipinlla llutarian* 'the wasps stick [to something] in a pile')
kipirina 'to hug someone'
kiras 'chin'
kiru 'tooth, teeth'
kishpichig 'rescuer'
kishpichina 'to save or rescuer'
kishpina 'to escape'
kiwa 'weeds'
kiwana 'to weed; to cut grass'
kiwina 'to twist or wring something out, e.g., clothes'
kiwirina 'to wring, twist, or sprain oneself'
kosana 'to roast food; to fire clay'
kucha 'lake, deep'
kuchuna 'to chop, cut down'
kukuyu 'lightning bug; click beetle'
kullki 'money'
kullki kara 'wallet; billfold'
kullkiyug 'a rich person; someone with money'

kulu 'tadpole'
kumal 'sweet potato; yam; camote'
kumari 'godmother or ritual co-parent'
kumbirana 'to invite, e.g., to a fiesta or a marriage'
kumishin 'termite; termite mound'
kumpari 'compadre'
kumu 'bent' (adjective)
kumulla 'bent over' (adverb)
kumurina 'to bend over'
kuna 'to give something other than food'
kunan 'today; now'
kunara (NQ) 'only now; belatedly' (i.e., *kunara wawara iyarin.* 'He only now thinks of his child [after it is too late]')
kunga 'neck'
kungarina 'to forget'
kungaylla 'to happen suddenly, or to be off one's guard, unaware of something going on'
kungaymanda 'unexpectedly; out of the blue'
kungukshi 'type of fish'
kunguri 'knee'
kungurina 'to kneel down'
kuri 'gold'
kuri shundu 'green gold scarab beetle'
kurta muyu (NQ) 'testicles'
kuru 'caterpillar, grub, maggot, worm'
kuruma (NQ) 'house fly'
kurzana 'to place something in a crossed fashion'
kurzashka 'crossed'
kusana 'to roast'
kushi 'happy; content'
kushillu 'kinkajou (a small primate hunted for food)'
kuska 'straight'
kuskata 'directly'
kuti 'again'
kutillata 'again'
kuwa 'frog'
kuyana 'to give; to love'
kuyuchina 'to shake; to make something move'
kuyuna 'to move; shake'
kuyurina 'to move oneself'
kwika 'earthworm, angle worm'; also *yana kwika* 'night crawler'

kwinta 'like, similar to'
kwintana 'speak; tell a story' (syn.: *rimana*, *nina*; Sierra Quichua uses *parlana*)
kwitsa (Sierra Quichua) 'girl, young lady'

L

lachuri (NQ) 'stepson'
lagarto 'caiman'
lala 'exaggeration; delicate; weak' (Orr and Wrisley 1961 translate the meaning of *lala* in the Tena dialect as 'complaint,' i.e., *quejumbre, quejarse*)
lala runa 'someone who habitually exaggerates'
lalana 'to exaggerate'
lalu 'a flowering planta: *Dieffenbachia*'
lamama (NQ) 'stepmother'
lañaña (NQ) 'stepsister of a female'
lansa 'spear'
lapani (NQ) 'stepsister of a male'
lapuna 'to fold'
laro 'next to, beside'
latsag (NQ) 'wet'
laturi (NQ) 'step brother of a female'
laushushi (NQ) 'step daughter"
lawawki (NQ) 'step brother of a male'
lawrachina 'to make something burn (as in acidic burning, rather than hot temperature)'
lawrana 'to burn (as in acidic burning, rather than hot temperature)'
layaya (NQ) 'step father'
lazu lazu 'the slithering movement of a snake or worm, or a vine that grows in loops'
libachina 'to punish'
libro 'book'
lika 'long net for stringing across a stream to catch fish'
likana 'to fish with a *lika*'
likchachina 'to wake someone up'
likcharina 'to wake up' (syn.: *(h)atarina* 'to get up')
likichina 'to cause something to rip, break, split'
likirina 'to split or tear lengthwise'
limpiyana 'to clean; to make shine'
ling 'the insertion of something into an enclosed space'
linzhurina (NQ) 'to be tangled'
lomo 'manioc' (also *lumu*)
lomocha 'squirrel' (probably Deppe's squirrel: *Sciurus deppei*)

lugar 'free time' (cf. Sp. *lugar* 'place'; i.e., *lunes tutamanda lugar ani*. 'I am free Monday morning.' The overlap of temporal spatial meaning is typical of classic Andean Quechua where *pacha* means both 'space' and 'time')
lugar kawsana 'to live free, i.e., to be in control of one's own time rather than being under a patron'
luk 'the sound of boiling'
luki 'to the left'
lulun 'egg'
lumarisu 'a cold' (syn.: *catarro ungwi*)
lumu 'manioc' (also *lomo*)
lumu paho 'a special gift for growing manioc'
lumucha 'guanta, paka'
lumukuchi 'peccary; javelina'
lumukuru 'a caterpillar that lives on manioc'

Ll

llachapa 'clothing'
llagllana 'to scrape, e.g., the bark of a tree, the burned carbon off toast, a canoe in the finishing process of making a dugout, etc.'
llaki 'a sadness or tragedy'
llakichina 'to cause sadness, empathy, love'
llakina 'to love, to have the power to affect and arouse peoples' empathy and love' (syn.: *munana* 'to want; to love')
llakirina 'to be saddenable'
llakiwag 'loveable, attractive, likeable, compatible' (e.g., *mana llakiwag* could be used to criticize a mismatch in clothing)
llakta 'place in general; area of concentrated population; city or town as a opposed to a rural area' (*llakta* may function as an adjective to describe something manufactured as opposed to rural or *runa* 'native, natural or wild')
llakta ala a humorous term for 'pasta' or 'fideo' (lit.: 'city mushrooms')
llakta atalla 'incubator hybrid chickens' (contrasts to *runa atalla* 'free range chickens')
llakta poroto 'store bought or imported red beans' (contrasts to *runa poroto* 'a kind of bean that Amazonians have always grown')
llandana 'to make firewood'
llandu 'shade, shadow'
llandu uras 'twilight (dawn, dusk)'
llangana 'to touch something; to caress'; also 'to work' (synonyms for 'to work' are *chausina* and *tarabana*)
llapina 'to squeeze, knead manioc mash with water to make *aswa*'
llashag 'heavy'

llatana (NQ) 'to undress'
llatanana (PQ) 'to undress'
llawkana 'to lick'
llawsa 'saliva'
lluchuna 'to peel, e.g., vegetables, skin of game animals, also clothing'
lluchurina 'to peel off'
llukana 'to crawl'
llukshichina 'to take or throw something out'
llukshina '"to emerge, exit, go out of"
llulla 'a lie'
llullana 'to lie' (syn.: *umachina* 'to deceive')
llullu 'green (as in unripe fruit); immature; recently born; tender'
llullu killa 'new moon'
llulluku 'newborn baby'
llushka 'slippery'
llushkarina 'to slip, slide'
llushti 'naked'
llushtina 'to peal, e.g., potatoes, manioc, bark from a tree'
lluw 'a shiny surface; a curved, meandering pattern'

M

machakwi 'snake'
machana 'to become intoxicated by alcohol or by hallucinogenic liquids (such as *banisteriopsis* or *datura*)'
machashka 'drunk, in an altered state of consciousness'
machin 'spider monkey'
machin araña 'tarantula'
machu (NQ) 'folded over'
machu ñawi 'blind'
machu singa 'bat' (lit.: folded nose) (syn.: *tuta pishku, tuta kara*)
makana 'to hit'
maki 'hand'
maki muku 'wrist'
maki pamba 'palm of hand'
maki pura 'in cash' (cf. cash-in-hand)
maki riru 'finger'
malki 'sapling; the sucker of a plantain or heliconia'
malta 'a young, unmarried person'
mama 'mother'
mama didu 'thumb'
mama kiru 'molar'

mana 'negative adverb'
mañachina 'to loan'
mañana 'to borrow'
manarag 'before'
manduru 'red powder from the plant: *Bixis orellana, achiote* (used for decorating the body)'
manduru machakwi 'coral snake'
mandzhana 'to scare, frighten, startle'
mandzharina 'to be scared, surprised, startled'
mandzhay siki 'scaredy cat, i.e., someone who is too easily frightened'
manga 'cooking pot'
manga allpa 'clay'
mankana 'to dig or hollow out a shallow round nest-like or pool-like space' (said of chickens or a whirlpool)
maria panga 'a type of leaf: *Piper bellidifolium*. Family: *Piperaceae*'
marka mama 'to be a godmother to a child'; also *markama* (NQ) 'godmother'; also term for 'praying mantis' (because if placed on the hair it will delouse a child like a godmother)
markana 'to carry in one's arms'
markayaya 'godfather'
masana 'to mix'
masha 'brother-in-law'
mashti 'used to indicate a pause in a sentence while the speaker searches for a word' (contraction of *ima shuti* 'what's its name?')
maskana 'to look for; to search, to hunt' (opposite of *tupana* 'to find')
matu 'flat or flattened down' (used for flat land, *matu pamba*)
mawka 'used up; tattered; worn out'
may 'where'
maykan 'which, whichever'
mayllana 'to wash' (exception: not for washing clothes. See *taksana*)
maytuna 'to wrap with leaves (and by extension paper or plastic wrap)' (usually of something edible, such as meat or *aswa* pulp)
mbwi 'type of frog'
mika 'honey'
mikuna 'to eat'; also 'to consume voraciously, e.g., by illness'
mikya 'aunt'
mimis (NQ) 'gums'
mimish (PQ) 'gums'
minga 'a work party'
mingana 'to have a *minga*'
mirachina 'to increase something (in number)'

mirana 'to grow'
miri banku (NQ) 'type of powerful of *yachag*'
misi 'cat'
mitikuna 'to hide (oneself)'
mitsa muyu 'wart'
mitsana 'to keep for oneself (said especially of food); to prohibit' (cf. Sp. *mesquinar*)
moreti 'type of palm tree'
motolo 'type of venomous snake'
muchana 'to kiss'
muchay 'a kiss'
mugllus 'cheeks'
mukaha 'drinking bowl made of clay'
muktina 'to sniff, smell something'
muku 'joint'
mukuna 'to chew, masticate'
muluk 'excessive stuff piled up'
munana 'to want; to love' (syn.: *nina* 'to want or intend'; *llakina* 'to love')
mundo 'a lot, very'
muru 'speckled, splotched, dotted'
mushuk 'new'
muskuna 'to dream; to have a vision' (syn.: *nuspana*)
musu 'a young man'
muti 'a thick soup-like consistency'
muyu 'seed, fruit'
muyurina 'to circle around'

N

nanachina 'to cause pain'
nanana 'to hurt'
nanay 'pain, harm'
nawa 'slip for wearing under a dress'
nda 'yes'
-niki 'sequencing suffix used with numbers, e.g., *shuk-niki, ishkay-niki,* etc.'
niktana 'to kick'
niktyana 'to trip'
nina 'to say; to mean; to intend; to want'
nina 'fire'; also *nina siki* 'fire side'
nitimuna 'to invade, as of forest or weeds into a *chagra*'
nitina 'to press on something'
nitirina 'to crush; to squash
nuspa 'crazy'

nuspachina 'to cause to dream'
nuspana 'to dream'
nusparina 'to get flustered; to panic; to go crazy'
nuyuchina 'to stir a liquid so that the dregs or solids that have sunk to the bottom become well mixed'

Ñ

ña 'then; now'
ñaka 'almost'
ñalla 'almost; any minute'
ñambi 'path, road'
ñambina 'to make a road, path'
ñaña 'sister of female'
ñankata (NQ) 'recently, just a little while ago'
ñañu 'narrow' (syn.: *utsun*)
ñawi 'face'; also 'the "eyes" on a manioc cutting'
ñawi iki (NQ) 'tears'
ñawi lipinshi 'eyelashes'
ñawi lulun 'eyes'
ñawi pura 'face to face'
ñawi wiki (PQ) 'tears'
ñawi wilma (PQ) 'eyebrows'; (NQ) *ñawi ilma*
ñawpa 'in front of; before; prior to'
ñawpachina 'to lead'
ñawpana 'to lead'
ñawsa 'blind'
ñawsayachina 'to blind'
ñawsayana 'to become blind'
ñuka 'I; me; my'
ñukanchi 'we, us, our'
ñuktu 'brains'
ñutu 'small pieces; small change'
ñutuyachina 'to divide something into small pieces'

O

ocho 'eight' (cf. Sp. *ocho*)

P

pacha 'blanket'
pachina 'a technical term from NQ for the ritual action of gently hitting manioc cuttings with a bundle of leaves to impart the qualities of the plants from which the leaves are taken to the manioc which is about to be planted'

pagarachu 'thank you'
pagarikta 'sunrise'
pagarina 'to be born'
paglla 'open; clear of obstruction (as in clear sky or a clear spot in the forest) (when speaking of clear liquids, *chuyag* rather than *paglla* is used)
pagllay 'openly; to speak or do something in the open'
pagri 'priest'
paho 'any kind of sickness; a special gift for healing particular kinds of sickness; the act or sound of popping a joint such as the sound made when cracking a knuckle'
pakalla 'secretly'
pakana 'to hide'
pakay 'type of guava fruit with long pods'
pakcha 'waterfall'
paki 'a piece of something that has been broken off; a piece of wood'
pakina 'to break something'
pakirina 'to break'
pakirinalla 'fragile, breakable'
paktachina 'to fulfill or complete'; also 'the engagement fiesta in Tena tradition'
paktamuna 'to arrive'
paktana 'to be enough'
palanda 'plaintain' (usually refers to green plantains)
pallana 'to gather; to pick (e.g., fruit); to harvest'
pallka 'a fork in a tree'
palo 'snake'
palta (PQ) 'avocado'; (NQ) *pina*
paltana 'to place something on top of pillars, beams; to place manioc on top of a row of plantains in a pot; to place meat on a rack over a fire'
pamba 'ground'
pambana 'to bury'
pambarina 'to sink; submerge in mud' (said of a car becoming stuck in mud)
panda 'a trap'
pandachina 'to cause someone to become lost or to make a mistake'
pandana 'to make a mistake'
pandarina 'to become lost'
panga 'leaf; a sheet (or leaf) of paper; a bill of paper money'
pangalla 'light; light weight'
pani 'sister of male'
papana 'to eat' (only used for children)
paramu 'drizzle'

paran 'the undulation of a canoe'
parihana 'to even something out'
parihu 'together; equal; even' (cf. Sp. *pareja*)
pasa pasa rikurig 'see-through; transparent'
pashin 'a species of fish that lives in still water and feeds on other fish'
pasiyana 'to visit'
paskana 'to open something'
paskarina 'to open (of flowers and buds)'
paspa 'rough or chaffed as of skin
pata 'floor; platform'; also *yaku pata* 'the shore or river bank'
pata haway 'upstairs; floor on a raised platform'
pata uku 'the space under the floor of a house raised on stilts'
patas 'cacao blanco'
patsak 'one hundred'
pawa 'generic term used to refer to various species of guan and currasow' (cf. Sp. *pava* 'turkey')
pawana 'to jump; fly'
pawshi 'paujil'
pay 'he; she; it'
paya (NQ) 'older sister'
payba 'his; hers'
payguna 'they; them'
pi 'who'
pichana 'to sweep; to clear a garden; also a technical term for ritual cleaning with leaves'
pichis 'silver beaked tanager'; also *nina pichis* 'masked crimson tanager'
pichka 'five'
pikun pikun purina 'movement of a fish's tail in water'
pillan 'lesser anteater; tamandu'
pilluna 'to wrap; to wrap a baby; to wrap a wound'; also 'a wrap around skirt traditionally used in Napo and Pastaza'
pilluri pilluri 'spiral or spiralled' (i.e., *pilluri pilluri fideo* 'spiralled pasta')
pillurina 'to wrap oneself, e.g., with strands of beads around the wrist'
pimpis (NQ) 'fin of a fish'
pina 'avocado'
piñana 'to express anger at someone'
piñarina 'to feel angry'
pindu 'river cane'
pingarina 'to be embarrassed; to be ashamed'
pingay 'embarassment; also metaphorical term for genitals'
pishi 'a small amount; less'

pishina 'to lack; to not be enough; to be insufficient'
pishku 'bird'
pishña 'river otter'
pita lala 'type of pit viper; possibly: *Viperidae Bothrops atrax* (Kohn 2002, 450)'
piti 'a piece'
pitikta rina 'to take a shortcut'
pitina 'to cut'
piton 'squash-like vegetable'
piwas 'anybody; whoever'; also *mana piwas* 'no one; nobody'
polang 'ideophone depicting emergence from underwater to the surface, or bobbing movements in water'
polo 'a puncture or piercing'
pu 'sound of a bird's wings as it flies' (undergoes multiple repetition)
puchan 'porcupine'
puchu 'left over'
puchukay (NQ) 'last' (i.e., *puchukay punzha* 'on the last day')
puchukaybi 'finally'
puchuna 'to be extra; for something to be leftover or to have leftovers'
pugllana 'to play'
pugru 'spring or pool' (*poclло* or *puquio* in Sierra dialects)
puka 'red'
pukanay 'pink' (lit.: 'desiring red')
pukayana 'to become red'
pukayashka 'reddened; something which has become red' (often said of a wound which is becoming infected)
puksiri 'a marsh bird which eats snails' (the name comes from its call which is said to sound like *puksiri, puksiri, puksiri*)
puktsi 'stunted'
puktsiyana 'to become stunted in growth'
pukuna 'to blow (smoke); to ripen'
pukuna 'blowgun'
pukushka 'ripened plantain'
pullu 'short'
puma 'jaguar'
punda 'first in a series' (opposite of *kipa* 'last')
pundzha 'day'
pundzhan 'brightly shining'
pundzhayana 'to dawn or to become day'
pungara 'tar; pitch; the sticky black material that is used on Kichwa/Shuar blowguns from Pastaza and Morona Santiago provinces; the material that is used to pave roads'

pungara muyu 'a sticky yellow fruit the size of an apple with a hard exterior'
pungichina 'to cause something to swell'
pungina 'to swell'
pungirina 'become swollen'
pungu 'door; entryway; the mouth of a river'
puñuchina 'to put to bed; to put a baby to sleep'
puñuna 'to sleep'
puñuy 'sleep'; also *puñuy (hapin)* 'sleepiness'
puñuysiki 'sleepy head'
punzu 'curly; frizzy' (describes hair after a permanent)
pupu 'navel'
pupu waska 'umbilical cord' (traditionally the *pupu waska* was always cut with *wamaj* 'bamboo' and never with a metal instrument)
pupuk 'the flower of the plantain, i.e., *palanda pupuk*'
pura 'between two or more persons' (i.e., *ñukanchi pura* 'among ourselves'; *maki pura* 'cash in hand'; *ñawi pura* 'face to face')
purina 'to walk, trek'
puru 'a bottle or container for liquid'
purun 'overgrown, uncultivated land'
puruntuna 'to prepare'
purus 'rustling movement (as of a dog digging in weeds)'
purutu 'beans, frijoles'
purutu pukunzhu 'the tropical screech owl, whose call sounds like its name'
pus 'sound of plucking something off of a stem'
pusak 'eight'
pushana 'to take, guide, or lead a person or group of people'
pushka 'thread; yarn'
pusku 'foam; bubble'
pusku shungu 'lungs' (lit.: 'foam, bubble heart')
puskuna 'to become sour; to spoil'
putan 'bee'
putan wasi 'bee hive'
putsik 'sizzling sound, as when water hits hot grease'
putung/potong 'resonant sound of hitting the ground without losing structural integrity'
putus 'fluffy, cottony'
puya 'lance'
puyu 'cloud'
puyu ñawi 'someone with blurred vision'
puyuyana 'to become cloudy'
pyulla 'mold'

R

raka 'vagina'

raku 'thick; fat'

rana 'to do' (see also *rurana*; *rana* also has the meaning of 'doing' sex. It is often avoided and replaced with *rurana* where it might be misunderstood or where a double meaning might cause laughter)

randi 'instead of; on the other hand'

randichina 'to sell'

randina 'to buy; to trade'

ransia 'a person of European descent'

rapana 'to criticize'

rapyana 'to twitch'

rayana 'to make lines; to scratch (as in to scratch a record or CD)' (cf. Sp. *raya*)

rayashka 'scratched (as in a scratched CD, record, or a marred wood table)'

raykay 'hunger'

raykuchina (PQ) 'to lower something'

raykuna (PQ) 'to descend, go down'

rayu 'thunder; sting ray'

rayu runa 'mythic thunder man whose actions lie behind the thunder'

rigra 'arm; wing of a bird'

rigra muku 'elbow'

riksina 'to know by experience; to be acquainted with; to know a person or place' (cf. Sp. *conocer*)

rikuchina 'to show'

rikuna 'to look or see; to read'

rikurina 'to appear; to look (good, bad, funny, etc.)'

rimana 'to say; to speak; to speak harshly; to take someone to task'

rina 'to go'

rinri 'ear (refers more to the internal ear)'; also *rinri isma* 'ear wax'

rinri kara 'external ear' (lit.: 'ear skin')

riparana 'to be aware of'

ruku 'old; big' (considered a positive quality)

ruku mama (NQ) 'grandmother' (syn.: *apamama* or *apama*)

ruku yaya (NQ) 'grandfather' (syn.: *apa yaya* or *apaya*)

rukuyachina 'to cause something or someone to age'

rukuyana 'to age'

runa ethnonym meaning 'civilized person'

Runa shimi 'name for Quechua language' (lit.: 'person's speech' or 'what a person speaks')

rupachina 'to burn something; to cause to burn up'

rupana 'to burn'

rupashka 'burned'; also in NQ *rupashka* refers to 'someone who is a little (but not very) drunk'

rupayachina 'to heat something up' (i.e., *Yakura rupayachin* 'She heats the water')

rupayana 'to heat up'

rurana 'to do; to make'

ruya 'tree'

ruyag 'white'

S

sacha 'forest; wild area' (partially synonymous with *urku* in a manner similar to Spanish *monte* and *bosque*); also 'wild' (in contrast with *llakta*)

sacha wagra 'tapir' (lit.: 'forest cow')

sachayachina 'to reforest'

sachayana 'to become forest; to become wild'

sakina 'to leave; stop; detain'

sakirina 'to stay behind; to remain'

saksana 'to be full or satiated with food'

salpikana 'to splash'

saltana 'to leap'

samana 'to rest; breathe'

samay 'breath; rest'

samba 'tired' (i.e., *Samba yachiwan* 'It makes me feel tired')

sambayana 'to become tired'

sambayashka 'tired'

sambulina 'to dunk underwater'

sangu 'thick or cloudy liquid; muddy or silty (water)' (opposite of *chuya*)

sapalla 'alone'

sapi 'root'

sapiyana 'to put down roots'

sara muyu 'pimple'

sargak 'a witch'

sargana 'to bewitch'

saro 'the other (i.e., *saro punzha* 'the other day')'

sasi 'taboo; something forbidden or proscribed'

sasina 'to fast (usually to fast from a limited number of things such as salt and hot pepper); to observe a prohibition'

satichina 'to make someone put something into a hole or enclosure'

satina 'to nail; to put something into an enclosure or a hole'

satirina 'to hole up; to enclose oneself in a hole or enclosure'

sawli 'machete'
sawna 'pillow'
saya 'traditional wrap around skirt used by Amazonian Kichwa women'
sida 'silk' (cf. Sp. *seda*)
sikana 'to climb'
sikayachina 'to raise (e.g., to raise prices)'
sikcha 'a generic name for a finch or finches'
siki 'buttocks; base of a mountain or tree; the East (in Amazonia)'
siki tullu 'tailbone'
siki uktu 'anus'
siku 'agouti'
silu 'sky' (Spanish *cielo*)
sillu 'finger nail; toenail; claw' (PQ)
sindi yura 'a type of tree: *Prunus debilis*. Family: *Rosaceae*'
sindichina 'to light a fire'
sindina 'to turn on a light; to light a candle'
sindzhi 'strong'
sindzhita 'strongly'
singa 'nose'
singa uktu 'nostril'
sintina 'to feel' (cf. Sp. *sentir*)
sipu 'wrinkle'
sipuyashka 'wrinkled'
sirina 'to lie; to be lying'
siririna 'to lie down'
sirtu 'certainly' (cf. Sp. *cierto*)
sisa 'flower'
sisu 'fungus'
sukta 'six'
suni 'long'
suniyachina 'to elongate'
supana 'to break up or liquify (e.g., a potato in soup)'; in Tiyu Yacu subdialect: 'to wash clothes' (syn.: *taksana*)
supay 'spirit; devil'; also used in superlatives: *tamya supay* 'tremendous rain'
supina 'to pass wind (to fart)'
surkuna 'to remove something'
suru panga 'a type of leaf used by *ayawaska yachaks* to fan or sweep their patients'
susurina 'to have an accident; to wound'
suyu 'swallow (the bird called *golondrina* in Spanish)'; also in the Quechua of the Incas *suyu* meant 'a quarter or region of the Tawantinsuyu'

Sh

shaka 'a tearing action or the result of a tear'
shamuna 'to come'
shapa 'a sliver'
shayana 'to stand'
shayarina 'to stand up'
shigra 'woven carrying bag'
shikitana 'to grate'
shikshina 'to itch' (impersonal verb)
shillkillu 'sap used to glaze pottery'
shillkillu wachan 'the bulge of *shillkillu* sap on the side of the tree that resembles the belly of a pregnant woman'
shillu 'nail, 'fingernail; claws' (NQ)
shimi 'mouth; language; voice; word'
shimi kara 'lips'
shina 'like, as'
shinki 'extremely black, shiny black; charcoal'
shitana 'to shoot, to throw'
shuk 'one'
shukta 'one group; some unspecified quantity of people'
shulla 'drops of liquid'
shullana 'to drip; to miscarry a baby'
shungu 'heart'
shushu ñawi 'sleepy eyed'
shushuna 'to strain (liquids) or filter'; also 'a strainer or filter' (i.e., *cafera shushuna* 'coffee filter' or *yakura shushuna* 'water filter')
shuti 'first name'
shutichina 'to baptize; to give a name while putting water on the child's head and becoming a compadre or a comadre'
shutuna 'to drip'
shuwag 'thief, robber'
shuwana 'to steal'

T

tak 'the sound of contact when two surfaces meet; typically, one surface is moved toward another'; *tak* may also be used to describe the complete fullness of a container, or a swelling within a body'
takana 'to tap; touch; hammer'
takina 'ritual song or chant used by a *yachag*'
taksana 'to wash clothes'

takta 'full'

talirina 'to spill'

talon 'the inside or underside of either the elbow or the knee'; borrowed from the Spanish term which refers to the back of the foot where the Achilles tendon attaches to the bone

tallutana 'to throw mud against a wall so that it sticks'

tamya 'rain'

tambu 'a temporary dwelling in the forest; a shelter for sleeping'

tamya añangu 'army ants'

tamya pishku 'nightingale wren'

tamya uras 'the rainy season'; also *sawan uras*

tamya yura 'type of tree'

tamyana 'to rain'

tanda 'bread'

tandachina 'to gather something together'

tandarina 'to gather together'

tangana 'to push, shove'

tanlla 'type of fish'

tapa 'a bunch of bananas'

tapana 'to close; to fill up with people' (cf. Sp. *tapar*)

tapuna 'to ask'

tapya 'an omen'

tapya pishku 'the squirrel cuckoo' (lit.: 'omen bird')

tarabana 'to work'

taripana 'to judge'

tarpuna 'to plant'

tawaco 'tobacco'

tawanas 'horse fly'

tawasamba 'feather headdress'

tawkana 'to pile up'

tawna 'long pole for maneuvering a canoe'

tawnana 'to maneuver a canoe'

taylla 'tough'

tigrachina 'to give back'

tigramuna 'to return to a point of origin'

tigrana 'to return'

tika 'sticking out' (i.e., *tika pichu* 'stuck out chest')

tiksina (NQ) 'to pinch'

timbuchina 'to cause to boil'

timbuna 'to boil'

timpu 'already; faster than expected' (i.e., *timpu mikwi pasan?* 'What? He finished eating already?') (cf. Sp. *tiempo* 'time')

tinaha 'large clay jar'
tinina 'to stain; to dye'
tinlachina 'to cause something to be stretched out; to stretch a wire or a rope from one point to another' (syn.: *chutachina*)
tinlana 'to stretch something out' (for a person to stretch is *chutarina*)
tiyana 'to exist; to be present' (overlaps in meaning with *ana* [*tiyana* corresponds roughly to Spanish *haber* and *estar*, while *ana* corresponds to Spanish *ser*]; opposite of *illana* 'to be lacking; to be absent; to not exist')
tiyarina 'to sit'
tiyu 'sand' (syn.: *tsatsa*)
toldo 'mosquito net'
tonsa 'a blind sardine'
trenchi 'fork'
tsak 'the sound of a shallow piercing into a resisting medium (e.g., a spear piercing a fish)'
tsaka 'rough, bumpy'
tsala 'pale'; sometimes used to designate light skinned people as in *tsala runa*
tsalakulun 'generic term for a lizard'
tsalayana 'to become pale'
tsambulina 'to swim under water'
tsar 'sound of scratching'
tsaras/taras 'rustling sound (e.g., paper, dried leaves)'
tsarga 'hoarse, (e.g., a hoarse voice)'
tsatsa 'sand' (syn.: *tiyu*)
tsawata 'tortoise'
tsingra pahu 'arthritis'
tsiya 'the eggs of lice'
tsungana 'to suck' (used to describe what a *yachag* does to suck out illness)
tsunglu 'wilted' (said of trees or plants)
tsuntsu 'raggedy and poor looking' (usually perjorative; *pugri* [cf. Sp. *pobre*] or *wakcha* 'orphan; someone with not relatives' would be used to describe the poor in a non-pejorative sense)
tuapurama 'face down'
tubi puma 'jaguarundi'
tukana 'to play an instrument (e.g., flute, guitar)'
tuklla 'a trap for birds'
tukllana 'to explode; for a river to overflow its banks, to hatch (from an egg)'
tuksina 'to puncture; to sting in the sense of bees, wasps, snakes; to inject with a needle'
tuktu mama 'a nesting hen'
tuktuna 'to nest'

tuku 'grub'
tukuchina 'to finish'
tukuna 'to become or to turn into'
tukurina 'to run out'
tukuy 'all, every'
tularina 'to cave in' (as of landslides or of a river bank caving in during a flood)
tuldu 'mosquito net'
tullu 'bone'
tullu uma 'skull'
tulluyana 'to lose weight (so as to become skin and bones)'
tultuna 'to cover completely' (i.e., *Wawara tultuy*! 'Cover the child!) (syn.: *killpana*)
tulumba 'a type of frog which sings loudly at night' (believed to be a messenger of harm sent by witches) (syn.: *sagra hambatu*)
tulun tulun 'sound of thunder (also *tuklun tuklun*)'
tulupuna 'to make noise'
tunshi 'type of bird'
tunu 'kind; color; quality' (cf. Sp. *tono*)
tupana 'to encounter; find; meet up with'
tupu 'a size or measure' (i.e., *caran tupu* 'every size')
tupu 'sound of the moment of falling into water, or of splashing through water while swimming'
tupuli 'a needle'
tupuna 'to measure'
tupuyana 'to subside; recede; calm down' (syn.: *aysarina* of a storm, a swelling, or an infection)
turi 'brother of a female'
turmindarina 'to suffer'
turmindus 'suffering'
turu 'mud'
turuyana 'to become muddy'
tushuna (Sierra Quechua) 'to dance' (*baylana* is the preferred verb for PQ and NQ)
tuta 'night'
tutakara 'bat' (syn.: *tutapishku*)
tutamanda 'morning'
tutapishku 'bat'
tutayana 'to become night'
tutayashkay 'dusk'
tuy tuy tuy shutuna 'the sound of dripping'

tyapi (PQ) 'to move toward something and stick to it'; (NQ) 'to be matted down or pressed flat and stuck together like a pillow that is crushed or like gum plastered on a surface'
tyas (NQ) 'alert' (i.e., *tyas rikuk allku* 'A dog that looks alert')
tyas (NQ) 'sound of cutting something hard (e.g., wood); sound of slapping or hitting a person'
tyu 'drop (of liquid)'
tyukana 'to spit'
tyukina 'to break off tender stems'

U

ucha 'sin; debt'
uchachina 'to blame'
uchu 'hot pepper'
uchu añangu 'tiny red ant that stings'
uchutikan 'a forest spirit or *sacha supay*'
ugllana 'to embrace, to hug'
uhuna 'to cough'
ukta 'fast, quickly'
uktu 'a hole'
uktuna 'to make a hole; to perforate'
ukturina 'to perforate oneself'
uku 'inside'
ukucha 'rat or mouse'
ukuchina 'to moisten or make wet'
ukupacha 'hell'
ukwi añangu 'leaf cutter ants'
ukwi paho 'the last week of September when the ants swarm and are collected for roasting'
ulu 'sound, inner feeling of gulping a liquid, such as soup, in a hurry'
ullu 'penis'
uma 'head; headwaters'; also 'West' (in Amazonia); also *wasi uma* 'roof of a house'
umachina 'to deceive; to fool' (syn.: *llullana* 'to lie')
umbi 'sweat'
umbichina 'to make someone sweat'
umbina 'to sweat'
unay 'a long time, a long time ago'
unayana 'to delay'
undachina 'to fill something, (e.g., a canoe, a basket, a tank, etc.)'

undana 'to become full; to flood' (said especially of liquids, i.e., '*Yaku undan*' 'The river is flooding or risin')
ungurina 'to become sick; to sicken'
unyana (NQ) 'to put fish poison in a pool'
upichina 'to offer someone a drink'
upina 'to drink'
urayta 'downriver'
urmachina 'to cause someone/something to fall'
urmana 'to fall; collapse'
urmarina 'to navigate downriver by canoe' (also used to describe animals going down to the river to drink)
usa 'small insect such as a flea'
ushi NQ 'daughter'
ushushi PQ 'daughter'
utsun 'narrow' (syn.: *ñañu*)
uyana 'to hear; listen; understand; obey' (syn.: [NQ] *kazuna*)
uyarik 'noisy'
uyarimuna 'to sound in a way that listeners perceive the sound coming toward them (e.g., a motor canoe or a plane arriving)'
uyarina 'for something to make its characteristic sound heard (e.g., for a bell to ring out, for a clock to tick)'

W

wa! 'expression of surprise combined with real or feigned disapproval'
wachana 'to lay an egg; to give birth (of animals)'
wachi 'coati' (racoon-like animal)
waglichina 'to spoil'
wagra 'cow'; also *sacha wagra* 'tapir'
wagra pishku 'cow bird'
wak wak 'sound and motion of a fan'
wakachina 'to make someone cry'
wakana 'to cry'
wakarina 'to rust'
wakay 'a cry'
wakay kuraga 'cry baby' (lit.: 'cry chief')
wakay siki 'cry baby' (when said of a child; when said of a woman it means a sensitive woman prone to tears; lit.: 'cry-butt')
wakaychina 'to put away for safe keeping'
wakcha 'orphan'
wakcha kari 'widower'
wakcha warmi 'widow'

waktana 'to hit'
waktarina 'to hit oneself'; also *maki waktarina* 'to clap'
walis 'kindling; small sticks for starting a fire'
wallka 'necklace,' also *wallka muyu* 'necklace beads'
wamag 'bamboo'; also *yaku wamag* 'the large bamboo used for making walls or beds' (*yaku wamag* wood is also preferred for firing ceramics, and it is used for cutting the umbilical cord since cutting flesh with steel [*iru*] is believed to cause the wound to infect and rot)
wambuchina 'to cause to float'
wambula 'hardwood medicinal tree with toxic bark'
wambula kuru 'caterpillar that feeds on the *wambula*'
wamburina 'to fly; to float on water'
wami 'a small conical fish trap woven of bamboo and lisan'
wandug 'datura'
wanduna 'to lift'
wangana 'peccary'
wangu 'a group of things tied together (e.g., a bunch of onions); also a stem with many fruits on it like *uwilyas*'; also *wata wangu* 'the Pleiades constellation'
wanguna 'to group together; to tie together in a group'
wangurina 'to stick together in a group; to be united as a group'
wanlla 'left overs (e.g., left over food)'
wañuchig 'killer'
wañuchina 'to kill; to put out a light or a fire; to turn off a light or engine'
wañug 'dead' (when used with a name, e.g., *wañug Maria*, it means 'the late___' as in Spanish *el finado___*)
wañuglla 'thick layer of fallen leaves and organic material stuck together; soil that is black and spongy from decayed leaves'
wañukta 'like dead; until the point of death; also 'deeply' (i.e., *Wañukta puñun* 'He/she is deeply or fast asleep')
wañuna 'to die; to be sick; to be very weak'
wañushka 'dead; severely debilitated, sick'
wañuy 'death; an agent sent by a *yachag* 'shaman' to cause death'
waranga 'a thousand; a class of soft trees with many small leaves'
warkurina 'to hang'
warmi 'female; woman; wife'
warmi wawa 'girl'
washa 'back; behind'
washa inyahuna 'descendents'
washa timpu 'future' (cf. Sp. *tiempu* 'time')
washa tullu 'spine, back bone'

washayachina 'to make late; to cause to be late'
washayana 'to be delayed'
washayashka 'late; delayed; running behind schedule' (said of a watch or a clock that is slow)
wasi 'house'; also *wasi uma* 'roof'
waska 'vine; rope'; also *iru waska* 'wire'; *kiru waska* 'dental floss'
wata 'a year; a knot; loose skin and fat (love handles) around the waist'
wata wangu 'the Pleaides constellation'
wata wata 'various species of gecko'
watana 'to tie or bind'
wawa 'child'
wawa mama 'placenta'
wawa wasi 'womb, uterus'
wawachina 'to impregnate'
wawki 'brother of a male'
wayku 'ravine'
wayra 'wind'
wayra shina (PQ) 'quickly, rapidly' (lit.: like the wind)
wayra wawa 'a child with no known father'
wayrachina 'to fan'; also 'a fan'
wayrashka 'a person who has been hit with winds sickness, often from a grave or from contact with the spirit world of the forest or river' (the symptoms of *wayrashka* are nausea and feeling faint or dizzy)
waytana 'to swim'
wichay 'pointed upward'; also *wichay singa* 'lying flat on one's back so that one's nose is pointed upward'
wikan 'the way something looks when it is positioned straight upward, and distinctive from its surroundings'
wiksa (PQ) 'stomach'
wilma 'fur' (see also *ilma*)
win (PQ) 'any group or collection of entities considered as a whole; any action done completely, comprehensively'; also (NQ) 'the sound of cleaning a *chicha* bowl' (e.g., *Win rasha tazon shimira pichai* 'Going *win* clean the lip of the *chicha* bowl')
wiñay wiñay 'always, forever' (used to translate 'eternity' or 'everlasting' in Christian or Biblical references)
wira 'fat; oil; grease' (has positive connotations as a desirable substance)

Y

yachachina 'to teach'
yachana 'to know'

yacharina 'to become accustomed to'
yachay 'knowledge; custom; religion'
yachina 'to seem, to feel' (see also *sintina*)
yakami 'trumpeter'
yaku 'water; liquid in general; body of water, such as a river, or pond'; also *chuchu yaku* 'milk' (lit.: 'breast *yaku*'); *laran yaku* 'orange juice' (lit.: 'orange *yaku*'; also the proper names of rivers in areas that are or were Quichua speaking often end in *Yaku*, e.g., *Napo Yaku, Chunda Yaku, Sarsa Yaku, Sara Yaku*. (In some dialects of Quichua the word *mayu/o* was used instead of *yaku* to designate rivers. In these areas *mayu* replaces *yaku* in the proper names of rivers [i.e., *Putumayo*]. In parts of the Amazon that have become Quichua speaking in recent decades or centuries, the proper names of rivers retain the word for river in the language that previously named the region. For example, the Shuar word for river *entza* can be found not only in the names of rivers in Shuar-speaking areas such as *Chupi entza*, but in the last syllables of river names like *Bobonaza* and *Pastaza* in areas that are now Quichua speaking. Similarly, in the Napo area many rivers end in –*nu/o* which is the word for river in Waorani [*Payamino, Arajuno, Cawandano, Cuyabeno*])
yaku paho 'a sickness that comes from the river that causes children to have significant diarrhea; also the name for a gift or ability to heal this sickness'
yaku runa/yaku warmi 'river man/river woman' (*yaku runa* are spirit beings that own the fish and water animals)
yakuyachina 'to liquify'
yakuyana 'to become liquid or watery' (i.e., *paywa nawi yakuyashka* 'her eyes watered or teared up')
yali 'greater than/more than'
yalig 'last' (i.e., *yalig semana* 'last week')
yalina 'to surpass'
yana 'black'
yana kwika 'night crawler'
yanapana 'to help'
yandana 'to cut or chop trees for firewood'
yanga 'useless; for nothing; without value'
yanuna 'to cook (usually by boiling)'
yapa 'very; a lot'
yapakta 'too much'
yapalla 'more'
yapana 'to augment'
yapanikta 'a little more' (i.e., *yapanikta churay* 'put a little more')
yarkay 'hunger'

yasa 'a fish trap of a larger size (with a larger mouth) than the *wami*'
yaya 'father'
yumingana 'to hex, curse'
yunurina 'to melt; dissolve'
yupana 'to count'
yutu 'tinamu'
yuturi 'conga ant'
yuyana (PQ) 'to pay attention to something; watch out for something; be aware of something'
yuyarina (PQ) 'to ponder; remember'
yuyay (PQ) 'thought'
yuyu 'heart of palm; a general term for a green herb'

Z
zambulina 'to immerse underwater'
zapatos 'shoes' (cf. Sp. *zapatos*)

Bibliography

Adelaar, Willem F. H., and Pieter C. Muysken. *The Languages of the Andes*. Cambridge Language Surveys. Cambridge: Cambridge University Press, 2004.
Bastien, Joseph W. *Mountain of the Condor: Metaphor and Ritual in an Andean Ayllu*. St. Paul, MN: West Publishing Co., 1978.
Drown, Frank, and Marie Drown. *Mission to the Headhunters*. Fearn, Scotland: Focus Publications, 1961.
Ennis, Georgia. "Remediating Endangerment: Radio and the Animation of Memory in the Western Amazon." PhD thesis, University of Michigan, 2019.
Grzech, Karolina, Anne Schwarz, and Georgia Ennis. "Divided We Stand, Unified We Fall? The Impact of Standardization on Oral Language Varieties: A Case Study of Amazonian Kichwa." *Revista de Llengua i Dret, Journal of Language and Law* 71 (2019): 123–145. https://doi.org/10.2436/rld.i71.2019.3253.
Haboud, Marleen, and Nicholas Limerick. "Language Policy and Education in the Andes." In *Language Policy and Political Issues in Education*, edited by T. L. McCarty and S. May, 3rd edition. Encyclopedia of Language and Education. New York: Springer, 2017. https://doi.org/10.1007/978-3-319-02320-5_32-1.
Karsten, Rafael. *The Head-Hunters of Western Amazonas: The Life and Culture of the Jibaro Indians of Eastern Ecuador and Peru*. New York: AMS Press, 1979 [1935].
Moya, Ruth. *Simbolismo y ritual en el Ecuador andino*. Otavalo: Instituto Otavaleño de Antropología, 1981.
Muratorio, Blanca. *The Life and Times of Grandfather Alonzo. Culture and History in the Upper Amazon*. New Brunswick, NJ: Rutgers University Press, 1991.
Nuckolls, Janis. *Quechuarealwords: An Audiovisual Corpus of Expressive Quechua Ideophones*. http://quechuarealwords.byu.edu/.
Nuckolls, Janis. *Sounds Like Life. Sound-Symbolic Grammar, Performance, and Cognition in Pastaza Quechua*. Oxford Studies in Anthropological Linguistics. New York: Oxford University Press, 1996.
Nuckolls, Janis B., Joseph Stanley, Elizabeth Nielsen, and Rosanna Hopper. "The Systematic Stretching and Contracting of Ideophonic Phonology in Pastaza Quichua."

International Journal of American Linguistics 82, no. 1 (January 2016): 95–116. https://doi.org/10.1086/684425.

Nuckolls, Janis, and Tod Swanson. "Earthy Concreteness and Anti-Hypotheticalism in Amazonian Quichua Discourse." *Tipití* 12, no. 1 (2014): 48–59.

Orr, Carolyn, and Betsy Wrisley. *Vocabulario quichua del Oriente*. Quito: Instituto Lingüístico de Verano Instituto Lingüístico de Verano, 1981.

Pierre, Francois. *Viaje de exploración al Oriente Ecuatoriano, 1887–1888*. Quito: Ediciones Abya-Yala, 1983.

Recio, Bernardo. *Compendiosa relación de la cristiandad de Quito*. Edited, prologue, notes, and appendices by Carlos García Goldaraz. Madrid: Instituto Santo Toribio de Mogrovejo, 1947.

Swanson, Tod, and Jarrad Reddekop. "Looking Like the Land: Beauty and Aesthetics in Amazonian Quichua Philosophy and Practice." *Journal of the American Academy of Religion* 85, no. 3 (2017): 682–708. https://doi.org/10.1093/jaarel/lfw086.

Uzendoski, Michael A., and Edith Felicia Calapucha-Tapuy. *The Ecology of the Spoken Word: Amazonian Storytelling and Shamanism among the Napo Runa*. Urbana: University of Illinois Press, 2012.

Whitten, Norman. *Sacha Runa*. Urbana: The University of Illinois Press. 1976.

Wroblewski, Michael. "Public Indigeneity, Language Revitalization, and Intercultural Planning in a Native Amazonian Beauty Pageant." *American Anthropologist* 116, no. 1 (2014): 65–80.

Index

abstract language. *See* concrete language
accusing, 60
action words. *See* movement, language about
adjectives, 55, 182; limitative. *See* limitative words
adverbs, 19, 27, 51, 151–53, 195, 210; ideophones. *See* ideophones; limitative. *See* limitative words; the suffix *–sha* and, 157–58, 159–60. *See also under* suffixes
advising, 104–5
affines. *See under* relationships, language about, 15
affirmative response, 18–19, 78–79, 124–25
agriculture, 48
animacy, 88
animals, 70–71
art, 6, 92, 130, 136, 197
aspect, 147; habitual, 145–49; progressive, 147
aswa. See food

basic interactions, 17–22
beauty, 92, 234–35
belief system of Quichua people, 2, 7–8, 78, 112, 117, 154
blame, 60

Bobonaza: river, 4, 5, 129, 145–46; Quichua. *See* Pastaza Quichua
body, language about, 69–72, 74–75, 76, 87–88, 165

causative. *See under* suffixes
celebration. *See* festival
collective nouns, 73
colonial period, 2–3
color words, 130–31
commands. *See* imperatives
complements, 182
concrete language, 7–9
conjunctions, 112–13, 219–20
contextualization, 7–9, 59–63, 222–23
conventions, written, 11
cooking. *See* food
criticizing, 60
culture, expressed through language, 1–2, 9, 60
culture of the Quichua people. *See* lifestyle of the Quichua people.

dialects of Quichua, 2–4
direct object, 35–37, 46, 82, 214–17. *See also under* suffix
direct speech, 225–27
directive. *See* imperatives

275

echo questions. *See under* interrogatives
economic status of Quichua, 2
Ecuador, Quichua in, 2–4
endearment, terms of, 66
environment, connection to, 1–3, 45, 64–65, 70–71, 74. *See also* plants *and* lifestyle of the Quichua people
etiquette. *See* sociability, importance of
expressives. *See* ideophones
evasion questions. *See under* interrogatives
evidential language. *See* perspective *and under* suffixes

family. *See under* relationships, language about
festival, 56–57
fictive kinship. *See under* relationships, language about
food, 64–65, 96–97, 117, 154, 218, 227; *aswa*, 56–57, 204; language about, 112; plants as, 28–29
future. *See under* tense

gender: culture and, 78; language about, 67
generalizations. *See* generic statements
generic statements, 8, 104
gesture, 42–43, 108–9, 126
geography of Quichua, 6–7
goals, study, 10
"goodbye." *See* social interaction, end of
grammatical sequence, 25, 35
greetings, 17–20, 32

habitual construction. *See under* aspect
happiness. *See* laughter
history of Quichua, 2–7
hm hm construction, 53–54
hospitality. *See* sociability, importance of
humor, 17

identity: collective, 9; expressed through language, 1, 9

ideophones, 43, 74–75, 125–26, 141, 158, 160; and gesture, 108–9
If/then construction, 169
imagination, language to aid, 74
imperatives: advising, 104–5; first person plural, 105–6; immediate, 98–102, 115–16, 135; negating, 102–3, 104–5; pluralizing, 101; politifying, 44–45
impersonal verbs. *See under* verbs
inappropriate speech, criticized, 9. *See also* lying
Inca conquest, 2–4, 32
indirect speech. *See* direct speech
infinitives, 24
influence on Andean Spanish, Quichua's, 6–7
instrumental nouns. *See under* nouns
intermarriage, effect on language, 4
International Phonetic Association (IPA) symbols, 11–13
international trade language, 1
interrogatives, 18, 26–27, 142–43; about family, 33–37; as greetings, 17–19; compound future and, 193–94; echo, 53–54; evasion, 53–54; for information, 39–42, 43–44, 93, 155, 165; negation in response to, 52–53, 79; open-ended, 47–48, 123–24; suffix. *See under* suffixes; unanswerable, 63–64; yes/no, 43, 49–50, 78–79, 164, 193–94, 223
intonation, 60, 74, 162, 217, 219–20

Jivaroan, 4–5

Karsten, Rafael, 4–5

language shift, 3–4
laughter, 20–21
leave-taking. *See* social interaction, end of
legends. *See* stories, traditional
lifestyle of the Quichua people, 2–6, 45, 48, 56–57, 70–71, 185; effect

on usage, 19. *See also* sociability, importance of
limitative words, 114–16
location of Quichua people. *See* geography of Quichua
locative words, 137–39
love, romantic, 37–38
lying, 9, 222–23. *See also* truth

magic, 38, 65, 117, 178
medicine. *See under* plants
migration, 3, 4
missionaries, impact on Quichua, 4, 6–9
moods, semantic, 211–12
movement, language about, 128–30, 160–61
music, 166, 235

names, 56
narrative. *See* stories, traditional
nature, connection to. *See* environment, connection to
negation, 51–53, 79
nonhuman bodies, 70–71
nouns, 55; exclusivity, 113–14; instrumental, 95–96; limitative. *See* limitative words; phrases, 35; possession and, 82–83. *See also* direct object *and* names
numbers, 92–94

obliques, 214–15
oral language, 11
orientation, self and others, 15, 59–66

paint, 92
Pastaza Quichua (PQ), 3; compared to Upper Napo Quichua, 4, 5–6, 19, 189, 221
perspective: articulating, 59–61; establishing, 8–9, 221–25; marking. *See under* suffixes; of nonhuman forms, 74; "other," 61–64, 65–66. *See also* contextualization
phonetics, 11

phrasal constructions, 55
plants: as food. *See* food; importance in culture, 22, 56–57, 92, 181–82, 190–91, 197; used for healing, 70, 78; *See also* beauty
plural, 54–56, 81, 101
politeness strategies, 44–45, 52–54, 222; ignored, 98
possession, 80–83
predictions, 188–89, 197
promises, 182–85
pronouns, 24–26, 29, 89; demonstrative, 55; personal, 24; possessive. *See* possession
pronunciation, 12–13, 55, 57n2, 75, 97. *See also* International Phonetic Association (IPA) symbols

questions. *See* interrogatives

reciprocation. *See under* verbs
references: for location, 22
relationships, language about, 15, 89, 112; *compadrazgo*, 21, 31–32; family, 31–33, 37–38, 65–67. *See also under* interrogatives; fictive kinship, 67–68; marriage, 32, 65–66. *See also* fictive kinship
remainder, 1
resources. *See* beauty *and* food *and* medicine *and* plants
rivers, 2–9, 45, 117, 128–29, 185, 190–91
rubber boom, 2, 6

semantics, 214, 216–17, 223
sensory language, 74
sentence construction. *See* syntax
sickness. *See* body, language about *and* plants
sociability, importance of, 17, 99–101, 204–5
social interaction, end of, 21–22
"soft" speak. *See* inappropriate speech, criticized

songs. *See* music
speaking well, 8
spirits. *See* magic
spread of Quichua, 2, 3–4, 6–7
standardization, 11
status, language indicating, 66
stigma, 2
stories, traditional, 92, 98–99, 126, 179–80; about animals, 51, 154, 227–30; about spirits, 65, 144, 158–59, 204; language about, 62–63, 74
stress: adverbial, 19; verbal, 18, 24
subjects, 29; implied, 25
suffixes: adverbial, 153–55, 158, 163–64, 216; affirmative, 18–19, 124–25, 164; attributive, 133–36, 145–49, 158, 198–99; body movement, 87–88; causative, 46–47, 109; cislocative, 149–51; cognitive, 86–87; comitative, 95; completive, 206–7; conditional, 211–14; conjectural, 222–23; conjunctive, 112–13, 139; coreference, 157–66, 168; despitative, 97, 126; direct object, 35–37, 76, 93, 155, 162, 214–16; directional, 40–41, 128–30, 212, 216; durative, 126–28, 139, 147, 151–52, 192; evidential, 59–64, 123, 126, 192, 212, 221–25; exclusive, 113–14; first person object, 76; future, 189–92; ideophonic, 136; imperative, 44–45, 70, 98–102, 105–6, 115–16, 135; inchoative, 230–32; inceptive, 208–9; infinitive, 24, 98, 104–5, 180, 202; instrumental, 95–96, 214–16; interrogative, 27, 33–34, 47, 63–64, 123; interrogative, information, 40–41, 93, 155; interrogative, yes/no, 18–19, 49–50; limitative, 114–16; locative, 29, 40–41, 137–39, 149–53, 214–16; low-animacy, 88–89, 136; narrative past, 178–80; negation, 51, 102, 162–63, 212, 233–34; nominalizing, 202–3; past, 180–81, 190; perfective, 126; plural, 54–56, 101, 134; present-perfect, 175–78, 207; purposive, 121–25, 139, 232–34; reciprocal, 109–12; representing "others," 61–64; reflexive, 86, 89; switch reference, 167–74, 199; topicalizing, 40, 47; translocative, 151–53

subject deletion, 209, 216
subject transposition, 209–10
surprise, 182
syntax, 43, 209, 214–18. *See also* subject deletion *and* subject transposition

temporal expressions, 195–96; linkages, 169–70
tense, 147–48; attributive future, 198–200; compound future, 192–94, 199–200, 216, 220; exhortative future, 194–95; future, 147, 187–91, 198–200, 220; historical present, 29; narrative past, 178–80; past, 1, 139–42, 147–49, 180–81, 198; present, 25, 27–28, 147; present perfect, 25–26, 175–78
threats, 182–85
traditions, Quichua: lost, 6. *See also* food *and* lifestyle of the Quichua people *and* resources
translation, 144, 148–49, 171–72, 205, 224–25
travel, 22
truth, 62–63, 222. *See also* lying

uncertainty. *See* truth
Upper Napo Quichua (NQ), 3–4; compared to Pastaza Quichua. *See under* Pastaza Quichua
usage, 19

varieties of Quichua. *See* dialects of Quichua
verbs, 27, 89–91, 139, 152–53, 214–15; auxiliary, 211–12; coreference

suffix and, 159–56; cognitive, 86–87; commands. *See* imperatives; compound, 201–4, 206–7, 208–9; compound phrases, 146–47; durative, 126–28; evidentially specified, 60–61; finite, 158–63, 168–69; future tense, 192; illocutionary, 225–27; imperative, 44–45, 98–105, 151–52, 203; impersonal, 76–79; limitative. *See* limitative words; locative, 149–53; main, 159–64; negating, 102–3, 162–64; nominalized, 202–4, 206–7, 208–9; past tense, 141–42, 143–44, 147; purposive, 121–25; reciprocal, 109–12; reflexive, 86; switch reference, 170–71; "to advise," 104–5; "to be," 23–24, 33–34; "to become," 203–4, 230–32; "to have," 36; "to say," 165, 225

visits, social. *See* sociability, importance of

vocabulary, 41, 65–66, 72, 89–90, 92–93

voice, shared, 9. *See also* environment, connection to

word order. *See* syntax

word-initial *h*, 57n2

written language, 11

written symbols. *See* International Phonetic Association (IPA) symbols

www.ingramcontent.com/pod-product-compliance
Lightning Source LLC
LaVergne TN
LVHW020342260326
834688LV00045B/1486